SPECIAL FORCES LIBRARY

This new series is devoted to the history of the world's special forces. These élite fighters shun publicity; they operate in small teams, frequently behind enemy lines, and cause havoc out of all proportion to their numbers. Today's special forces have achieved fame by the spectacular success of their exploits – the SAS at the Iranian Embassy siege, the Green Berets in Vietnam, and in countless actions throughout the world in the fight against international terrorism. But they have their origins in the Second World War. This unique series traces their development since that time.

Special Forces Library

PETER STAINFORTH

Wings of the Wind

GRAFTON BOOKS
A Division of the Collins Publishing Group

LONDON GLASGOW
TORONTO SYDNEY AUCKLAND

Grafton Books
A Division of the Collins Publishing Group
8 Grafton Street, London W1X 3LA

Published by Grafton Books in association with
Arms & Armour Press Ltd 1988

First published in Great Britain by
The Falcon Press (London) Ltd 1952

ISBN 0-586-07451-1

Printed and bound in Great Britain by
Collins, Glasgow

Set in Times

Who maketh the clouds his chariot, and
Who walketh upon the wings of the wind.
Psalm 104, v. 3

My wartime comrades of the First Airborne Division walked upon the wings of
the wind, and to them I dedicate this
book.

Acknowledgements

I wish to express my gratitude to all those who have helped in the production of this book.

I am indebted to Major-General R. E. Urquhart, CB, DSO, and Major-General G. W. Lathbury, CB, DSO, MBE, for access to official maps and records, to Lieutenant-Colonel J. D. Frost, DSO, MC, Major E. M. Mackay, MBE, RE, and many others who have supplied information, to Miss Mary Waddington for her invaluable advice, and to the Rev. H. M. A. Crawshaw, MA, for correcting the proofs.

Lastly, I thank my father for devoting so much of his time to research and revision of the manuscript, and for his very great help throughout.

Preface

This is the story of a small unit of the 1st Parachute Brigade during two years of action in Tunisia, Sicily, Italy and finally Arnhem.

It is not a military history, although dates and incidents are as accurate as possible. Instead, I have written it from the viewpoint of an ordinary soldier with his nose very close to the ground, in order to portray how every man lived and fought, suffered and endured. That these adventures are in some degree personal is immaterial – they were shared by many others, and might have happened to anyone.

There is one departure from a strictly true account. All characters drawn from the 1st Parachute Squadron, Royal Engineers, itself, have been given fictitious names; and occasionally in later chapters two identities have been merged for continuity. Whilst every episode refers to real persons, the more tragic events may have been altered, and sometimes omitted, for the sake of relatives. In the close conditions of active service there exists a particular kind of friendship which cannot be recorded, and death is a calamity in itself needing no elaboration.

PETER STAINFORTH

July 1949

Foreword

Foreword by Major-General R. E. Urquhart, CB, DSO, one-time Commander of the 1st Airborne Division

The author has had considerable experience with Airborne Forces in wartime. He was a member of the original Squadron of Royal Engineers in the 1st Airborne Division, and this Squadron expanded first into a Regiment and then into the Royal Engineers organization in Airborne Forces which was built up by the end of the last war.

Peter Stainforth was a Regimental Officer throughout his wartime service and in very close touch with the soldier. He speaks with accuracy and realism of the performance of junior Officers and Other Ranks in battle. Although he has been so intimately concerned with a small unit, and this is portrayed in his description of the various actions in which he has taken part, he does not forget the wider picture and the operations which are taking place around him.

This is a realistic and readable book. It adds yet more proof, if such be needed, of the versatility of the Airborne Sapper and of his ability both as a technician and as a fighting soldier.

R. E. URQUHART
Major-General

HQ Malaya,
Kuala Lumpur,
Malaya
18 April 1952

Contents

List of Maps

PART ONE
Introduction: Pegasus Tamed

1

Fledglings

May 1942

All eyes were focused on the dwindling basket. Then the winch motors stopped; the balloon had reached the jumping height, and it was time for the play to begin. A poignant silence fell.

We heard the instructor shout 'Go!' very clearly in the stillness of the early morning. Something like an Egyptian mummy fell away from the aperture, trailing an ever-lengthening cigar above its head. There was a peculiar whoosh of rustling silk, the parachute blossomed like an opening flower and floated away down wind. There was an audible sigh of relief from the spectators.

When all five had jumped the balloon was hauled down and another load went aloft. Very soon my name would be called, and I too should have to grit my teeth and launch myself into space.

It was only a fortnight ago that I had arrived at Hardwick Hall, the Airborne Forces depot, and at once I was in another world. That first evening in the mess I was the penguin among the eagles. Everyone else seemed to be on the instructional staff, and the room was filled with a conversation I did not understand – on oscillation and damping, of roman candles and thrown lines and other obscure terms. 'There's nothing in jumping,' the old hands all said. 'Just like stepping off a bus.' But it did not sound very convincing.

I was not, however, the only newcomer.

'You're Terrick, aren't you?' said a voice at my elbow,

and a heavily-built sapper subaltern propped himself up at the bar and ordered a couple of drinks.

'I'm Tony Miles. Major Drake told me you would be coming. Are you fixed up with a room yet? If not, why not have your stuff moved into mine? You'll have to share with someone, as they're crowded out.' So we struck up a partnership there and then.

We used to assemble after breakfast in the big gymnasium, and peel off gaberdine jumping-jackets, sweaters and trousers, to PT shorts and shoes. On the first morning we stood around blue with cold, but not for long.

'Squad, 'shun! Right turn! Double march!' Our instructor was hopping around, a ball of compressed energy.

'Form a wide circle! Come on, number six! Pick those feet up! Let's have more life, more bounce! Doubling with knees raised, begin . . . That's better! . . . Lower! . . . Now I want to see every man on the back of the man in front . . . Go! Why, you're like snails going in reverse! . . . Pull that man down!' He would indicate some victim for dismemberment, and we would all pile in, lest we too should be picked as the next.

The other exercises in the handbook, with horse, beam and the rest, followed one after another without intermission. We stretched, twisted, bent, heaved and sweated, while our tormentor urged us on relentlessly. Then we were passed on to the parachute sergeant-instructors, who chased us round the camp at the double for the remainder of the day. We went for long route marches, cross-country runs and gruelling run-walks which ended with a plunge into the lake below the camp. Afterwards we would return to the serious business of synthetic training, to get confidence and proficiency in 'exits' and 'air-control'.

Our ginger-haired sergeant would rave when we failed

to execute a perfect parachute landing in the sand-pit beneath the high trapeze.

'There you go again! What do you think you are? A spider? How many times have I got to tell you? I'm wore out knocking it into your thick skull! Get up to the top of those swings and shout twenty times "I MUST keep my feet and knees together!" Go on! Get up there before I come after you!'

And perched astride the horizontal cross-piece, thirty feet above us, the offender would do his penance.

This technique of landing with feet and knees together is the linchpin of parachuting. With one leg acting as a brace to the other, it ensures the weight of the body being taken equally on both feet, and prevents sprains and fractures on striking the ground. The complementary 'parachute roll' absorbs the speed to drift, and the shock of falling, on those parts of the body least liable to damage – the side of the leg, the thigh and the rounded back. As the feet touch ground, the body collapses like a falling chain and the feet swing up over the head, each movement flowing into the next with a rhythm rather fascinating to watch.

When a small mistake can mean serious personal injury and consequent danger to others, it is not surprising that our instructors were exacting in their standards. Our every action had to become instinctive; in a descent of thirty seconds there is no time for deliberation. We had to be able to take a landing forwards, sideways or backwards at speeds up to twenty miles an hour, and then free ourselves from the parachute harness instantly. Few faults, if any, went unnoticed.

Aperture drill took place in the big drill shed. A well-raked tan-pit ran the whole length of the building, and above stood the row of dummy fuselages on their trestle legs, looking like truncated grasshoppers. Here we were taught the Whitley exit from the sitting position, each man's feet swinging into the circular hole over the head of the previous number as he dropped through. When jumping from aircraft, the faster the 'stick' of men can leave the plane the less widely are they scattered on the ground, and the quicker their assembly for battle at the rendezvous.

And so to our last day at Hardwick, when we made two descents from the seventy-foot jumping tower. Though the drop was controlled hydraulically with no oscillation or drift, the sensation of falling free until the wires took up the slack gave us a foretaste of things to come.

We now went on to the RAF at Ringway for the final stage, which was to culminate in seven descents – two from the balloon and five from aircraft.

From the first we were instilled with the infallibility of our 'statichutes'. These differ from the rip-cord type in that they are operated by a 'static line', which is a stout piece of webbing about twelve feet long with a snap-hook at one end, the other end being strongly sewn into the parachute bag. Before jumping, the paratroopers hook this static line on to an anchor cable inside the plane, so that the parachute is automatically operated after they have fallen the length of the webbing, and should be fully open in about two and a half seconds. The aircraft must be flying level and at low speed, otherwise proper development is uncertain and accidents may happen.

We were kept hard at work during our first day or two, while the RAF instructors put us through our paces in a special hangar, where every phase of a parachute descent was reproduced on apparatus. The fan, the whirligig, the slides and the winch flung us at the earth from every angle and passed the time in a very exciting way. Then the evening of the third day arrived with unexpected suddenness, and nothing remained but to put theory into practice. The instructors gave us some last words of wisdom and informed us casually that the morning parade would be at five outside the main hangar. So the inevitable was upon us at last; we were to make a first jump at Tatton Park in the morning.

I slept badly that night and dreamt I was plunging down and down and down – a lonely comet in the nothingness of space.

'Your early call, sir! It's half-past four!' The guard had switched on the light and was shaking me ruthlessly by the shoulder. Tony stirred, turned over and blinked enquiringly at the light.

'What's all the noise about? Can't you let a bloke sleep in peace? Oh, what a ghastly hour to have to go and die!' We both felt that this was the day appointed for our execution.

We threw back the bedclothes with a gesture of resignation and dressed rapidly, pulling on an extra sweater in anticipation of the cold morning breeze high above the earth. Neither of us said a word.

We swallowed a mug of cocoa in the mess, picked up our gaberdine jackets and rubber helmets and plodded across to the aerodrome where we joined the crowd round the two camouflaged buses. It was chilly in the grey dawn and we stood with shoulders hunched and hands deep in pockets, stamping our feet to keep warm. Some of the heartier ones cracked a few feeble jokes, but for the most part our thoughts were already in Tatton Park.

After what seemed the shortest of journeys we swung in through the park gates and up the avenue of oaks, to alight by the YMCA hut. Even at this early hour there would be tea and buns for everyone after we had done our stuff. And there were the two balloons, wallowing on the ground like stranded whales beside their attendant winch lorries.

We walked across the five hundred yards of parkland, then queued up to draw our parachutes. The instructors went round the groups helping us to adjust our harness; fingers seemed all thumbs that morning. The chief instructor called out five names from his roll. Five luckless individuals waddled forward in their harness with resigned looks on their faces, and the day's business had begun. Very soon the parachutes were coming down, sudden puffs of drab and green appearing like shell-bursts beneath each balloon, and the parkland became peppered with men. We waited our turn in a daze while the group slowly dwindled.

'Sutcliffe, Swinburn, Talbert, Lieutenant Terrick, Turner! Next party, number two!' The voice crackled in the loudspeaker and jerked us back to reality. The balloon grounded, we climbed gingerly over the side of the basket and took up our stations round the hole.

The instructor stood at one end and hooked us up in turn to the 'strops' hanging from a steel bar above. He presented the fastened snap-hook to each man for inspection – a last attempt to persuade us that everything was going to be all right. Each one stared at the strop like a mesmerized rabbit. Meanwhile he chatted away cheerily, but his conversation was merely irritating. All the way up he kept this patter going, but I caught a look in his eye, a human expression which reassured me more than words. I liked him for that.

I did not dare look down through the hole but kept my eyes averted, staring fixedly at the silver bag above our heads – the one tangible thing in a world of imagination. This was truly hell on earth, I told myself, and nothing would induce me to go through it again. I felt horribly sick, and shivered and sweated alternately.

I sensed the balloon was rising, the air got colder, and the moan of the wind in the bracing wires changed to a dismal whistle. The sway of the basket increased, trying to tear me loose from my limpet hold. The breeze plucked at my clothing and whispered, as if telling me to go back before it was too late.

The instructor was looking over the side of the basket, watching for the winking Aldis lamp. This tells him that the winch has stopped paying out.

'All right, number one! Action stations!' The silence was shattered. Number one swung his legs into the hole with a crash. I gasped involuntarily.

'Go!' Number one went through the aperture rigidly, with a look of horror on his face. His strop jumped, snapped taut with a resounding crack and then hung limp. Somewhere below I heard the parachute whoosh open, and then again eerie silence.

'Lovely!' the instructor called over the side, and pulled in the static line and empty bag.

Now it was my turn. I wriggled to the edge of the hole, gripping the sides tightly. I was afraid to go too far forward in case I toppled out prematurely, yet could not sit too far back for fear of fouling my pack as I went down.

'Get nice and comfortable, number two! Take your time! OK? Right. Action stations! . . . Go!'

The word of command penetrated my numbed brain like a shaft of light. Then I was going down, limbs frozen stiff, jaws locked and finger-nails biting into the palms of my hands.

I have a dim recollection of air rushing in my ears, a growing feeling of nausea and contraction of the stomach-muscles, a jerking about my head as the rigging lines ran out, wind fluttering the silk violently, and then I was standing between heaven and earth, overwhelmed with relief and elated at my salvation.

'That was OK, number two! Make a good landing and finish it off!' A voice broke in upon my senses, and I felt pleased with myself.

I was struck up there by the utter silence and the feeling of detachment I acquired in an instant as I swung gently backwards and forwards. I was transfigured, I was a king seated on a throne high above the earth, and all my domains lay at my feet. Wherever I turned the whole world was mine – a paradise of unrivalled beauty bathed in a mist of gossamer, enchanting and very wonderful.

Down there beneath my feet a little crowd of mortals crawled over the earth like ants, so puny and so useless. I had only to put out my foot and I could crush them and rid my world of their scampering and tumult.

For ten seconds I was God!

Gradually the vision faded. The earth was rushing up, tilting first one way and then the other, revolving and sliding beneath with terrifying speed. I tried to remember everything I had been taught, but it was too late.

I landed somehow with a bump, a muddle of arms and legs. The canopy collapsed about me, shrouding me in rigging lines. I was bewildered but quite undamaged. I felt myself gingerly all over to make sure and lay on my back for a moment to collect my thoughts.

'That was quite good, number two, but don't just lie there! Get up, man!'

I was suddenly conscious of someone bawling through the loud-speaker. I struggled to my feet and rolled my parachute, ashamed I had allowed my thoughts to run away with me.

In a moment I realized I had to do it all over again. Once more the old terror clawed at my abdomen and turned my legs to water. Gone were the seconds of paradise in the sky, and I could only think of the agony of apprehension as I sat and waited, with six hundred feet of air below.

But as I hovered once again in that wonderful silence I was again translated, only to become mortal all too soon, as the earth rushed up, eager for my destruction. I had the hang of it now, however, and succeeded in marrying myself to the ground. I rolled with the swing, turned over and rose up.

Above me, two little mushrooms appeared against the blue and began to drift down wind. The tiny figures raised their arms and kicked about, as the chief instructor shouted directions and brought them safely down.

I stood and watched, entranced. My soul was up there too, soaring immortal in the sky.

2
Prelude
July–November 1942

'Here are Miles and Terrick, David,' said Major Drake, when we met Captain Westley, our new troop commander, in his office. We had just arrived after a fortnight's leave on completion of our parachute course, and this was our first morning in the 1st Parachute Squadron, Royal Engineers, at Bulford Camp.

'David has been very short-handed since Henry Walker became hors de combat,' he went on, 'and you two are going to be busy! We have an intensive training programme which has to be completed by the autumn, so you can expect no more leave for some time!'

We counted ourselves fortunate in our posting. David Westley was the finest type of leader – physically tough, a dynamo of energy, self-denying and quite impervious to hardship and fear. He was a slight, lightly built man, but his looks belied his strength and character. He was the only officer among us who had already done a parachute operation, having taken the Engineers detachment to Bruneval, an exploit of which we were to hear more.

Our training began immediately. Exceptional fitness was the first requirement, for we had to keep pace with our infantry comrades on the march, despite our heavy loads of explosives and stores. This was a tall order in itself, for the parachute battalions had developed a swinging gait with a long stride, which carried them over rough country at great speed.

Major Drake, himself over six feet and a one-time Blackheath Harrier, insisted it could be done with practice, and devoted much of our programme to this end. At his instigation we were supplied with the 'Everest' carrier, a device used by Sherpa porters in the Himalayas, and we would plod up and down Beacon Hill with two filled sandbags strapped on our backs.

The squadron, whose function it was to provide technical assistance to the parachute brigade, had an establishment of about a hundred and fifty officers and men and was organized in three troops, each commanded by a captain and capable of operating independently with its corresponding infantry battalion. For this reason we were specialists in assault demolitions, mine-laying and lifting, and improvised bridging. We made a study of enemy stores and equipment so as to be able to use whatever materials we found in battle, and were taught how to sabotage machinery so that it wrecked itself, and to make fire and water play their part. We were encouraged to develop our own ideas for light-weight weapons, in which pursuit Henry Walker, our predecessor in 'B' Troop, had fallen a victim to one of his own inventions which had exploded prematurely, and was now forced to accept a more sedentary role under Bill Stevens, our second in command, at squadron headquarters.

We were a growing unit, born of an embryo of officers and men known originally as the Air Troop, Royal Engineers; and in consequence each troop had a character of its own. 'A' Troop was already up to strength and fully trained, and its subalterns, Paul Mason, Ginger Hamilton, Paddy Roorke and John Pearson, were an exuberant quartet, well suited to the temperament of their men, the original volunteers eager for adventure and battle. And Kenneth Duncan, their commander, gave them plenty of rein.

'B' Troop, with David Westley and a sprinkling of

veteran NCOs, was still adolescent; but 'C' Troop, only lately raised, had a long way to go and again was rather different. Martin Brush and George Irwin were thorough and calculating, while Jack Burroughs was a man of few words and his orders were direct and to the point.

We were soon infected with the enthusiasm and esprit de corps which permeated all the airborne units concentrated on Salisbury Plain. Every man was a volunteer and had been subject to a rigorous selection. Discipline was strict, smartness was of the highest standard and the men were proud of it. It was as though they had brought with them all the finest of their regimental traditions and welded them into one, while the peculiar hazards of the work produced a comradeship of a very special quality.

Seeing these purposeful, finely trained battalions, it was hard to realize that only eighteen months had passed since a handful of volunteers from No 2 Commando had begun jumping with unsuitable parachutes from outmoded aircraft. But thanks to the prevision of Winston Churchill, from these few had emerged the 1st Parachute Battalion, then the 1st Parachute Brigade and later a full Airborne Division with the nucleus of a second.

Moreover, they had already been tempered in battle. In February 1941 there had been the Monte Vulture operation to destroy an important aqueduct in southern Italy. This action, although militarily successful, had unhappily ended in tragedy and captivity for the fifty officers and men who took part. But it had proved that the new technique was workable, and so assured the future of British parachute troops.

Any remaining doubts on this point were dispelled by the Bruneval raid of the 27th February, 1942, which was an outstanding success. The task of seizing a German radio-location station on the French coast – to enable an expert to examine the installations and bring away certain instruments for study – was given to the three all-Scots platoons of 'C' Company of the 2nd Battalion, under Major Frost.

On the night of the operation new snow and clear moonlight helped the aircraft in identifying the dropping zone. The parachutists quickly overran the station, so that David Westley and his sappers were able to dismantle the required parts before German reinforcements arrived. Naval landing craft duly put in to the beaches at the appointed hour, and the party was evacuated safely, with a loss of only two killed and six missing. Fortune had certainly smiled on this enterprise.

We had more or less settled down for the winter on Salisbury Plain, when early in October the 1st Parachute Brigade received orders for immediate mobilization and overseas service. Our destination was secret; we were to prepare for a journey by sea – all except the 3rd Battalion and our 'C' Troop who were to fly, ready for immediate battle.

Most of us were far too busy to feel depressed at leaving at such short notice. Paratroops possess a great quantity of specialized equipment to get them into the air, and all this paraphernalia had now to be shipped. Gangs of men went daily to Netheravon aerodrome to stow our heavier arms and stores in 'containers' which would be dropped from the bomb racks of our aircraft. The RAF packing section, which was accompanying the brigade, packed three thousand statichutes and container-parachutes in moisture-proof crates. Back in barracks we were issued with a plethora of jumping clothing and other equipment, and despatched the squadron effects in innumerable cases to the railway sidings. The Brigade were sailing in two troopships, and we now split up as we would fight, 'A' Troop and Bill Stevens going with the 1st Battalion, and the OC and ourselves with the 2nd.

When we marched out of barracks on the 29th of October for the last time, everyone was resigned and a little excited at what might lie ahead. England was already forgotten, and we were engrossed in a recluse life revolving round the unit and those who went to make it. The men were in a similar mood and sang with gusto the paratrooper's lament:

> 'Come sit by my side if you love me,
> Do not hasten to bid me adieu;
> Just remember the poor parachutist,
> Who is willing to die just for you-u!'

It was getting dark and drizzling steadily. The roads were almost deserted, and only two nursing sisters from the hospital waved us good-bye.

As our tender pulled out from the quay at Greenock the great concourse of shipping which made up our convoy came into view. There were cruisers, two large aircraft-carriers, a battleship and a cluster of destroyers; while about them all a dozen or more corvettes ploughed smoothly up and down. Then, as far as the eye could see down the roadstead, were giant liners, cargo vessels of every shape and size and a host of smaller craft dotting the grey lane of water. It was evident that something very big was in the wind.

We sailed the following night, and our last glimpse of home was of deeper shadows against the dark waters on either side. We still remained in complete ignorance of our destination, and it was not until we were two days out from the Clyde that our sealed orders were opened and we heard the details of the expedition to North Africa from our commander, Brigadier Flavell. We formed the second wave in the landings which were to begin on the 8th November, and we ourselves were due off Algiers four days later.

The plans which had been prepared necessarily provided for all contingencies, but it was sincerely hoped that the French armies would not oppose our occupation. Major Drake concluded our briefing by describing our actions in this event.

'If the French let us in without fighting,' he said 'the 3rd Battalion "air-lands" at Maison Blanche and takes off soon afterwards for Bône, near the Tunisian border. It is then proposed that the 1st Battalion shall jump on the El Aouina airfield near Tunis, and the 2nd Battalion at Bizerta. The Germans may, of course, get there first! These operations are pure speculation, and nobody can tell until the campaign begins what will happen. Impress on the men that once things start we may be sent anywhere!'

There was great excitement on the troop deck when David and his two minions, Tony and myself, arrived with armfuls of maps.

'Are we going to Burma, sir?'

'Bet you it's Dakar!'

Guesses were wild and entertaining. The news that Algiers was our destination was somewhat of an anticlimax.

We passed through the Straits of Gibraltar on the night of 10th November and, on hearing that the lights of Algeciras and Tangier were visible, groped our way out on deck. All around us the convoy was proceeding at half speed, completely blacked out. Dark hulks loomed out of the sea in a regular pattern, seemingly without motion on

the inky surface. From the Spanish shore three fingers of
light were probing the sky, crossing and recrossing; while
away to the starboard a multitude of twinkling stars were
floating on the water, throwing little daggers of gold
towards us. The sky was densely overcast, and those tiny
specks of light were like friendly worlds in a lonely void.

That night we left our slow freighters at Gibraltar,
while we raced up the coast of Africa at full speed. We
expected a hot reception from U-boats and dive-bombers
now that our destination was out of the bag, but the
following day went by without any alarms. Meanwhile
news was coming through over the ship's wireless that the
landings were going well and that Algiers had been
occupied by British troops. All of us were profoundly
relieved that we should not have to fight the French.

When we awoke on the 12th of November the convoy
was at anchor, scattered over a wide expanse of sea,
swinging slowly at anchor-chains. Balloon-kites were
flying and except for a wisp of smoke curling from a
funnel here and there, no sign of life disturbed the
morning's peace.

Turning towards the shore I was enthralled by its
unexpected beauty. From the green ribbon of Cap Mati-
fou in the east to the lighthouse and rocky crags of Cap
du Nord in the west the whole panorama of Algiers Bay
lay in a semicircular arc, with the early sun boldly picking
out the colours.

There were orange groves with black cypresses standing
behind like sentinels, palms nodding in the breeze, white
bungalows with brilliant red roofs, golden sands and a
mirror-like sea reflecting the sky; and then, the splendour
of the city cradled beneath the high ridge to the south.
From two miles out, Algiers looked fabulous, with its

—

concrete façades smooth as marble, and windows flashing like diamonds in the sun.

At sea level there was a forest of masts, derricks and cranes rising like cobwebs above warehouses and the grey harbour walls. Behind, the city rose in a pleasing geometrical arrangement of modern blocks, squares and parks, with the main streets and boulevards built in terraces, one above the other, parallel to the water-front. Large villas and houses peered out from among the trees and shrubbery of terraced gardens and covered the steep slope to the crest.

In contrast to the dignity of the modern city the Arab quarter in the west sprawled like an anthill. But for all its untidiness, the carefree jumble of streets, flat roofs and domes piled one on the other lent colour to the scene and added a touch of Africa and centuries-old romance.

I had been so absorbed that I had forgotten the war. Yet here we lay serenely under the very gun barrels of the Algiers forts. It seemed as though our thunder had misfired. Only the great fleet, with a sinister escort of grey-painted cruisers and destroyers patrolling across the mouth of the bay, reminded me that there was a reason for our journey.

PART TWO
The Red Devils in Tunisia
November 1942–April 1943

3

Maison Carrée and Maison Blanche
November 1942

We sat with our backs to some railings, listening to the insects singing in the undergrowth, and sucking oranges bought from a wayside barrow. The sun was getting up, and it was rather pleasant lolling on the pavement spitting our pips into the gutter. Now that we were on active service, time and etiquette did not seem to matter.

We had docked too late to go ashore the previous day and had only disembarked that morning. After marching up through vociferous crowds we were now halted outside the Botanical Gardens, on the coastal road east of the city. The water lapped the rough sea-wall on the other side of the road, and just beyond, an American assault ship was run up on the beach. Her stern had been ripped open in a raid by torpedo bombers two nights before and now she was guyed upright by hawsers, while her crew lounged about the deck and hung out their washing.

After a few minutes we hoisted up our mountainous Everest carriers again and turned into the gardens. We found 'A' Troop in a corner cooking breakfast in mess tins over tommy-cookers, and had a brief reunion. They had spent an uncomfortable night amongst the ferns, creepers and the ticks, having disembarked the previous afternoon; and they left us almost at once to march the sixteen miles to the airfield at Maison Blanche.

While we settled down to a 'brew-up' ourselves, David gave us the latest news and told us that the 3rd Battalion had dropped at Bône the day before without opposition.

Bône was three hundred miles away and about fifty

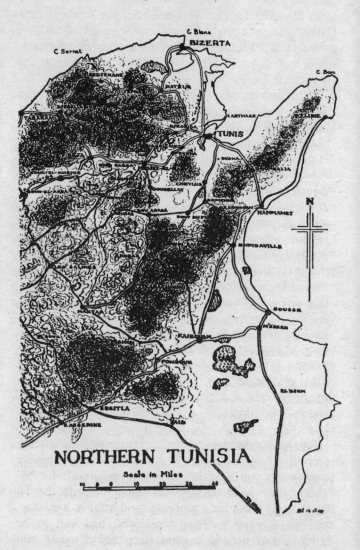

NORTHERN TUNISIA

Scale in Miles

miles from the Tunisian border. After the signing of the Darlan armistice the two infantry brigades which had preceded us had gone on, and were now hurrying eastwards to link up with the parachutists and to meet the Germans in Tunisia.

We ourselves were going into billets with the 2nd Battalion in Maison Carrée, about six miles this side of Maison Blanche.

Leaving our heavy kit to come on by truck, we made the march under the full strength of the African noonday sun. It was no great distance but it stands out in my memory as a prolonged ordeal. There was no shade, and our steel-shod boots slipped on the pavé which seemed to radiate the heat, adding to the blaze which beat down on our close-fitting parachutist steel helmets. When at last we staggered into our billets in the Collège Indigène as dusk was falling, we were interested only in bed and rolled out our blankets on the mosaic floors.

For the next three days we were occupied from dawn till dusk in moving our stores from the docks to the airfield and Maison Carrée. Brigadier Flavell had requisitioned a fleet of antiquated lorries running on producer gas, and the native drivers worked to all hours for a packet of biscuits or a tin of corned beef. We had little time for meals and lived mostly on oranges from the vendors who thronged our warehouse in the marketplace.

But on the first night, just after returning to billets, we received an urgent message from the OC to send a loading party to Maison Blanche, to bomb-up aircraft for 'A' Troop. They were off on their operation with the 1st Battalion the following morning; and after a hard day, had just finished packing containers, had still to be 'briefed', and needed a good sleep before going into battle. The whole of our troop at once volunteered, and we boarded our lorries and hurried up to the airfield.

We made our way to the one undamaged hangar, inside which we found the floor space filled with containers and the 1st Battalion settling down for the night. The interior was gloomy, with only two or three small electric lights high up in the roof. Men stood around in groups fitting parachutes, whilst others were laid out in rows, by platoons and companies, trying to snatch a few hours' rest amid the hum of preparation.

Ken Duncan and his four officers were in a huddle over a map; the others were already asleep, with the flaps of their sleeping-bags over their heads.

'Everything's ready for you, David,' Ken said. 'The aircraft numbers are chalked on the containers. You will find one of the American crew with each plane, and he will explain the release switches. For goodness' sake see that the parachute ripcords are fastened properly, as we are loaded up with mines and explosives!'

We got a load of containers on our trolleys and trundled them out to the airfield. The moon was just coming up over the cypresses behind the hangars, making the landing-ground look limitless in the half-light and the Dakotas seem very cold and lonely in their dispersal areas. We worked speedily by the light of torches, and the hours passed. At midnight there was an air-raid warning, so we were called off the field and sat and watched the graceful streams of red and orange tracer going up from the shipping in Algiers Bay, while the bombs rumbled in the distance. Eventually, we finished our task as the first streaks of dawn were in the sky.

Early that morning we watched the air-fleet take off, but they returned two hours later with the containers still beneath the planes. There had been a last-minute cancellation. They finally got away early on the 16th, disappearing like a swarm of gnats above the hills to the east. To us at Maison Carrée it seemed hard to believe that they were going off to war, while we remained so very much at peace.

That night we heard over the wireless that a parachute landing had been made on Souk-el-Arba airfield in Northern Tunisia. It was a long way from E1 Aouina and Tunis, which had been their original destination: the Germans had already landed in strength at both places.

A day or two later the 3rd Battalion group returned from Bône and went into billets about ten miles away. Their flight out had been uneventful; except that, on taking off from the short runway at Gibraltar, one of the heavily loaded planes had landed up in the sea. Then, after a night of great activity and preparation at Maison Blanche, they had flown on to Bône.

'We had a perfect drop,' Jack Burroughs told us when he came over. 'All the sticks were carrying extra rations in sandbags which we jettisoned on nearing ground. That preliminary bombardment softened up opposition considerably; the French civilians were delighted and ran about helping us out of our parachutes! I am afraid the battalion had one man killed through parachute failure, but our only casualty was George, who landed on his head as usual, with his feet caught up in the rigging lines!'

We heard later that the 3rd Battalion had only just won the race. A fleet of troop-carrying Ju 52s was on its way to the same objective, but turned back to Tunis when it saw our parachutes dotting the horizon above the airfield.

The paratroops were reinforced the following day by No 6 Commando, and their only trouble had been from persistent attacks by enemy bombers and fighters. When the Spitfires eventually arrived the Germans kept away during daylight, but bombed the harbour every night, sinking a number of ships.

Our own orders came at last on the 27th November while we were having lunch. We were to stand by for a parachute operation at forty-eight hours' notice.

'Suits me!' Tony remarked. 'I was getting fed up with this uncertainty and hanging about!'

Tony's mood was that of us all. Nevertheless, we had suddenly lost our appetites for any further lunch. The lack of conversation was also noticeable.

We spent the remainder of the day packing containers with arms and equipment. Major Drake also brought us over a quantity of incendiary bombs, the purpose of which we learnt at the briefing next morning.

The situation in Tunisia had altered considerably during the past week, as the enemy had been flying troops and aircraft over from Italy as rapidly as he could. Owing to our lack of forward airfields our men were being continuously subjected to air attacks, and the advance was temporarily halted at Tebourba. Whereas our nearest landing-ground was at Souk-el-Arba, the Germans were employing the many excellent all-weather airfields on the Tunisian plain. Our forward infantry in the hills round Tebourba could actually see the Stukas take off, come and plaster their positions, then fly back and land for another load. The effect of this unhindered bombing was very severe, and our transport and armour were largely immobilized.

It was thought that if we could disrupt these attacks, even for a day or two, our troops might be able to advance and establish our own fighters in a forward position. This was the task of the 2nd Parachute Battalion Group.

There were three airfields from which it was believed

the Stukas were operating. The first was an old French landing-ground at Pont-du-Fahs, only used in the dry season. The second was situated about twelve miles north-east of it near Depienne, a small market town on the plain west of Zaghouan. The last and most important of the three was just north of Oudna village, a halt on the railway about ten miles south of Tunis.

Our job was to land in the late afternoon of the 29th of November near Pont-du-Fahs and attack the landing-ground as dusk was falling. Everything on the field was to be wrecked – aircraft burnt with incendiary bombs, petrol dumps fired, motor transport destroyed and ammunition dumps and other installations blown up. Having completed our work we would slip away in the dark to carry out the same performance elsewhere.

We knew that our force was comparatively safe provided it worked by night, as the men were specially trained for it and preferred, if anything, to deliver that type of attack. Our tactics after Pont-du-Fahs were to march all night towards Depienne, lie up in the hills during the day and deliver another night attack. This was to be repeated against the airfield at Oudna. It was fully realized that these successive attacks would become increasingly difficult. But we expected our main forces to be advancing up the Medjez–Tunis road by then, and we were to rejoin them at Massicault on the third night.

Reveille on Sunday the 29th of November was at five, as there still remained a great deal of necessary work before take-off at eleven. We forced ourselves to eat something at breakfast in view of the strenuous business ahead. At six-thirty, 5-ton trucks arrived outside the billets, and we spent an hour getting our containers aboard, then collected our jumping kit and statichutes and clambered in on top. We kept up a pretence at cheerfulness during the drive to Maison Blanche, with the men singing 'Will ye no come back again?'

From the moment of our arrival at the aerodrome at eight o'clock everything seemed to go wrong. Recent rain had made parts of the aerodrome very soft and muddy. Then we discovered that at least half of our planes had not arrived and were not expected from Blida until about nine o'clock. Moreover, our lorries were urgently required for another job and had to dump us and our 300-pound containers on the airfield's edge, instead of taking them out to the planes. This very heavy work would now have to be done on our own shoulders. To make the whole thing more complicated it had not been possible to allot the Engineers a flight of aircraft on their own, and the sections were split up over the infantry aircraft with two men and a container on each. This meant that we now had five planes to bomb-up instead of one.

When the planes at last arrived they taxied in one after another and parked in a huddle just off the perimeter track. To our consternation we discovered that these aircraft were unnumbered, or else bore a legacy of several numbers from previous jumps, all different from those we expected. Officers milled around trying to identify their planes, and there was the utmost confusion. We actually bombed-up one aircraft in error before being vigorously disillusioned by one of the company commanders. It was very hot and steamy; tempers were equally heated.

When the first of the forty-four planes took off I was still working with my batman, Clarkson, under the belly of ours – number thirty-eight – endeavouring to fit the last container into an awkward bomb-rack. The engines of our aircraft turned over with a whistle of compressed air, then burst into life with a roar. The sudden blast of wind laid the grass flat and blew a cloud of grit into our faces.

Major Drake, who had been touring the 'B' Troop aircraft, came running up, very alarmed.

'Good heavens! Haven't you finished yet? Where's your 'chute and equipment?'

'Our stuff's inside, sir. I think we've just about finished now!'

'OK, leave it and get in.'

He pushed us in through the door, and the crew chief pulled up the ladder. The OC poked his head in and wished us luck.

Unlike the Whitleys in which we had trained in England there was plenty of room in the Dakota to move about and fit parachutes while the plane was in the air. The infantry gave us a hand and helped us into our jumping equipment.

I was flying in one of the 'C' Company headquarter planes under their second in command, Captain Measures. He would jump number one at the head of the 'stick'; I was going out in the middle, number eight. When the initial revving of our engines had died down he picked his way to the centre of the fuselage.

'Can you all hear me?' he shouted. We nodded in reply. 'OK number sixteen? I have got some important gen, so listen carefully! Colonel Frost sent me a message about five minutes ago to say we aren't going to Pont-du-Fahs. Got that? We aren't going to Pont-du-Fahs; British armoured cars got there this morning! Instead, we are flying straight to Depienne and dropping there. There hasn't been an air "recce" of the dropping zone, so the Colonel's going to pick one from the leading plane. He's flying a mile in front of the main formation and will jump when he sees a good spot. The rest of us jump where he jumps. OK? Any worries?'

'What about fighter escort, sir?'

'We get a squadron of long-range Lightnings – Yanks – to take us all the way there. Then we get an extra squadron of Spits from Constantine onwards to cover us over the DZ. I believe they've got an air strike laid on for German fighter 'dromes near Tunis, so we shouldn't have any trouble. The Colonel says it's going to be a cushy drop!'

The fact that we had one less enemy airfield to tackle encouraged us a lot.

Just as he finished speaking our engines opened up full throttle, and the plane shuddered and rattled, straining at the chocks. Then we moved forward slowly, bumping unsteadily on the uneven ground. We reached the runway and slewed round into the wind with starboard engine screaming. Suddenly we leapt forward, the tail came up, and we hovered uncertainly between heaven and earth, trying to rise but then sinking back to the tarmac. We were heavily loaded and would need a long run. All at once we bounded off the ground, the runway slid away beneath our wings and was left finally behind our tail – a black ribbon on the red Algerian landscape.

4

The Oudna Saga

29 *November*–3 *December* 1942

I
THE PARACHUTE LANDING AT DEPIENNE

The crew compartment door opened, and all the bodies sprawled in the seats shook themselves awake and began to fidget with their jumping equipment. The crew chief entered wearing steel helmet and rip-cord parachute and worked his way carefully aft over the static lines.

'We've crossed the frontier, men!' he said. 'Twenty minutes to go! Those of you who aren't hooked-up had better get ready. We may run into trouble from a bunch of Krauts any minute now!'

I came to with a start. The crew chief's words suddenly focused the full reality of our position on a brain which had been eager to forget it, and I felt horribly sick for the first time during the flight. In some embarrassment I called hastily for the bucket and parted company with the early breakfast I had eaten at Maison Carrée, nine hours before. I felt better immediately, but at the same time most annoyed that I should now have to fight on an empty stomach.

The flight had been most bumpy during the whole of the past two-and-a-half hours, but my mind had been so absorbed in the landscape that I had hardly noticed the airpockets, the yawing, the upcurrents rocking the wings, and the plane slewing, trying desperately to maintain our packed formation. Many of the men, however, had suffered misery from air-sickness.

Soon after taking off we had begun to climb, exchanging the rolling farmland of the coastal belt for the wild uplands which mark the foothills of the Atlas round Bouira. Algiers faded behind the mist hanging like muslin over the bay, and all at once we were above a tangled wilderness of rock and thorn, too uninviting for even the Arabs to attempt to till. The country grew wilder as we flew on, until, gradually losing the last traces of vegetation, it became a desolate world of saw-tooth ridges and scar-like ravines, hills, valleys, peaks and spurs, all heaped together in a chaos of earth and rock.

We stole in on the mountains, so that I was unaware of their presence until we were right amongst them. The lumps of rock grew bigger, more wild and fierce, and heaved themselves hungrily at our wings as we passed. Then a sandstone giant appeared beside us, reached out a jagged spur to knock us out of the sky, and turned his back on us as we flew on. After that the mountains were on every side, rearing terrible peaks high above the formation. Conscious of our own insignificance, we threaded our way carefully through their midst, following a natural pass.

This sight was so awe-inspiring that it baffles description. It was gigantic, terrible, wonderful and savage, all together – at times I felt as though we were trespassing upon nature. Huge buzzards wheeled and volplaned round the peaks, angry and defiant that their long solitude had been disturbed by a flock of winged creatures so much larger than themselves. They screamed their disapproval, but no one heard. The mountains bared their sandstone teeth and promised us a rocky grave at the bottom of a thousand-foot abyss if we dared go too close.

There was something so fascinating about the fierceness of their beauty that one felt lonely and frustrated when we flew out on the other side of the range on to low foothills and then rolling country covered with olive groves. The pygmy world of primitive cultivation below us, sandy cart-tracks, haphazard clusters of crude Arab dwellings, all appeared so futile and worthless beside the immortal mountains. My mind was still trying to retain something of their grandeur, even though it was now invaded by man's squalor. Then, to complete the transition from dreams to reality, there was the crew chief picking his way down the fuselage, shouting above the roar of engines that battle lay ahead, only twenty minutes away.

We took some little time to get each other hooked up. My next-door neighbour passed me the end of my static line over my right shoulder. I gave it a tug and pulled about six feet out of the parachute pack. I was unusually clumsy all of a sudden and had difficulty in fastening the safety-pin which secured the snap-hook.

Measures came round and checked our equipment.

'You all right?' he enquired, bending over me. I fingered my quick-release box, checked the snap-hook and strop and nodded in reply.

'How do you feel?' I asked him.

'OK so far! I'll feel a lot happier when it's all over! Look! There go the Spitfires! Whew! What a superb sight!'

I looked out of my foot-square perspex window and saw three dark furies rushing over the surface of the plain. They banked as one and rose silently to meet us, fast as shooting stars.

'Five minutes to go! Stand up!' Measures shouted.

We clambered awkwardly to our feet, fidgeted with our length of hanging static line, then crowded up in line behind number one who crouched in the doorway. We clung to the sides of the fuselage – the plane was bucking all over the sky in trying to keep formation – and waited for the red warning light. Everyone was silent, and there was an electric tension in the air. The seconds went by slowly. Then the red winked on and shone like an evil eye.

A few seconds later, number one had plunged out, and his static line cracked against the rear edge of the door. The line surged towards the tail and melted before the square of sunlight. Almost before I knew what had happened I was scrambling for the aperture and lunged outwards into space.

I stood up, slipped out of my parachute harness and jumping-jacket, then clipped a thirty-round magazine on to my Sten machine-carbine.

Everywhere other figures were getting to their feet and moving across the dropping zone. The last flight of three aircraft came over and dropped their bouquet of coloured parachutes, followed by the train of men. The canopies sank earthwards gently in the hot afternoon and joined the harvest of mottled parachutes already abandoned on the ground.

We had landed in a field of hard plough divided by a muddy stream. About three hundred yards away lay a large Arab farm surrounded by a high cactus hedge, and a dusty road, marked by a row of telegraph poles, ran north and south.

We were in the middle of a plain of sun-scorched earth, broken only by cactus hedges and clumps of camel-thorn. All around the open country there ran a wall of rocky hills, rising steadily in a jumbled mass. In the south-east towered a massive needle of sandstone, the Djebel Zaghouan, the highest mountain in Tunisia – over seven

thousand feet. After the warmth of colour and rich
fertility of Algeria, this frizzled landscape looked a desert. ¢

Clarkson joined me a moment later, and we hurried off
to look for our container. We found it at last among the
reeds, lying half under water in the stream. Two or three
men with containers in a similar plight came and gave us
a hand, and we dragged it to dry land by the rigging-lines.
The contents were fairly dry, thanks to their protective
coverings.

'C' Company headquarters and rendezvous was marked
by a white star on a large red sheet. The wireless section
was installed in a ditch beneath a cactus hedge and was
reporting to battalion headquarters. Most of the infantry
had already arrived, and the platoons had taken up
defensive positions around the farm.

The rest of my section came along in a moment. Two
of my men were missing, together with half a platoon of
'C' Company, with whom they had been. We heard that
their plane had become bogged down in the mud at
Maison Blanche and had been unable to take off. My
wireless set had been smashed in the drop, and our
trolley, too, was in bits, as its parachute had failed to
open.

The battalion had suffered about fifteen to twenty
injuries, mostly 'concussions' and sprained ankles and
wrists, from heavy landings in gullies and plough. But
there had been one fatal accident, due, in parachuting
jargon, to a 'roman candle'. One of David's sappers had
been killed by rigging-lines getting thrown over the
canopy, causing it to stream out like a wind-sock, too
hopelessly entangled to develop.

The landing-ground was not occupied by the enemy. In
fact, there was little evidence that the airfield had ever

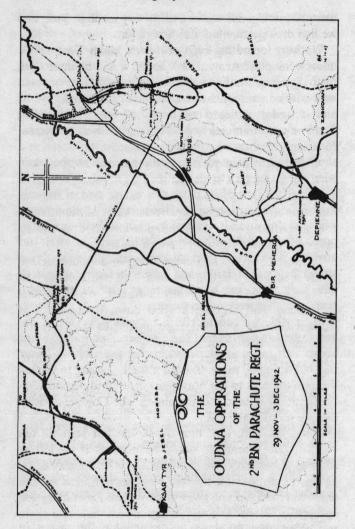

existed. Intelligence seemed to be very much at fault, and we had drawn a blank at our first covert.

We were operating on Greenwich Mean Time – two hours behind 1st Army time – and it would be quite dark by four o'clock. In the two hours of daylight that remained we collected our parachutes and containers into the barns, and foraging parties went round all the neighbouring farms to procure mules and carts for our march to Oudna. Meanwhile our padre, Murdo Macdonald, officiated at a short burial service of our dead comrade at the place where he had fallen to his death.

We left our dropping casualties in the care of friendly French farmers in Depienne. Buchanan of 'C' Company – whose half-platoon it was that had not arrived – stayed to protect the injured with the rest of his men, to await our advance-guard from Pont-du-Fahs. But the next day a strong column of tanks and lorried infantry appeared, and, after a hopeless battle lasting an hour, all those who remained alive were taken prisoner.

Meanwhile we had received a report from one of our armoured car patrols that the Germans had a road-block about four miles up the road in the direction of Tunis. But our 1:50,000 maps showed a track leading to Oudna through the hills to the north-east of us, and, in consultation with the company commanders, the Colonel decided that we should take this.

It was decided, too, that we should not start till ten o'clock. Our intentions would be obvious if we left as soon as it was dark; we should stand a better chance by giving the impression that we were staying here for the night and then slipping away quietly when the countryside had settled down. The men could have a meal and some rest before the next phase, for they were now very tired after their long day and the strain of the jump.

The temperature dropped suddenly after sun-down. We were, of course, only lightly clad under our smocks and were thankful for the parachutes we had salvaged during the afternoon. We wrapped ourselves in the heaps of silk, to snatch what was to be the last real sleep for four days and nights.

When we moved out of cover shortly before ten and formed up on the road facing north, a wonderful array of Arab carts, donkeys and mules had been added to our cavalcade; and on to these we bundled our heavy explosive and incendiary packs, our mortars, anti-tank rifles and wireless sets. Major Ross, OC 'C' Company, gathered all his officers together and pointed out our route on the map with the aid of a shielded torch. I totted up the kilometres and reckoned the distance to be about eighteen miles.

The column moved off. We marched in silence, and except for the occasional jingling of harness and creak of carts there was nothing audible save the dull murmur of a thousand padding feet.

Soon we turned off up a broad and well-trodden track, and the column straggled out into single file. Our numbers quickly faded with the background, and it now seemed that I was alone with two or three companions among the rocks and scrub. Occasionally, there would be the rustle of clothing close at hand and the slither of feet as though the hills were peopled with ghosts.

The moon came up about midnight, and we could see the tail of our column winding like a snake far below, whilst above us the advance-guards had just topped the ridge and were moving like flies across the skyline. In the silvery half-light there appeared to be no end to our force.

The moon did not help us much, for the track rapidly got worse and sometimes petered out altogether. Marching became impossible over the layers of rock and stone, and the men swore, floundering and slipping at every step. Animals heaved and grunted as they dragged the creaking carts over boulders and scrub. Often they would be jerked to a stop, as wheels jammed in a crevice or stuck on a rock ledge, and the carts would have to be man-handled forward to an accompaniment of shouts and curses. The work became heavier as the hours went by and the track deteriorated further. Every cart had to be hauled up the steep hills, and this added to the exhaustion which had already laid its hold on the battalion. When a halt was called we lay face downwards in the heather and sobbed for breath, until the night air dried our sweat and chilled our bodies, and we were glad to be on the move again. When the track disappeared we plunged straight through the undergrowth in front of us, too tired to look for a better way. Progress was intolerably slow, and sometimes it seemed as though we floundered in a quicksand, getting nowhere but merely sapping our strength. The hills were bewitched that night.

By four o'clock in the morning when the moon was beginning to wane, we estimated that we had come ten miles; neither men nor animals were in any condition to go further. We had put the worst of our march behind us, so the Colonel called a halt until dawn. We dragged the carts off the track into the undergrowth and lay down on the cold earth, falling asleep immediately.

II
THE BATTLE FOR OUDNA AIRFIELD

We awoke just before dawn, chilled to the marrow, limbs aching and eyes smarting with fatigue. Gradually, however, as the first streaks of day appeared, our circulation returned. We stamped about the hillside to ease our cramped muscles.

The horizon was now ablaze with a lurid wash of orange streaked with fire, and fierce crimson fingers splayed over the eastern sky.

'Talk about shepherd's warning!' I heard someone exclaim as he sat up and rubbed his eyes.

Just at that moment we heard a low moan in the air, which grew louder as a plane approached rapidly from the north.

'Get down, everybody, and don't look up,' I heard the Colonel shouting. 'Don't show anything light!'

We turned over on our faces and lay still in the heather where our camouflaged smocks blended with the scrub. A fast German light-bomber roared low over the crest of the hill with a snarl of powerful engines. Only when the hum had died away again in the distance did we dare come out of cover. We tried to hope that our presence had not been noticed.

We had a hasty and unappetizing cold breakfast of dry biscuits and chocolate and then re-harnessed our pack-animals. Even though they were unhobbled, our mules and donkeys had been too exhausted to move away from the carts, but dozed dejectedly with their heads hung low. We pushed them awake, induced them back into the shafts and hauled the carts back on to the track. The column assembled and set off briskly.

The route now lay along the crest of a long ridge which ran north-east towards Oudna, and the agonizing climbing of the previous night was past. The surface improved, too, as we went along, and when the sun came up we forgot our troubles and believed that the worst of our mission was over.

As if in confirmation, we were suddenly greeted with a sight which set our spirits soaring. The plain lay before us, and there in the distance not more than ten or twelve miles away lay Tunis, a radiant city of dazzling white in the early morning sun. The dawn mist hung over the coast, hazing the coarser outline of the suburbs and only revealing the graceful domes and more prominent buildings against the deep blue of the lake and bay. The general effect was mystic and exhilarating; it was like a new discovery. To us Tunis appeared like the goal of our ambition, our symbol of victory. The men laughed and joked, a very different atmosphere from the misery of the night before. There could have been no finer tonic at a more opportune moment.

As the sun rose higher we came upon a primitive settlement of Arab farms and olive groves, and here we rounded up further mules and carts to supplement our baggage train. Then the track began to slope downwards, and we knew that we were nearing our objective. At eleven, we calculated from our maps that we were within three miles of Oudna Station; and, on coming to a large Arab well – marked Prise d'Eau – in a hollow surrounded by a rim of hills which afforded a good laager and defensive position, the Colonel decided to halt for an hour before beginning the attack in the afternoon. Contrary to our original plan of a night attack, the assault on the airfield would now have to be carried out with the least delay, for we did not trust the Arabs and knew that the enemy plane could not have failed to observe our vehicles. We flopped down in the gullies out of the sun, had a little food and a brew of tea, and then a short but deep sleep in the pleasantly warm air.

I was awakened a little later to go to 'C' Company Headquarters, where Major Ross gave us our orders. The Colonel had been up to the top of the hill on our left, and had identified the airfield just to the north of Oudna Station. 'A' Company was to attack on the right, down the valley, and we were going down the spur on the left. 'B' Company was in reserve with Battalion Headquarters.

'The airfield looks very disappointing,' Major Ross said. 'Not a sign of life on it at the moment. There are four erections on the southern side which might be emergency hangars, and there also appears to be one aircraft crashed on the edge of the field. Well, you'll just have to do the best you can. Smash up everything you can find!'

We sat and chatted for a few minutes, then went off to rejoin our men.

'C' Company formed up and set off down the track to the starting positions. The other companies watched us as we passed through their ranks, and shouted pleasantries after our heavily loaded men. We passed Tony's section sitting beside the track with 'B' Company Headquarters, and a little farther on there were David and his men among the carts and wireless aerials which marked Battalion HQ. The fourth section of the troop was out in front with 'A' Company. The sappers laughed and joked as we went by, and everyone seemed to be in holiday mood.

'C' Company moved round the back of the spur and began to climb the low ridge of hills with the two leading platoons spread out in open order. As we gained the top we looked right down into the plain stretching away towards Tunis. In the middle distance ran the white strip of the main Pont-du-Fahs–Tunis road until it was lost amongst the white houses and cluster of farmsteads marking the village of Oudna. Behind the railway line lay a flat open space, and beyond that a line of Roman ruins, presumably an aqueduct which had once carried water from the hills to Carthage on the bay.

We moved slowly down the spur into a fold, and then up the other side on to another small hill crowned by a few olive trees and a dilapidated Arab farm. From this position we could watch the other forward Company working like ants round the base of the spur in the valley to the right. Meanwhile our own two platoons had reached the far end of the ridge and were moving rapidly towards a group of large farm buildings at the bottom.

All at once the drowsiness of the afternoon was shattered by a crash, followed by five others in quick succession. Six little puffs of smoke had appeared among the extended ranks of 'A' Company, and now two shadows lay huddled on the ground.

'Damn! Now the cat's out of the bag!' shouted John Measures with whom I was walking at that moment. 'Did you see that mortar? . . .' He was already scanning the farm buildings and cactus hedges with his binoculars. 'I've got it!' he exclaimed. 'See that small olive grove beside the big farm? Nine o'clock from that is a cactus hedge – you'll see the cone of smoke go up if he fires again!'

He sent a message over his wireless set to warn Ken Morrison and Henry Cecil, the forward platoon commanders.

Meanwhile 'A' Company had moved on and had gained the broken country near a large white building. The platoons rushed the last forty or fifty yards under cover of their own Bren guns and drove the Germans northwards. The hidden mortar did not fire again.

Our attention was now attracted by a white cloud of dust coming down the main road from the direction of Tunis. This finally materialized into a German 8-wheeled armoured car, and we watched it turn and drive towards us. It swung off the road to the left, bumped a few yards over the plough and stopped behind a small embankment in a hull-down position. We could just see its squat turret peeping over the top.

Suddenly there was a flash, and a 75-mm shell came screaming over, to land with a crash and a pall of black smoke a hundred yards away. It then scattered shells in quick succession over the ridge, but with little effect, and drove off again at high speed.

By this time the forward platoons of 'A' Company had cleared Oudna Station, and 'C' Company had reached the south-western edge of the airfield. The four large objects which we had imagined to be hangars were straw-stacks. Except for a crashed Ju 87 lying forlornly by itself, the landing-ground was empty.

But our men had no time for disappointment. No sooner had they left cover on the southern side of the field than a veritable blizzard of machine-guns opened up from the far side, completely drowning our own ineffectual reply. Red, blue and white tracer zipped through the cactus and whined off the rocks. In the lull which followed we could hear the unmistakable clatter of tracked vehicles manoeuvring for position. Unknown to us the enemy had concentrated a force of three tanks and four more armoured cars in ambush, and these now had the two forward companies practically at their mercy.

One of the platoons of 'C' Company attempted, with

the greatest bravery, to engage the tanks at close range. About ten men and their commander, Ken Morrison, advanced stealthily through the broken ground on the west of the airfield and succeeded in getting close enough to one of them to engage it with anti-tank grenades. Very few of them got away again.

The Colonel now gave the order for the battalion to withdraw to Prise d'Eau, the hill position we had vacated at lunch time, as we could not withstand a tank attack here. 'A' Company and the remains of 'C' were successfully extricated from the area of the landing-ground, and the German tank commander made no attempt to follow up his advantage.

Enemy aircraft were our chief source of worry during the withdrawal. As we retired from Oudna Station four Stukas with fighter escort flew over from the west and looked as though they were about to land. The leader peeled off and began his circuit of the airfield. But the ground staff put up such a barrage of warning Very lights that the planes sheered off in the direction of Tunis. The leader dropped an answering flare which burst near the ground in a cascade of red balls.

Two of the fighter escort saw their wards out of the danger area and then came streaking back at us. A winking light in the propeller boss of the leader heralded a stream of cannon shells which swept our spur from end to end. The second, following close on the other's tail, raced down in a steep dive and let fly at the Arab hovel in which we were sheltering. For one awful moment the stones seemed to explode, the wall crumbled, and the thatch caught fire – then the hurricane had passed as quickly as it came. The planes wheeled away in a climbing turn and came back at us again and again with cannon and machine-guns blazing. We could make no reply, as our Bren gun ammunition was too precious to waste. Instead, we relied upon our camouflaged smocks and veils to hide us as we withdrew; and although the aircraft blasted the ridge along its whole length, giving us some excessively unpleasant moments, we had no casualties during the move back to the hills.

The dusk was now gathering fast, and this evidently decided the German tank commander against pursuit. Under the cloak of darkness the battalion reformed slowly at the foot of the hills, and the casualties were collected in what remained of the mule carts. The enemy planes had caught part of the baggage train beneath the spur; and many wagons and mules had been blown to bits or scattered by the cannon shells, including ours with the section's packs containing the rest of our food.

The wounded arrived in a pitiful trickle and were directed up the pass to an Arab farm, where the surgical team of the 16th Parachute Field Ambulance had established their dressing-station. While searching – in vain – for our cart, I came across the convoy of makeshift ambulances jolting up the uneven track. It made a gruesome scene – the tumbrils swaying and pitching behind grunting mules; the unnatural postures of the wounded sprawling helplessly in a heap of bodies, arms and legs; the heart-rending sight of hopelessness written on every face. Both we and they knew that the war was over for them; if we ever succeeded in getting back to our own lines it would be impossible to move the more badly wounded men.

Padre Murdo Macdonald was in charge of the collection of wounded, and was leading one of the mules.

'How are things going, Padre?' I asked him as I passed.

'Not too good, I am afraid.' He spoke in a hushed

voice. 'Not too good! There is so little we can do to help these brave lads.'

'Are any badly hurt? Is there anything I can do?'

'No, old man! Mac will do what he can up at the dressing-station. There're two men very badly wounded. And there's nothing we can do about it except give them morphia and make them as comfortable as possible.'

In the small Arab farm which passed as a dressing-station the surgeon and his half-team toiled under very difficult conditions. The second surgeon and the remainder of the medical orderlies had been in an aircraft which had had to return to Algiers with engine trouble, and the greater part of the theatre equipment had gone back, too, slung in the bomb-racks beneath the plane. So MacGavin and his men had to improvise with what they had got, operating on a makeshift table by the light of pocket torches. The Padre held the tray of instruments and totted up the swabs. Those men performed a wonder beyond all praise that night. They gave us confidence for one thing – a man always fights best when assured of good medical treatment on being wounded, and we had a very high regard for our Parachute Field Ambulance.

As we were moving into our new positions I looked back down the pass towards Oudna, the graveyard of our hopes. A fire was burning fiercely on the edge of the airfield with leaping tongues of flame and a red glow. Every now and again the conflagration would swell, and fountains of exploding cannon and tracer shells would go up in twinkling festoons. An enemy ammunition store must have caught fire during the battle. It was too far away for us to hear the noise; we could only judge from the puffs of flame which blazed up intermittently like an incandescent light.

III
THE BATTLES OF SIDI BOU HADJEBA

The companies spent most of the night digging-in with entrenching tools and then camouflaging the holes with undergrowth to offset their lack of depth. The ground was a mass of roots and rock, and, after breaking a couple of entrenching-tool helves, we had to content ourselves with the cover of a beggarly two or three feet. We settled down in the bottom of our pits for an hour's rest at about four o'clock in the morning; by this time we were all dead tired and feeling the strain. But it proved almost impossible to sleep owing to the cold, and at the first signs of daylight we crawled out of our holes, feeling utterly miserable. For a moment we were too stiff to move and sat huddled on the rocks while our teeth rattled uncontrollably.

David found us in this state a few minutes later. He was making a round of the sections before it was fully light.

'I've brought you a couple of tins of bully,' he said. 'My section heard that your chaps had not got any breakfast, and so pooled their rations and asked me to give you these. And Tony's section sent this bag of biscuits.'

We were more than grateful. Apart from a small loaf of bread between the eight of us the night before, we had not eaten for eighteen hours, and food was the thing we needed at this moment more than anything else.

L/Cpl Dory divided one tin into eight slices with his jack-knife, and we swallowed them down ravenously with a handful of biscuits each. The rest of the other tin of bully I ordered them to keep.

While we were eating, David continued: 'The first job

is to send two men to fill your section's water-bottles from the big well down the track. Each company is sending a watering-party before it gets too light.'

After the men had gone, David enlarged upon the plan. 'We stay here for the present,' he said, 'as local information suggests the enemy may be withdrawing on Tunis. The Colonel thinks we should be able to hold this pass until tonight, for it is a naturally strong position. "B" Company are holding this big hill on the left; "A" Company and Battalion Headquarters are on the heights to the east of the track. "C" Company are protecting the rear of the position from this ridge here.'

'Do you think the enemy will come after us and try and dig us out?' I asked.

'The Colonel thinks he may send up some lorried infantry; and then there are those tanks and armoured cars down at Oudna. The plan is to wipe out their armour in an ambush if they come up the pass. We've laid some mines across the top to prevent the tanks getting out, and Tony and his section will bottle them up at the bottom!'

'Sounds a bit tricky!'

'They've got a very good site – a deep gully on one side of the track and a steep cliff on the other. They let all the tanks go through, then pull the mines across on a necklace behind the last one. They've got anti-tank rifles posted farther up, and men hidden in the gullies with Gammon bombs.'

The news over the battalion wireless was not so encouraging. The Signal section had put up their twin-masted aerial and long-range set in a hollow between two peaks of the hill opposite my position and had been in contact with Brigade Headquarters at Algiers. Early that morning they received the uncomfortable news that our Armour had been delayed in its push eastwards. Colonel Frost received instructions to fight a delaying action throughout the day, then to rejoin our main forces the following night. Everything depended upon our being able to hold our own in the hills, until darkness gave us the cover to get away.

The Germans began to probe our positions soon after sun-up, at eight o'clock. Look-outs on 'B' Company hill reported a long cloud of dust coming up the track from Oudna, and soon enemy armoured fighting vehicles were identified. The Colonel and his Headquarters Staff were standing in a little group in the vantage point of the hollow, watching the approach of the German force through their binoculars. There appeared to be a couple of heavy armoured cars leading the way, three big tanks following, and then two lorries towing light guns bringing up the rear. The Colonel followed them up the track with satisfaction – at their present rate of progress they would run right into our ambush within a minute or two.

Everyone had forgotten the watering-party down at the well, a slip which upset all our calculations. The leading armoured car spotted the men hiding in the gullies when it was about level with the well and pulled up hurriedly. Someone threw a Gammon anti-tank grenade at it, but missed, and the enemy vehicle withdrew in some confusion to the protection of the heavier tanks. These quickly took in the situation, closed their visors and depressed their guns. The first shot blew the well to bits, but the watering-party succeeded in getting away under cover of gullies and broken country without loss.

Any chance that we might have had of ambushing the column had now flown. The tanks and lorries immediately deployed to hull-down positions and opened fire haphazardly with a rain of explosive bullets and their heavy guns at the face of the pass. They were well out of range of our limited anti-tank weapons, so there was nothing that we could do. But our camouflage proved effective, and we suffered little material damage.

'Mortars!' shouted the Colonel. 'Sergeant Godfrey! Bring your mortar section up here as quickly as you can! All your guns and ammunition! We'll give them something to think about!'

The mortar section struggled up the hill under their heavy loads and got into action. They bracketed the range nicely on the third shot and opened rapid fire. The tanks scattered like a flock of frightened hens in every direction, churning the sandy soil into powder and sending up clouds of white dust as they pivoted on their tracks. Then they withdrew and left us in peace for a little while.

Twenty minutes later another column of armoured vehicles was reported on the track behind us. They advanced slowly round the winding hill road until they were about two hundred yards from our nearest position.

'You know, I believe they are some of ours!' I heard Major Ross talking to his second in command. 'Look, they've all got yellow recognition triangles! The tanks have got them flying from their wireless aerials, and the cars are plastered with them – on their bonnets, on the sides, and on the turrets as well! Funny! I don't recognize the type! They may be American Staghounds and Honeys – difficult to tell at this angle!'

One man in the section nearest to them seemed to be satisfied with their identity and got out of his hole waving his own Celanese triangle furiously. A moment later he was joined by a second man, and together they set off down the slope to meet the friendly armour. The arrival of Allied tanks at Oudna put a very different complexion on the situation.

My section position was in a slight dip, so I was unable

to see exactly what happened. But two minutes later one of the two men came running back towards Company Headquarters, flushed and very out of breath. When he was about thirty yards away he stopped, gulped for air once or twice, then shouted across to us:

'They aren't our tanks at all, sir! They're Jerries! The officer sent me back to tell you to surrender or else he will wipe the lot of us out!' We now guessed, by their yellow triangles, what had happened to Buchanan at Depienne!

The tank commander had kept the second man as a token of good faith. Meanwhile, the column had advanced another two hundred yards and had overrun the farthest section covering our rear.

'Open fire!' shouted Major Ross. 'Tell that forward platoon to open fire!'

A Bren gun suddenly broke the hypnotic effect of the enemy's trick, and then every weapon blazed away. This proved a little too hot for the thin-skinned armoured cars, which backed down the track a little way.

Both tank forces now opened up a barrage from either end of the pass, but made no attempt to come in close. They spotted the twin masts of the battalion wireless set, and 20-mm explosive shells plastered the top of the headquarters' hollow, where the aerial was pulled down hurriedly. Then one of the heavier tanks, from the north end, started with its 75 and made the air hum with fragments. Tracer flickered all over the track and up and down the sides of the hill above our heads, forcing us down into our pits. The dry heather caught fire in one or two places, and black smoke drifted across.

After enduring this for about twenty minutes without being able to make any effective reply, the Colonel decided to withdraw from this trap while we could. If

lorried infantry came up to support the two tank forces
we should be in a hopeless situation. So orders were given
for 'C' Company to withdraw first and take up position
behind the hill to our left rear, where we should be out of
the fire of the tanks. 'B' Company would follow, with 'A'
Company acting as rear-guard. After a little while the
enemy fire eased and gave us the respite we desired for
the move. 'C' Company slipped away with a few machine-
gun bursts over our heads as a parting present, and the
others disengaged themselves without any trouble at all.
Both tank commanders remained very cautious and made
no attempt to interfere.

There were two unhappy circumstances connected with
this withdrawal. The first was that all our wounded of the
previous day's battle were left in enemy hands, together
with the Field Ambulance surgical team and the Padre.
The force of armour coming up the track from the south
overran the farm and made them all prisoners before they
could be evacuated to a safer place. The second was the
destruction of all our heavy equipment. Our wireless sets
were now dead, our mortars were out of ammunition, and
the men were already too exhausted to carry anything for
which we had no immediate use. We made a big pyre of
them in a gully and blew up the lot with the remainder of
our explosive and incendiary bombs.

We then fell back southwards from the pass, keeping
out of sight of the main track by withdrawing along a goat
path winding through the hills. We struggled along in
single file, with a point company out in front and a couple
of screening platoons on high ground to the flanks. We
descended slowly into a valley, across a deep gully, then
began to climb the almost precipitous face of the hill in
front of us. We scrambled up the rocks on our hands and
knees and eventually fell gasping and sweating on the top.

The rest of the battalion was taking up new positions, and the remnants of 'C' Company were getting their breath before moving on. This feature formed a bastion of three high peaks dominating all the surrounding valleys, and it was here that we were to make our stand until nightfall. On my large-scale map the place was shown as Sidi Bou Hadjeba, the name given to a small well two hundred yards farther on.

Each company took up a defensive position on one of the three peaks – 'A' moving on to the height to the south, 'B' on a great domed hill overlooking the plain to the west, and 'C' and my section on the crown of the massive bluff up which we had just struggled. Battalion Headquarters and the First Aid Post, now tended only by the MO, Captain Gordon, and a handful of stretcher-bearers, were in the hollow between the three peaks. When these dispositions were complete we had a rest. By this time the sun was well up, and everyone was quite exhausted, suffering acutely from heat, strain and lack of sleep. We scratched ourselves little holes in the ground with entrenching tools and lay and dozed in the heather with weapons close at hand.

I was roused at about one o'clock in the afternoon, after half an hour's sleep, by somebody shaking me violently by the shoulder.

'Wake up, sir! Wake up!' he said hurriedly. 'We're standing to! Look-outs report German infantry debussing from a dozen lorries on the main track half a mile to the north! They've got tanks up there too, sir!'

'OK. Watch your front!' I shouted to the rest of my section, who were now fully awake. After the glorious peace of sleep the thought of battle filled me with dread. We crawled forward into our allotted fire positions and waited for things to happen. We were on the extreme northern end of the bluff just back from the crest, covering the flank of 'C' Company and the track along which we had withdrawn.

We judged that the German force totalled about four hundred men, approximately our own strength, after our casualties from previous battles. But whereas we were nearly exhausted, the ememy was fresh and had the added fire-power of his tanks. The German armour, finding the pass unoccupied, had come up in strength on to the track opposite our positions and was now manoeuvring into suitable fire positions.

For the first phase of the battle the Germans occupied all the high ground around Sidi Bou Hadjeba, on to which they dragged their heavy machine-guns, mortars and an apparently limitless supply of ammunition. Having settled themselves in they opened a concentrated cross-fire which swept the crests of our hills from end to end. The bullets crackled shrilly above our heads and sighed with an unpleasant swish, swish, through the heather, terrifyingly close. One drew back instinctively, but as they were falling everywhere, kicking up spurts of dust, we could only wriggle a little deeper into our furrows and pray for the best. We could not spare ammunition for ineffectual reply.

More and more guns were brought into action, until there was a continuous roar, and the air one stream of tracer; ugly ricochets whined off the rocks and flew screaming away over the hills. A man a few yards to our right was hit in the thigh. He lay still for a moment, bewildered by the sudden paralysis of his legs, then hoisted himself on to his elbows and dragged himself gasping and sobbing down the hill. At last he lay across the slope and rolled over and over, until stretcher-bearers found him and he was pulled to safety. Another was hit in the side and lay moaning quietly to himself. Clarkson and I crawled over and lay beside him to bandage his wound. We turned him over and cut away his smock with my fighting knife, then saw that he was dead.

Owing to the incessant hail of bullets it was impossible to look around and see how the struggle was progressing. We could only gauge its ferocity by the hurricane which howled above our heads, churning up the ground on either side and scarring the rocks with weals of white. We were taking severe punishment; four men out of about a dozen near me were either killed or wounded. Sapper Mallam got machine-gun bullets through both legs and smiled ruefully as though apologizing for being hit. While his wounds were still numb Jones and Gregory, on their stomachs, grabbed him by the arms and hauled him down the hill. The fear of death fell like a shadow on us all, dulling every emotion except an overwhelming desire to live.

The enemy attacked at about three o'clock, advancing behind their tanks from the track to the east. Our own Bren guns suddenly burst into life, and I heard the heavy cracks of the anti-tank rifles firing away to our right. I was told afterwards that one of these gunners accounted for two light tanks, handling his weapon with the greatest bravery and crawling to a new position after each shot to confuse the tank commander. But they got him in the end.

'Watch out!' a man shouted from the crest of the hill on the right. 'Tank coming through on the left! He's coming up the hill!'

'Stand your ground!' Major Ross bellowed, and came scrambling across the slope like an ape. 'Gammon bombs! We'll give him hell! Come on!'

As I heard the deep roar of the tank on the hill below

us, I primed my anti-tank grenade with feverish fingers, suddenly very much afraid.

In another moment a squat turret appeared over the crest and opened fire blindly with its machine-gun. But the tracer flew harmlessly yards above our heads, as we were on the reverse slope well below the crown. A second later we hurled our Gammon bombs in a shower.

The tank disappeared behind a thick cloud of black smoke and blinding thunder-claps. The machine-gun stopped suddenly, and the monster halted as though bewildered.

'Come on!' yelled John Ross. 'Give him another dose! Close in and finish him off!'

A groping hand came out of the turret of the tank and clutched around wildly for the anti-aircraft machine-gun mounted on top.

Having nothing more effective to throw I pulled a hand-grenade out of my smock pocket and yanked at the pin. I must have let the lever go in my excitement, for to my horror I saw the thing fizzing in my hand, eating up a four-second fuse. I flung it from me wildly and ducked back for cover. By the greatest of luck it went in the right direction and burst directly above the open turret. The hand sank out of sight, like a wilting flower.

'Oh, good shot!' shouted Ross, feeling the tank in his power.

Again the tank erupted under another shower of bombs. That was the end of it, and it ran backwards down the hill under its own weight, leaving a broken track like a cast-off scale.

After the failure of the tank attack the machine-gun barrage came down again, supplemented now by intermittent mortar fire. I saw a section of 'A' Company crawl forward on the farthest hill to repulse an attack. An officer or NCO led them on bravely, and the German infantry went down under their fire. Suddenly the little group disappeared behind three puffs of black smoke. One man staggered back, the others lay still. All around us this drain of dead and wounded went on, and it was becoming a race with darkness as to whether we should be overwhelmed before the sun went down.

The enemy made further attempts, covered by their tanks, to move forward against our positions. Once, a big tank and a body of infantry came round a spur, five hundred yards to our north. Jones opened up with our Bren gun, and the tracer bullets ricocheted off the armour plate amongst the infantry on either side. The Germans ran back for the cover of a gully, and the tank turned round and lumbered off hurriedly.

But in the end Providence came to our aid in an amazing way. Towards nightfall when the battle was at its height, two bomb-carrying Messerschmitt fighters appeared and flew low round our positions. We realized that this was to be the coup de grâce.

The pilots picked their targets and dived; we shrank breathless into our furrows. Seconds passed, and then came the sickening crash of the bombs. But we still lived. We raised our heads in fear, to see the planes wheeling away and the track and pass blotted out with smoke and dust. Then, to our astonishment, the planes returned again and again to strafe *their own* concentrations of tanks and infantry, completely ignoring the galaxy of light signals which seemed to beg them to stop. At once the enemy fire slackened and gradually died away.

The obvious explanation of this strange stroke of fortune only occurred to me long afterwards. Many of the German tanks were still displaying our yellow recognition triangles, for they could have had no opportunity of removing them during the battle, and these would have provided the most damning 'identification' from the air.

Soon it started to get dark. As dusk fell all firing ceased, leaving a pregnant stillness over the hills. A runner crawled painfully across to my position and slid down to where I was lying.

'Is that Mr Terrick?' he enquired. 'Major Ross wants to see you, sir. Is there anyone else farther over?'

I found myself replying in a whisper, as though awed by the silence. The guide led the way, and I followed on my hands and knees for about fifty yards.

Major Ross was sitting with a knot of about ten men just below the crest of the hill. Their eyes were bloodshot and stared horribly out of faces streaked with grime; all seemed too tired to speak and sat leaning forward with heads resting in their hands, dozing warily as though mistrusting the lull.

'Hullo!' he said, looking up. 'Glad to see you're still OK! I brought you over to tell you that we are going to withdraw in a moment. The signal will be two long notes on the Colonel's hunting-horn – the "Gone Away!" As soon as you hear that, collect as many men as you can see and get out quick. Meet me in the hollow between the three hills. I'll wait a minute or two for you, but don't be any longer because I don't want to hang around here after dark!'

'What happens then, sir? Where am I to make for if I miss you?'

'The Colonel thinks we had better go to Massicault as planned; it's only twenty miles or so. We must get there tonight! Each company is going off independently. Small bodies of men may be able to slip through, whereas the whole force together would attract too much attention.'

I looked around at the remains of 'C' Company, a

gallant little band of ten men and Major Ross. They were all that were left of 'The Jocks'. All the other officers, except Buchanan at Depienne, were dead.

I felt suddenly very overcome by the catastrophe of the Battles of Sidi Bou Hadjeba and crawled back to my section with a heart almost too heavy to speak.

Darkness engulfed us quickly, and a night breeze rustled the heather. Suddenly the notes of the hunting-horn rang out in the silence.

'Come on!' I whispered hoarsely. We scrambled to our feet and slithered as fast as we dared in the failing light down the hill to our rendezvous with 'C' Company.

We arrived at the bottom and looked around, but found nobody. Major Ross and his party seemed to have vanished. Then we saw some figures moving; we watched them carefully, wondering whether they were friend or foe. More arrived, and we heard a word of command in English; Major Ashford and about sixty men of 'A' Company were forming up in a hollow.

'You had better come along with me,' he said. 'I'm afraid John's gone by now. Tack on to my Headquarters.'

The greatest of all the tragedies of Sidi Bou Hadjeba was that we had to abandon our wounded. After the loss of the surgical team in the Arab farm the battalion MO, the only remaining doctor, could not be spared to stay behind, and we had no means of taking them with us. Instead, a small guard under Lieutenant Playford remained to cover our withdrawal, and to these, together with half a dozen medical orderlies, fell the task of tending them until daylight and then getting help from the Germans. We left them with heavy hearts, knowing that lacking adequate drugs, blankets or shelter, many of the more seriously hurt could not survive the night.

* * *

Our departure was unnoticed by the enemy. We moved off stealthily down a sandy watercourse and crept along in single file, listening with strained ears for the first suspicious sound.

We crossed a series of low ridges forming the lesser foothills of the Djebel Bou Hadjeba which we had just left. There was no path to follow, so we set our compasses north-west and marched straight across country, taking all obstacles in our stride. We soon found ourselves involved in a maze of gullies, which slowed down our progress considerably and caused us to make rather more noise than we intended. But after an hour's hard work, we had left the worst behind and seemed to have slipped through the enemy's ring.

The foothills now gave way to rocky cultivated strips of land, with an occasional Arab dwelling. As far as possible we left these well alone, but our presence was always betrayed by the maddening bark of dogs. These started their howling about a mile before we reached them and did not cease until we had passed a mile beyond.

We reached the main road half an hour later. Fearing that the enemy might have standing patrols along it, we slipped across in small groups and formed up again in the shadows on the other side.

We were now on the plain and consequently expected our route to be easier. But we had hardly left the road when we encountered an enormous belt of ploughed land. We could not risk any delay in trying to find a way to skirt it, and there was nothing for it but to plod straight across.

In the dark this ploughland was a fearful obstacle to exhausted men. The Arab blades had thrown up enormous chunks of soil which had baked rock-hard in the sun, leaving a furrow nearly two feet deep. We tripped over every gigantic clod, we stumbled into every ravine-

like furrow, we pitched forward on to our faces, too tired
to save ourselves and almost too weary to rise.

Eventually we felt our way forward step by step, testing
every foothold, and emerged from the belt bruised and
smarting from many falls. Then we halted for a rest, and
every man sank to the ground to lie panting or more often
fall asleep. After a brief ten minutes we rose and struggled
on, only to encounter another hellish belt about a quarter
of a mile farther on. As the hours passed we lost count of
the endless fields and got used to a plodding stride, as
though walking on the sea.

But at midnight we straggled out over an open patch of
thorny waste, and our forward section reported that they
had reached a river. This was good news, for, even with a
rigid water discipline, our water-bottles had been empty
since midday, owing to the excessive strain of battle and
our general exhaustion. All the afternoon we had lain
under a wicked sun, and now our mouths were dry, with
tongues like lumps of uncured leather, and our bodies
craved moisture.

Major Ashford gave orders for the platoons to cross
one at a time, fill their water-bottles on the way, and take
up a defensive position on the other side until we were all
across. That river saved us all. The men waded in silently
up to their thighs and let the water swish round their legs,
cool and invigorating, while they rolled up their sleeves
and washed away the clinging sweat and dust. When they
emerged on the other side they were like men reborn.

We set off again, but the going was very much easier
and we seemed to have left the plough behind. The moon
was now well up, and we were moving over a flat open
plain of coarse grass and clumps of thorn. There was a
screen of ten men out in front, with the OC in the middle
steering the course, while the rest of the company fol-

lowed in a dense column behind. The men were too far gone to maintain any formation, and stumbled along blindly in a pack. Gradually they sorted themselves into little knots of particular pals; they got along better that way and prevented each other from straying.

We had come about three miles after leaving the river when Jones passed out. He had been plodding along with the rest when he suddenly collapsed. Clarkson picked up the Bren gun, and Stewart and I hoisted him to his feet. He was a big man, and it was all we could do to hold him up. Some water was thrown in his face, but his eyes remained closed and his head lolled. We put his arms over our shoulders and dragged him along between us. His toes trailed behind and dug two little furrows in the dusty ground. After half an hour, however, he recovered sufficiently to take his own weight, and in another thirty minutes he was able to walk without further assistance. Up and down the column that night there were many men being dragged along in this way.

At half-past three in the morning we came to a wide sandy ravine, and the OC called a halt. With twenty miles behind us, and another black mass of hills looming directly in our path, there was nothing to be gained by attempting to cross them before daylight, with the men in their present condition.

'Get the men down into the ravine,' Major Ashford ordered, 'and we'll have a couple of hours' sleep out of the wind. Wake me up at half-past five without fail!'

IV
THE BATTLE OF EL FEDJA – CACTUS FARM

Just before dawn Major Ashford decided to push on and
get into the cover of the hills before it was fully light. It
was difficult to rouse the men. They were so dazed and
numb with fatigue and cold that it took some time to get
them to understand what was required, but once they
were on their feet and fully conscious we moved on again
at quite a good pace.

As dawn was breaking in its lurid African way we heard
very distinctly the unmistakable notes of the Colonel's
hunting-horn. It sounded very close at hand, but owing to
echoes and our own dulled senses it was quite impossible
to tell from where it had come. We waited a moment,
keeping stock-still and listening intently, hoping that the
call would be repeated; but there was nothing, only a
cock crowing lustily in a nearby farm. I wondered
whether, in my exhaustion, I was beginning to have
hallucinations.

We saw a large farm in the general direction of our
march, so set off towards it rapidly, hoping that we should
find the Colonel's party there. It turned out to be a French
farmstead, standing at the junction of three tracks, with a
well-built house and several large outlying barns. But,
most cheering of all, we found a large well standing in the
open about two hundred yards down one of the tracks.
An Arab farmhand in one of the barns went off immediately to fetch an ox to draw water for us.

He returned a few minutes later with a great white
beast and a large iron bucket. The ox was harnessed to a

rope passing over a pulley, and after the bucket had been lowered, was propelled into the distance with a smack on the rump.

The first bucketful of crystal-clear water had just come up when the French farmer himself came out to us in a state of great agitation. He explained that German armoured cars and tanks patrolled the district and it was very unsafe for us to remain in the open. He offered us a large barn in which to rest and lie up, while he personally would see that we had everything that we required. We left the well as though it were infected with the plague.

He showed us an outbuilding with sliding doors at the back of his farm which would just comfortably take our party of seventy men, and then instructed his farmhands to bring several bales of straw for our comfort. He brought us water in a galvanized water-cart and said he would get his wife to boil us a large kettle so that we could make tea. Finally, he gave orders for a meal of kuskus to be prepared for the whole party. We asked him what this was, but beyond saying that it was an Arab dish containing corn as its main ingredient, further description defeated him.

That French farmer was goodness itself. He gave us valuable and very accurate information regarding German activities in the neighbourhood and pointed out on our maps exactly where the Germans maintained posts and standing patrols. Above all, he strongly advised us against going into Massicault, saying that, although British patrols had once or twice visited the place, the town was more likely to be occupied by the enemy. Our main line ran much farther to the west – exactly where, he could not say for certain. He also undertook to supplement our own lookouts by keeping watch from one of his upstairs

windows – where his activities would not arouse suspicion.
We were by now entirely satisfied as to his bona fides, so
gratefully accepted, and lent him a pair of binoculars.

We had finished our drink of tea and a very rough and
ready meal of biscuits and had just fallen into a delightful
doze when suddenly we were awakened to find the farmer
bending over us.

'Do not wake the men,' he said slowly in French, so
that we might understand his meaning perfectly, 'it may
only be a canard – a false alarm; you understand? I have
just seen four German motor-cycles with soldiers on the
road half a mile from here. They are coming this way!
Get your weapons ready and do not make a noise!'

The four other officers and myself got up quickly. We
seized a couple of Bren guns and some grenades and had
a cautious look out of the doorway, keeping well in the
shadows.

The patrol consisted of four motor-cycles and sidecars,
each carrying three men fully armed. They passed by on
the road, then stopped, turned round and came back,
halting about four hundred yards from the farm. One
detached itself from the others and came down the track
and into the farmyard not fifteen yards from where we
were hiding. The driver stopped his engine, and they all
dismounted. The senior NCO questioned the farmer in
bad French, while the other two stretched themselves and
went off behind a haystack with little show of modesty.
They were going from farm to farm, asking at each
whether any English parachutists had been seen! If they
had not been so thoroughly idle they would have found
out rather quicker than they expected!

Apparently satisfied with their mission they remounted
and drove off to rejoin the rest of the patrol waiting at
the head of the track. We could easily have opened fire

and written off the whole lot, but we dared not take the risk. In the first place these were probably an advance patrol of an armoured car force, in which case a search of the area was sure to be made if they were missed. Secondly, if we had fired and one cycle had succeeded in making its getaway, we would have brought a hornets' nest about our ears. Again, there might be enemy troops in the area who would almost certainly come and investigate any shooting or sound of a skirmish. Finally, the farmer had treated us with the greatest kindness and without any thought of the consequences for himself and his family if the Germans discovered that he had been harbouring British paratroops. So we let them drive off unmolested, with our presence still concealed.

We were now in rather a dilemma. We could not overlook the possibility that the patrol could come back – this time with an escort of armoured cars and tanks. The farm itself afforded a hopeless defensive position. It stood alone in the middle of a plain completely bare of trees or cover of any sort. To try and fight tanks on such terms would be suicide; they would stand back well out of range and blow the farm to pieces with their heavy guns.

We had just made up our minds to move when our problem was solved to everyone's satisfaction. Some passing Arabs informed the farmer that there were English soldiers in the next farm about half a mile away. Immediately, he sent his foreman over on a mule to confirm this story. The man returned in a little while with Charteris, the battalion intelligence officer, perched uncomfortably on the animal's withers. Charteris told us that the Colonel and about fifty men of Battalion HQ were in a farm close by and we were to join him there immediately. His place offered a much better hide-out and a perfect defensive position.

We roused all the men quickly and then left the farm in open order as fast as we could go, as we had no idea who might be watching from the hills. Soon we started to climb into the foothills by a narrow sandy track, and then quite suddenly came upon a small Arab farm standing on a slight rise and screened from the rest of the country by a convenient rim of hills. Thus it was that we came to Cactus Farm.

The farm itself was a sprawling Arab building with corrugated iron roof and strong stone walls. On the south side lay a cobbled courtyard and a large stone trough out of which gushed a spring of clear water, the beginnings of a stream which trickled down the hill towards the plain. Around the farm and courtyard ran a thick cactus hedge, denser and more impenetrable than any barbed wire entanglement. Beyond it, and really surrounding us on three sides, lay a large orchard of olive trees, stretching down the hill for about two hundred yards. Around the whole ran another cactus hedge, even denser and more formidable than the inner one, providing the outer defence to the fortress.

Besides the Colonel and a small party of his battalion headquarters I found David Westley with two sections. It was like coming back amongst old friends.

'Why, hullo, Peter!' said a voice behind me, and there was David smiling all over his face. 'How on earth did you get here? We heard that you had been killed on Sidi Bou Hadjeba!'

'Far from it – and you aren't looking at my ghost now, either!' It was rather cheering to be able to laugh at one's misfortunes. 'I got separated from Major Ross in the withdrawal, so tacked on to "A" Company, and here I am!'

'Oh! I'm thankful John Ross is still OK then.' David

and he were close friends. 'I suppose you haven't seen or heard anything of "B" Company on your travels? I hope Tony is with them!'

'No, I haven't. The last time I saw Tony was yesterday morning. What news of him?'

'He was all right up to about two minutes before the hunting-horn. He went off to find 'B' Company, so I feel pretty confident that he's all right.'

We arrived in this new position at about midday. As we were all very tired after three days and nights with hardly any rest at all, we took turn and turn about to settle down and get some sleep. Lookouts were posted all the way round the farm, and with the aid of binoculars the whole countryside was kept under observation. It seemed that I had hardly got off to sleep before I was roused and told that enemy troops were approaching from the east. My watch showed that it was two o'clock in the afternoon.

I found David already outside the farm, looking through his binoculars. I followed suit and, sure enough, there was a body of men in extended order coming over the crest of a ridge about a mile away.

'What do you make of them?' I asked, still with the binoculars glued to my eyes. 'They seem to be wearing khaki drill; they couldn't be our blokes by any chance?'

'Not a hope, I am afraid,' David replied quietly. 'They're wearing sandy overalls right enough, but with black leather equipment; Afrika Korps almost certainly!'

'Damn!' I exclaimed. 'They don't give us much peace, do they?'

'Oh, well!' David said, as though resigned to the unpleasant business ahead. 'Get your section together with all their arms and equipment, and I'll meet you here in half a minute.' Then he suddenly focused his glasses on the skyline. 'Quick! Look at that! The devils! It was those Arabs who gave us away!'

I could see two or three white-robed figures at the head of the force pointing and gesticulating in our direction, no doubt the same party of Arabs who had told us of the Colonel's whereabouts. We heard afterwards that the enemy was offering five hundred francs for imformation leading to the death or capture of each British parachutist.

As ammunition was very low we made a rapid count of what we held between us and divided it out at about ten rounds a man, with fifty to each Bren gun. This was really worse than we had imagined. The Colonel ordered that no man was to open fire until the enemy had approached within sixty yards, so that every bullet should be effective. Men armed with Bren guns were to use their weapons on 'single shot' unless presented with an exceptional target.

Fortunately the Arabs only knew of the small party, fifty or so strong, originally in occupation of the farm. The Germans obviously had not the least idea that the party had been reinforced by a further seventy. Had they known it they would never have sent so small a force to clean us out, nor would they have walked down towards the farm so confidently and with such complete lack of caution.

At their head strode a very tall officer a little in advance of the rest. The remainder of his party followed in three extended lines. David and I watched them approach through our binoculars from the cover of the inner cactus hedge. The force continued down the long slope from the ridge into another shallow dip and up the other side on to a large open space of waste land covered with knee-high clumps of camel thorn. When they were within one hundred yards of the outer hedge they must have thought that the farm was unoccupied and that they had been called out on a wild-goose chase. The afternoon was basking in the drowsy warmth of a sun nearly at its zenith, and everything was still.

Crack! The tall officer toppled over and lay screaming, a hideous retching noise dreadful to hear. There followed a scattered fusillade; two of his machine-gunners dropped, and the rest went to ground behind whatever cover they could find in the open field. It had happened so suddenly that the peace of the afternoon was hardly disturbed by the shots. There were only the terrible groans of the wounded German, and they, too, gradually died away.

The Germans made no move for about half an hour. Once or twice a machine-gun opened up, sending a stream of tracer crackling through the cactus, but this was merely to cover the withdrawal of the force still in the open. Occasionally there would be a dull bump, and several seconds later a mortar bomb would come whistling down, to land with a crash and scream of fragments among the olive trees. The enemy mortar-team was ranging on the farm buildings; the bombs crept closer to the cluster of stone barns, until at last they were landing in the cobbled yard. Then they came in groups of three at a time, spattering the walls with fragments and setting the hay-stack on fire. Sometimes a heavy machine-gun would open up at long range from the ridge a thousand yards away, chipping long splinters from the olive trees and making the cactus collapse about our heads. I called out the names of my men to see if they were all right. L/Cpl Dory? OK! Stewart? OK! Clarkson? OK! Golding? I called again, then crawled over to find Golding lying with a bullet through his head.

Meanwhile the enemy had evidently brought up the rest of the battalion. Towards four o'clock they attacked in earnest, opening the assault with a sudden rain of mortar bombs and a heavy machine-gun barrage from the surrounding hills.

While we were cowering beneath the storm and waiting for them to appear I became aware that it was rapidly getting dark. With a little luck we might slip away as before.

During a short lull David crawled over to my position and flopped down beside me in a shallow ditch.

'Open fire as soon as the enemy start to leave the broken ground ahead, and don't waste ammunition. We've got to hold them off until dark!'

'Same drill as last night?' I enquired.

'Yes; exactly! The Colonel will blow his hunting-horn as soon as it is dark enough for us to make a getaway. When you hear it, collect your section together and go like smoke for the big gate in the farmyard. I'll be waiting for you there. We have to get into the hills as fast as possible. OK?' He crawled away to warn his own section.

The enemy was now closing in fast from the north, south and east. Small parties of Germans were advancing through the scrub and clumps of thorn in the half-light and were slowly creeping up to the first cactus hedge. Our men were firing now – a sudden burst easily distinguishable above the shriller crackle of shots coming the other way – and were picking off shadowy forms whenever they detached themselves from the dusky background. Above the din we could hear shouts and fire-orders in German, and it was only a matter of time before they would be in amongst us.

Suddenly, the hunting-horn sounded. We leapt to our feet and went like the wind down the cactus-lined paths and into the cobbled farmyard.

'This way!' shouted David, standing beside the massive iron gateway. 'Keep going hard up the hill and don't stop until you get nearly to the top of the saddle! There don't seem to be any Germans up there – the Colonel sent a patrol. Wait for me near the top!'

As we went out of the farm at the west end, the Germans came in through the cactus at the other. A small party of the enemy appeared through a gap in the hedge, and our rearguard turned and met them with a hail of grenades. As the covering party went out three more came over the wall into the farmyard and wilted under the contents of a tommy-gun magazine. The next moment the farm was behind us flickering in a glow of the burning haystack, and we were among the shadows of the rocks and hills, plunging deeper into the night.

About sixty of us had kept together in that mad rush from the farm. David took command and led us north-westwards up a rocky goat track winding into the heart of the Djebel Mengoub. All were so exhausted by now that it was necessary to move very slowly and to halt every half-hour. Directly the word to halt was passed, the men sank in their tracks and were immediately asleep. It was a most incredible phenomenon: the column would suddenly keel over like a line of skittles and melt into the ground.

We took it in turns to stay awake at every halt and rouse the others when those fleeting minutes were up. This was the most unpleasant duty of all. The men were so far gone that they had to be kicked awake and then hacked to their feet with pleas and curses to jolt them into consciousness. Mere shaking was useless. One could shake a man by the shoulders until his teeth rattled and one thought his neck would break, but he remained inert and fell snoring as soon as he was released. Once on their feet they stood dejectedly in a coma and only rubbed their bruises.

I can now scarcely believe how it was possible to

administer such terrible treatment, but these were extraordinary circumstances, and it was vital to put as much ground as possible between ourselves and Cactus Farm before daylight. Some, when they dropped, would crawl away a few yards into the darkness, so that they would be left alone and not wakened. It would be unfair to blame them; the craving for sleep had stolen their will and overpowered even the strongest sense of discipline. When we moved on again they were left sleeping among the rocks and bushes just off the track. It was impossible to check numbers in the darkness, and we were too tired to search the surrounding ground. Those that fell by the wayside were lost and not seen again.

Our route led us right through the heart of the mountains and down into the plain beyond. The track broadened out and the surface improved. We were approaching a large Arab farm when a dog started to bark, and set up such a maddening incessant howl that in our exasperation at betrayal it was quickly traced and ruthlessly silenced. Then all at once there was the light ribbon of a dusty road.

Taking the French farmer's advice we had given up all idea of going into Massicault and were making for Fourna, some miles farther west. As far as we could tell we had hit the main road somewhere between the two. It was considered too dangerous to march straight down the road, so we struck off across country, intending to make a loop to the south and rejoin it on the other side of Fourna. But almost immediately we ran into an enormous belt of plough, in which we floundered helplessly. After an hour of negligible progress we gave it up. The men were so weak that it was now imperative that we should get through to our own lines as soon as possible. We could no longer chance having to lie up for another day, with the possibility of being caught again by a superior German force. So we decided to risk the road after all and cut across to its nearest point.

When we reached it we sent a scout section of about ten men a hundred yards ahead and followed in column of threes. If we were unlucky enough to run into an enemy post the section would give us adequate warning and would stand a good chance of slipping away in the darkness themselves.

We found marching on the smooth road surface a wonderful change. We had not gone very far, however, before we realized from the kilometre stones that we were not on the main Tunis road but on another running parallel, a few miles south. That was all to the good, for although we were going away from Fourna we were still going in a westerly direction and were very much safer on this minor road.

Then, one of those almost unbelievable things happened. At about four o'clock in the morning we met the Colonel and another large party coming across the open. Both parties had covered about eight miles over mountain country by different routes, and the odds against our meeting must have been a matter of infinity.

We went on together down the road, moving westwards for another two miles. As the time was about four-thirty, and it would be getting light in an hour, the Colonel decided to look for another farm where we could lie up before it was fully daylight. The first suitable one was a large French farmstead standing in a grove of poplar trees. In the dim half-light of the waning moon it appeared to have large outhouses and barns which would answer our purpose well.

The Colonel sent me on ahead to investigate. I pulled a heavy bell chain in the porch and the deep clanging at the back of the house seemed to make an appalling commotion. Presently one of the shuttered windows opened, somebody looked out quickly, then pattered down the passage. The bolts were drawn, and a middle-aged lady in dressing-gown and slippers opened the door a crack. In spite of the apparition standing on the doorstep, armed and covered in grime, she recovered her poise almost immediately and asked me politely of what service she could be.

'Madame,' I explained as well as I could in my limited French, 'we are British soldiers on our way to Medjez-el-Bab.' (I said the first thing that came into my head; gossip travels fast among Arab farm-hands, and we wanted no repetition of Cactus Farm.) 'We are very tired, having marched a long way. We should be very grateful if you would let us sleep in your barns for a few hours before we continue our journey.'

'Why, yes, Monsieur! Anything you wish!' The next moment David Westley arrived and explained more precisely what was required.

As our weary column stumbled into the farmyard, farm-hands showed the men to the least occupied of the barns. Nothing was too much trouble; bales of straw were produced and spread thickly on the hard earth floors, water was brought in large containers, and almost immediately the men collapsed into an exhausted sleep. Finally, the foreman showed us a small outhouse round the back and went off to get a bundle of straw. I fell down and went to sleep on the concrete floor at once. I have only a vague recollection of being lifted and later covered with straw to keep me warm.

V
OUR RETURN TO MEDJEZ-EL-BAB

I awoke to find David Westley bending over me.

'Sorry to have to wake you up, but we are moving on again shortly. The Colonel wants to see all officers in the house immediately.'

'OK. I'll be along in a moment,' I said, fumbling under the straw for my equipment. 'How long have I been asleep?' Sunlight was streaming in through the open door.

'About two hours, I think. It's seven o'clock. We're moving off at eight.'

I struggled to my feet feeling almost worse than before. Throwing my equipment over aching shoulders I stumbled out in the glare of sunlight and round to the front of the house.

The French lady had prepared a wonderful breakfast for us in the living-room, where all the other officers were collecting. I was shown to a seat, and a huge plateful of ham and eggs was placed in front of me. This was followed a moment later by a cup of black coffee, rolls, butter and jam. Madame and her three daughters served us themselves, forcing food upon us with a gentle insistence.

I must have been too far gone; the very thought of food was nauseating. I picked at the fried eggs and washed the mouthfuls down with coffee, but soon had to confess that I was defeated. Madame urged me, but I could only sit and shake my head in a dazed, stupid way and mumble that I felt tired. In spite of my gaucherie they understood and smiled in sympathy, while Madame murmured softly after each refusal, 'Le pauvre fatigué! Il ne peut pas manger! Comme il est fatigué!' She clicked her tongue and shook her head sadly.

One of her daughters was about twenty and very attractive in a dark, Latin way. I think she was slim and tall, with dark hair falling to her shoulders – but I was too tired to notice even that.

The Colonel, who had not been to bed, told us that he had explained everything to the French lady, who had given him much information. There were no German troops actually in the district, but occasionally they sent armoured car patrols round the country. Several times they had passed her farm. We were in a sort of no-man's-land between the lines, controlled by neither side but patrolled frequently by ourselves as well as the enemy. The Colonel had decided not to risk wasting a day lying up, but to try to get through to our own troops round Medjez-el-Bab before evening. It was impossible to cover the tracks of our large force; nor, again, did we want to jeopardize our benefactress by remaining longer. Medjez-el-Bab was only about sixteen miles away, and there was now less risk in moving in daylight; we were already through the enemy's main positions and we should have to take our chance of a German patrol.

We said good-bye to our charming hosts. No words of thanks could have been adequate for all their assistance and kindness, but we did our best, from the bottom of our hearts.

'Méfiez-vous des indigènes! Beware of the natives!' Madame warned us as we were leaving. We needed no words of caution in this.

We marched out through the big iron gates and back on to the road. After about a mile we turned off to the south up a sandy cart track which led towards a low ridge of rocky hills. We started to climb almost immediately, leaving the Massicault plain behind us. The sun was just getting up in a cloudless sky.

David was limping very badly and obviously in pain as he endeavoured to hobble along with the column.

'It's my knee!' he explained. 'I had a nasty fall last night in the Djebel Mengoub.'

Eventually, as we climbed farther into the hills and the track got worse, he had to give it up and sat down on a rock beside the path.

'I'm afraid I'll have to stop here for a little,' he said as I drew level. 'Doc Gordon is crocked, too, and is staying with me. We'll find a donkey or something. Don't you worry! I'll come along all right.'

We had to go on without him. As we reached the crest of the ridge I saw David and the MO sitting beside the track far below.

We had a short rest at the top, then turned west again and began to descend into the plain on the other side. Very soon we reached cultivated land at the bottom of the slope. Here we split into two parties moving parallel to each other in extended order, so that we covered a large frontage of ground.

But our progress was terribly slow. Every one of us was now in a really pitiful condition, and the strain was beginning to tell on the nerves; after our earlier experiences of being caught in the open by enemy tanks the men were in a very jumpy state. Someone would see through swollen eyes a large dark object moving on a ridge a thousand yards away and give the alarm. The column would be galvanized into action and scatter for cover amongst the olive trees. Usually it turned out to be mere hallucination, or the object was identified through binoculars as a harmless Arab horse and cart. Every donkey became a motor-cycle patrol, and every cart a

tank, until we reached such a pitch of alarm and false
alarm that we almost ceased to care. We plodded on like
men walking in their sleep.

At about two o'clock in the afternoon we met the
Medjez–Tunis road at the junction of several tracks. We
learnt from some Arabs that a force of American light
tanks had passed that way only a few hours before.
Medjez-el-Bab, our goal, was now only about ten kilometres down the road, and we felt certain that we were
now inside the domain of Allied influence. Spirits began
to rise, and the men to sing and whistle. For the last two
days I had heard no laughter and hardly seen a smile. We
now had a good tarmac surface beneath our feet; it was
like walking on thistledown after the slough of cultivated
land.

The sun was just dipping behind the hills when suddenly
the column halted, then melted into the ditches beside the
road. I was in a dream and looked around enquiringly.

'Get down, sir! For God's sake get down!' Clarkson
was shouting from the ditch. I suddenly came to life and
dived into the ditch in panic.

'What's up?' I asked.

'Just have a look over there, sir!' My eyes followed his
pointing finger. On the horizon about five hundred yards
away was a large half-tracked vehicle crawling round a
spur of sandstone. It was slowly followed by a second,
and then another and another, until six had lumbered into
view. We were completely hypnotized. The road was
devoid of any adequate cover, and we had little ammunition to keep them off for longer than a minute or two.
We just sat and waited.

Then the leading vehicle appeared over the crest of the
dip a hundred yards away. There was the large white star
on the bonnet, and we knew that we were safe. Everyone

shouted and cheered, a wild elation succeeding our paralysed dread. The Colonel got to his feet waving his yellow identification silk above his head and walked over the field to meet them.

The column was a patrol of the American 1st Armoured Division operating in the zone east of Medjez-el-Bab. They had no room to take us all on board, but managed a score of walking wounded who had come all the way without complaint. After a minute or two they drove off down the road towards Medjez in a cloud of dust. The Colonel went along with them to make his report and to arrange billets and hot food for us. He hoped to be able to get transport to come and pick us up.

Those last few miles were, perhaps, the worst part of the whole march. At first we started off singing and swinging along at a good marching pace. After the last five days of great exertion and mental strain, relief buoyed us up. We had accomplished what had looked so impossible. We had fought off the enemy in four engagements and passed right through his screen in front of Tunis, with a march of seventy miles on little food and water and hardly any sleep.

We were in this elated mood when a pony and trap came trotting briskly up the column, and a tremendous wave of cheering broke from the rear and rippled to the front. Seated in the back with a French farmer were Captain Stark and Lieutenant Crawley, the latter with his eyes heavily bandaged. 'B' Company had been ambushed after withdrawing from Sidi Bou Hadjeba, we learnt later, and these two were almost the only survivors. Crawley had been blinded during the battle, and Stark had led him by the hand over difficult mountain tracks and past German patrols to safety. Now the picture of the blind man in the pony trap, laughing and joking with everyone as he passed, seemed to symbolize all the courage and endurance of our achievement. Our emotions were brimming over, and we cheered until they were out of sight.

Gradually the reaction set in as the miles dragged on and on, and we again experienced the full effect of our exhaustion. We had felt so sure they would send transport for us, but as each kilometre-stone went by our spirits sank lower and lower. The ranks wavered and straggled out and finally lost all cohesion as they stumbled and strayed over the road. At last we were too tired to raise foot from the ground and slithered along as though skating, making the sparks fly in the darkness.

So at last, late in that evening of the 3rd of December, we came to Medjez-el-Bab. We passed a big concrete and steel-rail road-block, and tottered through the defences of a French tirailleurs regiment. No doubt they looked at us in wonder, marvelling at the sight of half-dead men pitching and reeling from one side of the road to the other, like drunks incapable of steering a course.

5

The Struggle for Medjez-el-Bab
December 1942

We were awakened the next morning at about seven o'clock. Although I had slept for over ten hours I felt dazed for several minutes and incapable of movement. I got my socks and boots on at last and crawled downstairs to find the rest of my equipment. The billet-owners, a sapper maintenance party on the Bailey bridge, had made a dixie of tea for us on their hydroburner, and there was David, of all people, standing in the throng.

'Don't look as though I'm the ghost this time!' he laughed. 'I came in after you had gone to bed. The Doc caught a donkey, so I rode into Medjez like Sancho Panza!'

We were being taken to a Rest Area, and after a short drive of twenty minutes found ourselves at Sloughia, a small Arab hamlet about ten miles south-west of Medjez. It was built on two low hills, the warren of streets and houses rising one behind the other in terraces, and was crowned by the white dome of the mosque. Each house had its own small compound within a ragged hedge of cactus; and below, the land was divided up into groves of olive trees, vineyards and vegetable plots, a pleasing patchwork of systematic cultivation. Farther down the hill a concrete bridge spanned a wide shingly river bed, with the stream curling lazily down the centre. Beyond, groves of pomegranates and olive orchards covered the plain to the north with a carpet of green, out of which rose a range of distant hills. Everything was quiet and peaceful in the stillness of the morning, and even the heavy guns round

Medjez were silent. It seemed as though Nature smiled and welcomed us to this haven.

Soon the fires were going for breakfast, and afterwards the morning was spent leisurely in making the place comfortable.

We were just having lunch at midday, sitting on a terrace above the river, when a 3-ton truck crossed the bridge and drove towards us up the hill.

'Hullo! I wonder who this is,' David said, looking up. 'By Jove, I believe it's some more of our blokes!'

There were some dozen men wearing camouflaged smocks and red berets in the back of the truck.

'It's John Ross!' David exclaimed and ran down the hill to meet them.

The next moment we were clustering round the party as they clambered down, all dusty, haggard and unshaven.

'Well done, John!' Colonel Frost said, pushing his way through. 'Come and have some food right away. Don't start asking questions now, you lads. Take them over to the cookhouse and see that they get something to eat!'

'C' company had put up such a marvellous show at Oudna and Sidi Bou Hadjeba, and it was wonderful to see these few survivors get home safely.

There was still no news of Tony Miles and his section, and I was feeling anxious for his safety, but David remained convinced that he would turn up. There was still hope that there were other parties unaccounted for, and strong patrols of light tanks, armoured cars and trucks went out daily to scour the countryside and bring them in. But the final tally, about two hundred and fifty officers and men, was disappointingly small – a pathetic remnant of the grand fighting force, nearly six hundred strong, which had started off for Depienne only a week before.

Fifteen officers and three hundred and one other ranks did not return.

In the afternoon of that first day we gave ourselves a good clean up in the river. It was surprisingly hot for early December and the water quite warm, so we were able to take our time and make a thorough job of it. Then we got to work on our filthy garments, and lay and sunbathed while these were drying. It was very pleasant basking in the sun while I stared at the sky and thought how glorious life could seem after the abject misery of the last few days. It was hard to believe that this was Africa and there was a war not more than ten miles up the road.

We went to bed as soon as it was dark, for we were still drugged with an overwhelming weariness. I was intrigued by the quaintness of the Arab houses, which were built round a central courtyard entered by a massive wooden gate in the surrounding wall. Each room had a low doorway not more than four feet high, and was closed by a grass mat which hung from the lintel and kept out the cold night air. The very simplicity appealed to me and produced a feeling of ease and security, rare in a mechanical age.

But the carefree bliss of the Sloughia Rest Camp was not to last. At about eleven o'clock the next morning a large staff car flying a General's flag came slowly up the hill and drew up opposite our cookhouse. The Colonel got up hastily, straightened his beret and walked quickly down to meet the personage who emerged. Talc-covered map boards were produced, and a low and earnest conversation ensued. After a quarter of an hour the General's car drove away, and the Colonel came back up the hill with a long face.

'I'm sorry, chaps, but we are going back to Medjez this

afternoon. The Germans have broken through at Tebourba, and the situation is not too good! They are now moving up to attack Medjez from the east, where our defences are comparatively weak. Our job is to protect the small landing-ground outside the town.'

We had an early lunch and at one o'clock began the weary march back in the sweltering afternoon sun, trying to shut the pleasant memories of Sloughia out of our minds. Our muscles had stiffened up from the two days' inactivity, and by the time we entered Medjez every man was dead-beat, in spite of frequent halts along the route.

We picked our way through the ruined streets just as the sun was setting, then out along the Massicault road down which we had stumbled two nights before, and came to a halt among the stumps of plane trees and cactus hedges half a mile outside the town. Suddenly a powerful aero-engine spluttered into life on the flat country below us, and a Spitfire roared into the air. We watched it wheel away to the north and disappear over the hills – the last plane to use the landing-ground before the tide of war swirled over the plain.

Our position lay on the south-eastern edge of the airfield, where a table of high ground commanded all the low-lying country to the north and north-east, as far as the Arab village of Grich-el-Oued about five miles away. The place had been occupied by the enemy before his withdrawal in the middle of November, for there were well-dug weapon-pits lined with straw and, here and there, abandoned grenades and boxes of mortar ammunition. At first we treated these with care, thinking they might be booby-trapped, but the Germans had left in too great a hurry to prepare any surprises.

Early the next day David came and sought me out, a piece of red-hot news burning his tongue.

'Tony's turned up! Came in about an hour ago with all his section and about twelve other men.'

'The fact is,' Tony told us, after a long sleep, 'I got left behind on Sidi Bou Hadjeba when the battalion retired. I was told to meet "B" Company in the hollow between those three peaks, but somehow I missed them. I got a bit anxious when nobody came and everything was so deathly still and quiet. Suddenly I heard some chaps scrambling about in a ravine about forty yards away. I whispered as loudly as I dared, "Is that 'B' Company?" . . . No answer! Then I heard someone speaking German, so I whispered to my blokes to follow me, and mice could not have been quieter going down that hill!'

Tony struck due west instead of going towards Massicault, having decided to play safe. They marched by night and lay up during daylight. Being a fluent French speaker he gathered information about enemy movements from the French farmers en route, who helped him to avoid enemy reconnaissance forces and any roads and tracks on which the Germans were maintaining standing patrols. 'My job now,' he asserted, 'was to get my lads home without any further casualties, and I was not very concerned with how long I took to do it!'

Even so, they had one very narrow escape. They were sleeping about midday in an isolated farm, when the French owner roused them with the news of the approach of a German armoured patrol. They just had time to dive out of a back window and into a nearby clump of thorn bushes which the farmer had indicated, when the tanks roared into the yard and encircled the buildings. The Frenchman admitted to the German officer that British troops had been there, but maintained at the point of the pistol that they had left some six hours earlier in a northerly direction. Discovery of the party's bully-beef tins merely appeared to support his story, so the tanks went off up the track by which Tony and his men had come in. The farmer gave the all-clear in the evening, and they emerged painfully from their bed of thorns. Bits of the four-inch spikes remained in their arms and legs for weeks, causing septic sores.

'On the farmer's advice,' Tony concluded, 'we went south-west to Goubellat and were picked up there yesterday by British armoured cars.'

All of us felt the greatest admiration for the complete loyalty of the French. Although we were on the run, they did everything in their power to help, knowing full well the penalties if this were discovered. They looked for nothing in return – and we had nothing to give beyond profound gratitude.

We were now experiencing the first hints of a belated African winter, and almost overnight the skies changed from their customary blue to a murky overcast, black with rainclouds. Then the heavens opened and water drenched down, leaving the countryside running with new watercourses and streams and turning the rich red soil to a gluey morass. At first it was a respite from the glare of the sun; but, as the thunderclouds banked up before an icy wind, we felt acutely our lack of greatcoats, blankets and warm battle-dress, and shivered under the deluge in our summer clothing, wet to the skin. When we manned our trenches at dawn and dusk during the ritual stand-to we used to count the minutes and curse the raindrops, appalled by the sudden onrush of winter which had caught us so unawares.

Until the middle of December Allied forces in Tunisia were very small and were all included under the command of the British Fifth Corps. The original dash from Algiers to Medjez-el-Bab had been executed by Blade Force, an armoured spearhead consisting of some artillery and tanks from the 6th Armoured Division and a small column of lorried infantry from 78th Infantry Division. This column was reinforced by the 1st Parachute Battalion, after their drop at Souk-el-Arba in November. In support of this force, 78th Division had advanced rapidly into Tunisia along two roads, the 11th Infantry Brigade by the inland road through Constantine to Medjez, and the 36th Infantry Brigade along the coastal road from Bône. The intention had been to capture Tunis and Bizerta before the Germans could concentrate large enough forces to oppose our advance, but here we suffered great disappointment; the enemy poured in troops and succeeded in halting both thrusts.

We were now very short of troops to fight a static campaign through the winter. The two brigades of 78th Division were more or less isolated from each other, pending the arrival of further troops to fill in the gaps. Meanwhile, the bulk of 6th Armoured Division were moving into the Teboursouk area south-west of Medjez, and the 1st Guards Brigade had disembarked at Algiers and were expected to arrive daily. Until the beginning of January the 1st Army in Tunisia could not have numbered more than thirty thousand men.

On the 13th of December the storm broke, and the Germans – having completed their concentration first, owing to their vastly shorter communications – launched their counter-offensive. I was attached to 78th Divisional headquarters as a liaison officer at the time, and so was able to watch the blue arrows creep across the battle map as the Germans came on.

The first indications of the attack came from the 11th Brigade, eight miles up the Tebourba road. They reported that a force of about twenty tanks and a long column of lorried infantry had gapped their protective minefield under cover of an artillery and mortar bombardment, and were attacking the main position. But here they met with no success, beyond forcing us to withdraw our advanced posts.

At midday the French tirailleurs on the eastern side of Medjez reported another German force of equal strength advancing down the Massicault road, and, in the early afternoon, a third enemy force moving up the Goubellat road from the south. The Medjez salient was being attacked simultaneously on three sides.

The Germans made no progress against the 11th Brigade, but they succeeded in moving a considerable force down the east side of the Majerda river, occupying Grichel-Oued and capturing on the way the light tanks and half-tracks of an Amercan armoured combat team which had been patrolling in the area. The main French positions in the centre held firm, but German tanks and infantry had reached the high ground overlooking the airfield and were shelling Medjez with their long-barrelled 75-mm tank guns from a range of half a mile.

The 2nd Battalion, now dug in round Medjez Station to the north of the town, were not being seriously engaged, but their patrols had encountered intense fire from German troops across the river. Enemy long-range artillery sent over occasional salvoes of heavy shells which threw up towering geysers of black smoke and mud near the road.

The most cheering news of the day was that the Guards Brigade had arrived and were marching up from the Souk-el-Khemis with guns and transport. Meanwhile,

Major-General Eveleigh, commanding 78th Division, had decided to withdraw the 11th Brigade that night from their exposed position up the Tebourba road to a new one in the neighbourhood of the River Zarga ten miles farther west; turning Medjez into a redoubt to be held by the Guards Brigade. At the same time, Blade Force was to be disbanded, and the 1st and 2nd Parachute Battalions were to be withdrawn to Souk-el-Khemis for rest, provided there was no new development.

In the evening the General made his tour of the battlefield, and we followed on our motor cycles to a rendezvous near Medjez, threading through the guardsmen who were filing up on a two-mile stretch of road.

The battle died down as we arrived. The Germans had withdrawn their tanks from the aerodrome for the night, no doubt intending to renew the attack in the morning. Long-range shells still came whining over, to land harmlessly with a crump and fountain of wet mud in the water-logged fields; but, as the shadows lengthened and observation diminished, the German artillery, too, packed up. As dusk fell it was apparent that the line was safe, and General Eveleigh confirmed the new dispositions.

In the gathering darkness the Guards Brigade moved into the town, took over the positions covering the railway station and re-occupied the important ground to the east. The Germans had lost their last chance of capturing the Medjez bastion and the key to the Tunisian campaign.

After an interminable night our vehicles stopped at a large French farm a little outside Souk-el-Khemis, at about four o'clock in the morning. We saw the men into straw-filled barns, and as it seemed rather pointless to go to bed at daybreak, Tony and I sat up with a number of 2nd Battalion officers, and fried eggs on the kitchen fire.

At dawn the 1st Battalion advance party arrived, and we fell upon their news hungrily. Our only link had been through the Army battle reports, and these were sketchy and impersonal. Almost at once our spirits fell; the sappers had had a bad time, they said. Several officers and a large number of men were killed or missing. We confirmed the barest details shortly afterwards: Kenneth Duncan, Sergeant Muir and half a dozen men were known to have been killed; John Pearson and half the troop were missing.

We had to wait in suspense until 'A' Troop returned later in the morning, and we had it from Paul Mason at first hand.

'It happened during a night raid on an enemy strong-point near Mateur,' he told us. 'Ken took half the troop to lay mines on the road behind the position to prevent reinforcements getting through while the attack went in. Well, the engineers went off round the flank while the infantry formed up, and that was the last that was seen of them. Suddenly there were some tremendous explosions, and then hell was let loose. When it was all over they found Ken and the other bodies at the bottom of a ravine, but of the others there was no sign.'

What became of John Pearson and twelve men no one has ever been able to discover: the Tunisian hills hold the secret.

The 1st Battalion Group had done an outstanding job, following their landing on Souk-el-Arba aerodrome in the afternoon of the 16th of October.

The purpose of the operation was political as well as strategic; first, to establish themselvs at Béja and persuade the scattered French garrisons to fight for us and then to harry and delay the enemy while our own forces were moving up through the Algerian mountains.

The battalion went into the air after the sketchiest of briefings; they knew only that their immediate objective was to secure Souk-el-Arba aerodrome and after that a guerrilla campaign of uncertain duration. Colonel Hill in the leading plane picked the dropping zone from the air and led the jump, the success of which was marred only by another fatality through a parachute failing to open. Within an hour they entered the town, and negotiations with the local French commander began.

The garrison had been in two minds as to what they should do in the event of one or other of the opposing armies arriving in the area. Already the Luftwaffe was much in evidence, a melancholy procession of Stukas and Ju 88s on their way to bomb the advancing British force on the frontier passes. Also, German armour was in the offing, and there were murmurs that it was useless to resist without adequate arms. But when the British paratroops dropped from the skies, with every appearance of modern efficiency and armed might, the French commander decided to throw in his lot with them.

The French were induced to part with their local bus service – a collection of charabancs running on producer gas – and after nightfall the battalion set off, arriving on the escarpment above Béja at midnight. Here they bivouacked among the rocks, but they had to keep walking about owing to the bitter cold. In the town below, the nervous garrison of Tunisian tirailleurs were standing to arms, reluctant to make any move until the matter had been thoroughly discussed.

There were three thousand troops in the town, and parleying went on all the following morning, during which our strength and possession of secret weapons were duly exaggerated. Meanwhile, preparations for our entry were made and carefully rehearsed.

At dusk the Colonel marched his men down through the town in single file with large gaps between the platoons which then doubled back out of sight and tacked on to the rear of the column again. In this way it was made to appear that a very powerful force had passed through the streets. The garrison was suitably impressed.

The French had outposts on the Mateur and Tunis roads – at Sidi N'Sir, Oued Zarga and Medjez – so one company of paratroops was sent off at once to Sidi N'Sir, while the rest of the battalion prepared Béja for defence.

At Sidi N'Sir the advanced company had further arguments with the French, but were eventually allowed to clear a gap in their minefield and pass through. They were going to seek out the Germans, and demonstrate that they were a match for the enemy – *and* his armour. In this they had amazing luck.

At dawn on the 18th of November a German column of six heavy armoured cars and reconnaissance vehicles suddenly approached at speed from the east and roared past in the direction of Sidi N'Sir. The parachutists hastily arranged an ambush against the enemy's return, the engineers mining a culvert and laying mine necklaces, and the infantry lying in wait with anti-tank rifles and Gammon bombs.

After an hour or so, back came the enemy column as hurriedly as before, fell straight into the trap and was completely destroyed – all except one armoured car which was taken intact with a few prisoners.

Their immediate job done the company returned to Béja with their prize and their prisoners, and the last vestige of French hesitancy disappeared.

But the Germans quickly retaliated, with repeated

bombing of Béja and an attack on the French outpost at Medjez-el-Bab. One company was sent up to support the French in the Oued Zarga–Medjez area and was soon at close grips with the Germans. At this point advanced elements of the 11th Brigade arrived, together with an American armoured battery.

Meanwhile the French reported a German–Italian column of infantry and armour, four hundred strong, approaching Soudid, about ten miles north-east of Sidi N'Sir. At dusk on the 23rd the rest of the battalion moved up in their buses to Sidi N'Sir and then made a difficult approach march of twelve miles over the mountains in rain and darkness, to attack the enemy encampment before dawn. Unhappily some mines exploded while they were forming up, so that the battle opened prematurely and there was much confusion, with our mortar barrage coming down amongst our own men; nevertheless the enemy position was overrun, and a number of prisoners was taken.

But the battalion had lost its commander through enemy treachery, and it was in this action that 'A' Troop had their heavy casualties. Colonel Hill had himself captured an armoured car; then, as the crew tumbled out with their hands up, an Italian officer suddenly produced a small pistol and shot and critically wounded both the Colonel and his adjutant.

The success of this operation imposed great caution on all other Axis columns, and the battalion, now under Major Pearson, hastened to follow it up. After reorganizing at Béja they set off once again for the mountain country flanking the Mateur road. Tanks from Blade Force had arrived to give them armoured support, and this enabled them to establish company strong-points in the hills to block this line of advance.

They now began a very vigorous private war. The only way in which they could maintain their positions against growing enemy pressure was to attack again and again in a series of quick, elusive thrusts, and every night saw them embroiled in some minor action or patrol clash. Sometimes tanks from Blade Force helped them to clean up a troublesome infiltration, but for the most part they operated on their own. It was during this month in the Tunisian hills that the whisper 'Die Roten Teufel – The Red Devils' went round the enemy army, and the wearers of the maroon beret came to be held in some considerable awe.

This campaign of nerves was highly effective, but it was very hard on the men taking part. Approach marches through rain and pitch darkness were long and exacting, and our wounded suffered great hardship through exposure and exhaustion before receiving proper medical care. The battalion was living under appalling conditions of wet and cold. As in our case, they had gone into the air in hot weather, wearing only string vests beneath their smocks, and had no greatcoats or blankets – the humble amenities of the ordinary infantry soldier. The cold, combined with the excessive discomfort of soaked and rotting clothing continually next to the skin, made sleep impossible at night; and their sorties came to be regarded as a welcome alternative to sitting huddled and miserable in the dark.

Rations were short or never arrived at all, and the battalion had to live chiefly off the land. At one time the parachutists were reduced to one meagre meal of turnips a day and counted themselves lucky when a German tank was knocked out and they were able to supplement their wretched fare with the provisions of the dead crew.

At last the enemy became very sensitive about these activities and decided to put up with this beard-singeing no longer. For days German troops had been steadily working southwards through the hills against our positions, and now threatened to isolate the battalion from Sidi N'Sir and their life-line with the 1st Army. Then at dawn on the 12th December two battalions of glider troops began an attack with artillery support. They advanced towards our company positions across a low, rocky ridge, but were driven back with the help of a troop of tanks. In spite of this check they returned to the assault in the afternoon.

The parachutists, however, were now thoroughly roused. Their armoured support returned, and the whole battalion went over to counter-attack furiously. The open ridge proved a death-trap to the enemy on the defensive, the Germans being caught by the tanks as they withdrew up the forward slope. One battalion was annihilated except for a score of men who succeeded in surrendering from the cover of a ravine. The survivors of the other were hounded down by the victorious paratroops until darkness made further pursuit impossible.

This successful action fittingly rounded off a most distinguished month of hard fighting, and they were withdrawn to Souk-el-Khemis for a well-earned rest. Their privations had been most severe, the actions fierce and desperate, and casualties by no means light; yet their achievements had been great. For three weeks the enemy had been kept on the defensive, in an area which guarded the vital Medjez flank.

6

Christmas in Béja

December 1942–January 1943

Troop trains rumbled into Souk-el-Khemis station during the night of 17th December, and when we awoke the next day there was a pile of kitbags stacked in the square under the guard of a 'C' Troop sapper. He told us that 3rd Battalion, brigade headquarters, the remainder of the squadron and parachute field ambulance had all arrived and had been spirited away by truck to Béja.

It was now clear that no further parachute operations were contemplated and that for the present the parachute brigade was to be used as ordinary infantry to help hold the long mountainous front. But this prospect did not worry us unduly: we still had a week's rest before us; Paddy Roorke had found us luxurious billets in a deserted house in which the electric light, radio and hot-water system worked; and now the arrival of clean clothing and warm battledress put us in better relation to the change in weather.

Tony Miles, being mechanically minded, unearthed an old car in a bombed garage, and we lost no time in making the twenty-mile trip to Béja to see the remainder of the squadron.

We found them in a tumbledown shack on the Djebel Abiod road. Jack Burroughs and Martin Brush were out on a mine-laying expedition with 'C' Troop, but Henry Walker had just arrived from England with the rear party, and with him were two new officers, Tom Slater and Roy Coleman. Over lunch they told us all the news. Major Drake was away on a reconnaissance to locate an enemy

tank harbour near Mateur, which was to be dealt with by
the sappers and the 3rd Battalion. George Irwin had gone
off with a sergeant and a sapper the night before to squirm
through the German lines and reconnoitre the roads and
tracks to the south of Tebourba, and they were to be
away three days on the investigation. No doubt the
division to which the squadron was attached regarded
these sorts of jobs as coming within our repertoire.

George and his two companions duly reappeared at the
appointed time. The most frightening experience, he said,
was when they were trying to re-enter our own lines and
were nearly shot by French sentries who were unfamiliar
with the garb of the British paratroops.

They had spent the first night getting through the enemy
positions opposite Medjez and moving up into the hills of
the Djebel Aoukaz. Here, many German and American
light tanks and half-tracked vehicles lay derelict and
abandoned, evidence of the skirmishing earlier in the
month. Our party had so much to do that dawn caught
them on a scrub-covered hillside, with no better hiding-
place within reach. They lay down in the undergrowth,
camouflaged themselves and prepared to spend the day
sleeping and watching.

George woke up to hear German being spoken close at
hand. Turning his head very carefully he found himself
looking straight at a pair of jackboots only two or three
yards away. A German sentry, rifle slung on back, was
gossiping to a fellow over a cigarette, completely unaware
of the three Englishmen lying so close at hand. George's
sergeant had frozen into an unnatural attitude on the
approach of the two enemy soldiers and was now forced
to hold this position on a bed of sharp, pointed stones as
long as they remained. The Germans sat down on the

rocks and chatted for a couple of hours before they finally wandered off.

On the second night the party went across country towards Tebourba. Before the moon was up they unwittingly walked into the middle of a battery of heavy guns. George said he actually touched the barrel of a huge piece of ordnance – a 155-mm Long Tom, he thought – before he realized where he was. It was drizzling hard, and the sentry had his back to them, huddled in a greatcoat with upturned collar. Again they slipped away undiscovered.

During the last day they watched columns of German infantry filing up over the hills and then digging in along a ridge behind Grich-el-Oued. That night, as they were wriggling back through the lines, they came on a section of enemy troops asleep in straw-lined trenches, but they let them lie.

The Guards' Brigade commander was very enthusiastic over George's story and all but sent out a strong fighting patrol then and there to deal with the guns which had been plaguing him for days. The Chief Engineer, 78th Division, was no less pleased with the report, and George received an immediate award of the Military Cross.

But the days went by, and Major Drake did not return. It was not until the end of the war that we learnt from his batman, the sole survivor of the patrol, that they had been ambushed, and that our fine OC lay buried on some wild hillside.

At the end of a week he was posted missing, and Bill Stevens took over the squadron. David Westley's field experience was now too valuable to lose, so, although nominally second in command, he remained with 'B' Troop, and Henry Walker filled the administrative gap in squadron headquarters. At the same time Paul Mason was confirmed the new 'A' Troop commander.

The 1st Battalion went back into the line on the 19th December, and when the 2nd followed on the 21st, 'A' and 'B' Troops moved up to Béja. This wrecked the plans we had made for Christmas. A local farmer had promised us four turkeys, and we had laid in a good stock of wine from the monastery at Thibar. Though we had to leave the live-stock behind we packed our wine and other provender in the car, in the hope that things would remain sufficiently quiet for celebrations to be held elsewhere.

But no sooner had we arrived in Béja than we received orders on the 22nd to prepare for an immediate operation. Disregarding the tradition of peace and goodwill the High Command had decided on a last big offensive, to capture Tunis before the winter really set in. So we threw a party in the Arab shack on the Djebel Abiod road to dispose of our wine and drown our sorrows at the same time. The Chief Engineer brought along his piper to play laments at our departure for battle. The night sky emptied a deluge on our leaking roof, while, round a guttering candle, we put aside thoughts of the morrow to the maudlin strains of 'Come sit by my side if you love me.'

The next day we loaded our stores for our move to Medjez after dark, and were briefed for our part in the offensive which was that of assault engineers clearing mines and booby-traps. Ginger Hamilton was selected, from among volunteers, for the very hazardous one-man job of making his way by night to an enemy bridge near Grich-el-Oued and removing the demolition charges.

The success of the offensive depended mainly upon the condition of the roads and tracks leading to Tebourba, which George Irwin had pronounced suitable for heavy traffic during reasonably dry weather. But the incessant rain entirely altered the situation and eventually put an end to all hopes of spending the New Year in Tunis. Our artillery, so necessary in each bound of the attack, was bogged down to the axles and could not be moved forward, and the offensive was abandoned. Back in Béja we heaved a sigh of relief – no one more so than Hamilton – and turned our thoughts to more seasonable ways of spending Christmas.

The weather cleared up a little on Christmas Day, and occasionally the sun broke through the pall of watery cloud and sparkled on the white houses and tree-lined streets.

Even with so little time for preparation we made it as near to a real Christmas as we were able. The arrival of mail from home assured our success – these were the first letters we had received since our arrival in Africa, and everyone had been rather despondent at being so out of touch. We purchased a pig from a local farm and the 'compo' ration produced a very good substitute for Christmas pudding, which was duly decorated with a piece of holly sent out in a parcel. The officers served the men's Christmas dinner in accordance with custom, a local school serving as a makeshift dining hall. That evening we had an impromptu concert and sing-song, with plenty of red wine to make the party go. One of the parachute battalions made themselves rather unpopular – both with our own artillery and no doubt the Germans – by causing a general stand-to when they got very tipsy and fired all their mortar flares in a most impressive firework display, spelling a confusion of success and disaster to the silent night.

We now settled down in Béja to routine engineer work in the neighbourhood. We exchanged our inadequate and muddy barns for three small villas in the town where a bombing raid, despite several near misses, did not upset our comfort unduly.

Béja had been badly knocked about by air raids, and there was little left of the centre of the town. Many streets were closed with barbed-wire entanglements to prevent looting, and long queues stood for hours outside the Mairie to draw a meagre ration of bread. The only thing that distinguished Béja from all the other war-stricken Tunisian towns was the Moorish castle standing high on the escarpment behind. This old fortress, guarding the road which wound down the hill to the town, was remarkably well preserved, and its picturesque, pointed battlements and high, loopholed towers were in strange contrast to the ruins below.

There had been rumours that we were moving to another sector. The brigade transport was loaded up with rations and petrol for a five-day journey and set off for an unknown destination. The 3rd Battalion was withdrawn from the line unobtrusively and departed by lorry. Only the 2nd Battalion, which was still seriously depleted, was to remain behind under the command of 78th Division.

Then on the night of January 7th we were packed into cattle trucks at Souk-el-Khemis Station, in company with the 1st Parachute Battalion and the 16th Parachute Field Ambulance, and knew that our destination was Algiers. The only possible explanation for our return to base was that further parachute operations were expected.

The 3rd Battalion did not return with us, but followed three or four days later. When the story came out we heard that they had been specially chosen for an important attack, with a battalion of the Buffs, to capture Green Hill – a mountain feature on the Bizerta road and the key position to Mateur.

Conditions for the assault of 4th January were very bad indeed. After the heavy rain which had persisted for the past fourteen days the ground was soggy, and most of the approach march had to be made through fields deep in mud. In spite of a driving drizzle, the blackest of nights and determined enemy opposition, the parachutists stormed Green Hill, forcing the Germans out of strong concrete defences back on to a secondary feature known as Baldy. Baldy lay a little to the south-east of Green Hill and was to have been dealt with by the Buffs. But this battalion, after floundering through waterlogged fields, were completely exhausted by the time they went in to the assault, and their attack was broken up by fierce German resistance.

The enemy quickly reorganized on Baldy, and the first counter-attack came back almost immediately. The German infantry advanced shoulder to shoulder, yelling like maniacs and chanting a Nazi war song. But this incredible bravado was of no avail in the face of our withering fire, and the counter-attack was cut to pieces.

Just before dawn the Germans counter-attacked again with fresh, more experienced troops, following a devastating mortar barrage. Enemy infantry poured round the flank of Green Hill and more or less isolated the parachutists. 'B' Company was forced out of its main position, but somehow managed to cling to others less favourable for defence. The remainder of the battalion were in a similar plight, and all were now running out of ammunition which it was impossible to replenish.

With the approach of daylight the position became hopeless, and the order was given to withdraw. The enemy was sweeping the western face of Green Hill with intense machine-gun and mortar fire, and this death-ridden slope was the only line of retreat open to our men.

But the withdrawal was carried out with perfect discipline. The men were not to be hurried out of the positions which they had defended so stubbornly, and not one wounded man or weapon was left behind.

7

Interlude at Boufarik

January 1943

There is something fascinating about life on a troop train, especially under the primitive conditions of sixty trucks labouring along the single track across the North African countryside. The weather, although cold at night, cleared after the first morning, and most of the five-day trip was in bright sunshine punctuated by an occasional shower. The men pulled back the sliding doors, and sat dangling their legs, watching the scenery drift by. Some played a hand of cards, staking cigarettes or their next pay, some 'brewed-up' over a biscuit-tin brazier hanging outside on a piece of wire, others slept under greatcoats and khaki blankets – enjoying the spell cast by the rhythm of the wheels and the satisfaction of an undisturbed rest at last. Our train rolled westwards at a leisurely pace, halting for many hours in country sidings to let the ammunition and reinforcement trains for the front rattle by at speed; we were infected by the happy-go-lucky atmosphere and cared little how long we took to reach our destination.

During the frequent halts we stretched our legs and did all the necessary jobs of the day. There was always great activity first thing in the morning, and as soon as the train jolted to a stop the trucks disgorged a human avalanche which swarmed over the area bordering the track. Within a minute smoke was going up from a colony of camp fires with dixies of tea already on the brew; lathered faces, frilled with towels, were grouped round a tin of hot water from the engine; and on the perimeter the odd-job men collected firewood, replenished their jerricans of water and bartered cigarettes and ration biscuits with the Arabs for eggs and bread. Meanwhile, the engine puffed off down a siding to refill its boiler.

But we never knew how long we were stopping. Sometimes the engine would come trundling back after five minutes instead of the expected half-hour, re-couple with uncanny speed, and with only a short, malicious whistle, go lumbering down the track. Then pandemonium would break loose as improvised kitchens were hastily abandoned, braziers, dixies and cooks swung unceremoniously aboard, and a stream of late-comers charged after the train with towels flying in the wind; while the men cheered and laid odds on the last man in the field.

Haggling with the Arab population was always a popular pastime; and as news of the British soldiers' bounty had been spread by other trains going east, whole communities turned out on our approach and thronged the track. The children ran along beside us, yelling, tumbling over each other and piling into a scrimmage as somebody threw some hard-tack into the surging mass.

The scenery was ever changing. There are the rolling hills round Ghardimaou, blanketed in olive groves, the wild sandstone heights near Guelma and then the twenty-mile run through the gorges before reaching the big junction of Kroubs.

The Guelma Canyon is magnificent; the railway winds down the valley bottom following the course of the Majerda, and one is awed by the green mountains which tower on either side. The thousand-foot crags threaten to topple into the cleft, and the train scuttles up the canyon, like a lizard seeking a crack in which to hide. The farmsteads and groves of trees which dot the valley look like toys on an emerald carpet – a Lilliputian community in a land of giants.

After the confinement of the mountains the vast wheat-growing prairie-land on the high plateau round Setif appeared wind-swept and devoid of life. One saw an occasional Arab settlement far away beneath a ridge of hills, but generally there were only remote colonies of native farmers, for whom a train meant companionship and contact with the outside world. While we were toiling slowly up the long incline under the combined power of two enormous Trans-African locos a fine-looking Arab galloped along beside us on a chestnut pony, standing in his stirrups and shouting in salute. His stallion bounded effortlessly over the ground, with head held high and golden mane and tail flying in the breeze.

When darkness blotted out the landscape the glimmering lights from scores of braziers dangling outside the trucks went out one by one as the men turned in, and we rolled ourselves in blankets and greatcoats and slept. When we awoke in the morning we were eighty-odd miles nearer home, and the scenery had changed again, like the turning of a page.

We passed through the foothills of the Grand Atlas by the Bouira Gap and descended into the Algiers plain. In sharp contrast to the heat of the sun the peaks of the mountains were crowned with snow. And now we were in familiar country – the rich coastal strip thickly covered with farms and intense cultivation, the red earth and the green walls of orange plantations, the friendliness of the blue sky and sparkling sea – all of which had seemed so desirable in the Tunisian hills. We stopped for two hours in Maison Carrée Station, and nothing appeared to have changed during the two months we had been away. In the wretchedness of battle conditions it is hard to grasp that the permanent things of life have not moved at the same pace as one's own transient existence at the Front. There was the Native College on the hill, our first billet on African soil; the air was heavy with the nauseating smell of goatskins drying in the tannery across the way, a reminder of visits to the town. There was even the same old beggar sitting by the footbridge intoning a prayer as a coin rattled in his bowl, and then his quavering cry, 'Alms for the love of Allah!'

When we arrived at Boufarik, our new Base, we found that our heavy kit and parachute equipment had been brought up from Algiers, thirty miles away, and our oddments of personal luggage and sleeping-bags were awaiting our return.

With the help of the local mayor we found a very charming farm in the middle of a vast orange plantation, tucked away at the bottom of a half-mile drive flanked with olive and poplar trees. Two fruit-storage barns and outbuildings provided excellent accommodation for the men, while the Officers' and Sergeants' Messes installed themselves in a modern villa behind, at the end of a creepered carriageway. It had large, shuttered windows and a wide stone verandah which kept out the glare of the sun. The brigade quartermaster supplied tables and collapsible forms, hurricane lamps and wash-basins, and with our chest of crockery, unopened since leaving England, we made this our semi-permanent home.

We grew quite fond of our picturesque farm at Boufarik; there was an atmosphere of peace and serenity in its cradle of orange and tangerine acres. Two families of storks nesting on one of the barn roofs sat for hours on a ragged platform of sticks and clicked their beaks with a peculiar whirring noise, or flapped ungracefully round the buildings, volplaned on a huge span of wing and landed with a flurry after an awkward glide approach. Then there was the soothing rustle of the breeze through the orange trees, the lowing of cattle in the stalls and the pleasure of the soft January sunshine touching up the colours on the plain. Boufarik was a garden-paradise after the slough of winter in Tunisia, and war.

It was not merely revulsion from ugliness and misery that made us appreciate our surroundings. During those first few weeks in January the Algiers coastal area was in the ecstasy of an early spring. Boufarik lies in the centre of the orange-growing district, and for miles around estates were laden with fruit at the peak of the harvest. Regimented groves of tangerines and oranges, clementines and nectarines, grapefruit, lemons and passion-fruit, lined every road and studded the green with gold. In the distance the hills round Blida hung between plain and sky, a blue and purple smudge. The enchantment of this lovely place had us all enthralled; we used to sleep on the verandah on warmer nights and watch the African full moon come up and peer inquisitively through the line of poplars. The crickets chirped in chorus among the orange trees, an owl hooted from the sycamore grove, and finally the nightingales filled the perfumed night with song, warbling a potent spell.

It was only after the plans had been put into the waste-paper basket that we heard the purpose of the brigade's return to Algiers – a parachute landing in support of the Eighth Army's attack against the Mareth Line. Our objective had been the port of Sfax, where we would link up with armour from the American 2nd Corps attacking from Gafsa. But the German Kampfgruppe-Süd-Tunesien put up fierce resistance against the Americans, and the assault on the Mareth Line made slower progress than had been hoped. So our part in the operation was cancelled.

Directly we heard that the show was off we settled down to enjoy a period of real rest and re-equipment and hoped that a new operation would not be forthcoming for some little time. We confidently assumed that the 2nd Battalion, now on the Robaa front, would be withdrawn and would rejoin us at Boufarik for reorganization after its heavy losses. In the meantime, we undertook easy training with route marches to the Blida hills, run-walks and PT and an occasional 'liberty truck' to Blida and Algiers for baths and recreation. Brigade headquarters prepared training programmes for February and March, and our future looked very happily settled.

Our complacency was short-lived. At the beginning of the fourth week in January we were sitting round the Mess table finishing supper when orders suddenly came for us to be ready to move that self-same night. But just when the frenzy of preparation was at its height, we received a further message which gave us a little breathing-space.

We spent the whole of the next day in packing up the farm and had our final orders that evening for the move to Algiers docks at midday on the morrow. When we left we were wearing full battle order, carrying ammunition, grenades, shell-dressings and weapons ready for immediate action. There was the usual speculation as to the nature of our mission – a seaborne landing behind the German lines, perhaps, or an attack on Pantellaria. But the majority picked a last helmet-load of oranges for a long journey and left it at that.

Excitement was heightened when we drove in through the dock gates and saw two assault ships alongside the quay. The trucks drew up directly beneath the grey

landing-barges slung from the ships' derricks, and the
men alighted agog with the prospect of an operation a
little different from their usual line of business. We
staggered up the gangway under groaning Everest carriers, across the deck and then clambered down on to a
destroyer moored alongside. The Navy took charge and
showed us where to stow our kit, then led the men away
to the nooks and crannies which were to serve as their
accommodation for the voyage. We were directed down a
companionway to the wardroom, which was already foggy
with tobacco smoke and bulging with a dozen officers of
the Field Ambulance.

'What's all the mystery about, Percy?' I heard David
asking one of them. 'Everything seems to be very hush-
hush! Does anybody know where we are going?'

'Yes – you'll be disappointed when you hear,' the other
replied. 'We're going to Bône! Nothing more exciting
than that. We're going back into the Line!'

We put to sea that night after dark, and began the
thirty-six-hour journey back to Tunisia. We were a small
but fast convoy, with two assault ships and two destroyers
carrying the brigade, and we arrived at Bône the following
evening after a pleasant, uneventful voyage. We had
steamed up the African coast in brilliant sunshine, with
the brown rocky headlands sliding past on the horizon,
eight miles away. But inland, black and sulphurous rainclouds shrouded the mountains, and we disembarked
under the familiar conditions of drizzle, cold and overcast
skies. The harbour was a depressing sight in the rain and
dark – masts of sunken ships rising like gallows out of the
water, the bomb craters on the mole filled with stagnant
water, the torn-up railway lines, the mangled skeletons of
dockside cranes reeling drunkenly along the quay, and
everywhere rubble, mud and litter. There was indeed a

gulf between Algeria and Tunisia – warmth and peace: bleak winter and war.

Our onward progress further emphasized this. After an uncomfortable night on the flagstones of a disused hospital we 'embussed' in the late afternoon in *open* 3-ton lorries. The convoy set off slowly along the coast road, but then it swung inland and began the tortuous climb over the mountain road to Souk-el-Arba. Several hundred vehicles made up our jolting, labouring procession, and, as night came down, our twinkling lights shone high above us near the head of the pass, with others far below in the depths of the mountain mass – an uncertain, wavering, luminous centipede.

We entered the black misty blanket of low cloud, and it came on to rain with a steady persistence. We wrapped ourselves in groundsheets and oilskin coats and huddled together for warmth and protection in the bottom of the truck. But puddles collected in the crevices and folds and quickly penetrated our clothing, so that we were soon soaked through and through. After a while the silence of depression fell upon us all, while we dozed and shivered through the interminable hours in a semi-conscious state.

The transit camp at Ghardimaou, where we arrived at dawn, was only a stepping-stone on our hundred-mile journey. After a day of inactivity among the muddy olive groves we moved on again, this time in over-packed troop carriers. After the previous sleepless night we slumbered as much as cramp, the swaying truck and sprawling bodies would allow.

Shouts and violent bumping brought us to. Six trucks were drawn up on the verge of a rough road, while ours negotiated an uneven track up the side of a hill. The engine roared, and the wheels spun in the mud.

'Jump off, and lend a hand!' Major Stevens shouted over the tailboard.

It was about five o'clock in the morning by the time we had manhandled the trucks up the track and camouflaged them with branches among the thickets at the top. The air was frosty, and a heavy dew on the rocks glistened like mercury in the waning moonlight.

All around us a shadowy countryside of jumbled hills covered with pine bushes and heather took shape as dawn broke over the German lines to the east. Men stood watching the gold fire gild the skyline, and flayed their arms against their sides, trying to induce warmth and life into frozen limbs. The cooks' hydroburners were roaring farther up the hill, and there were shouts and the thudding of mauls among the bushes as camp was pitched.

8

The Battles of Djebel Mansour and Bou Arada

February 1943

The weather cleared for a week, with a cloudless sky and a warm Spring sun; and all the wilderness came to life with a sudden sprinkling of wild flowers and shoots of corn. The rocks ran with lizards, and the ground crawled with tortoises, fooled into believing that winter was at an end.

Our camp was in a reserve position just behind the village of El Aroussa, on the main road running east to Bou Arada, Pont-du-Fahs and Zaghouan. To our north lay a wild hill-country of rock and heather, through which a road ran from Bou Arada to Goubellat and the great British salient of Banana Ridge adjoining the Medjez sector, some twenty miles away. We were practically on the right flank of the British line in Tunisia. To our south lay the French Corps round Robaa, and beyond that the theatre of operations of the American 2nd Corps in the desert round Gafsa and Tebessa.

From El Aroussa the road runs straight down a restricted valley narrowing to a bottle-neck at the small country town of Bou Arada. The 1st Parachute Brigade (now including the 2nd Battalion) had taken over the hill feature, the Djebel Bou Arada, which secured the southern side, while to the north lay the positions of the 38th (Irish) Brigade on a series of bald lumps of rock and heather known as The Grandstand, Paddy's Hill, and Two Tree and Three Tree Hills. Bou Arada itself was not occupied by our troops, but all the open country was

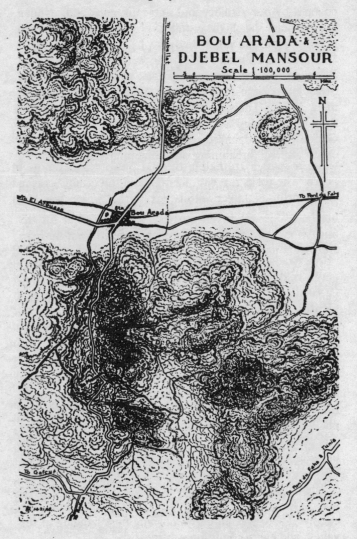

covered by our artillery and anti-tank guns and, as long as we held the high ground, no enemy force could penetrate into the valley below.

On the 1st February 'A' Troop were sent off to the 1st Battalion to take part in an attack which was to be the prelude to a large-scale offensive. South-east of us lay the main Robaa–Tunis highway, running across the plain through Pont-du-Fahs. It was down this road that the Germans had advanced recently and now held a considerable salient threatening our communications centre of Robaa and the most direct route to the American 2nd Corps. The keystone of the German position was formed by the mountain mass of Djebel Mansour and El Alliliga; but once this was taken the way would be clear for the 6th Armoured Division to push through to Pont-du-Fahs and Zaghouan.

The 1st Battalion were to attack at dawn on 3rd February and seize Djebel Mansour before it was fully light. A battalion of the Guards would follow through and assault the adjoining peak of El Alliliga in the afternoon, while a company of the French Foreign Legion moved on to the western peak of Djebel Mansour to reinforce the parachutists. The task of 'A' Troop during this operation lay on the supply communications from the Bou Arada–Robaa road, where a branch track wound round the base of the mountain, across a deep gully by a rickety plank bridge and finally up the lower slopes to end in an Arab farm. The engineers were to widen this track by blasting, and build it up so that armoured carriers could take ammunition, food and water to the forward troops.

The companies formed up silently in the pitch darkness just before dawn, without any interference from the enemy. There was an early morning mist hanging in the valley, and every condition was ideal.

Without the customary artillery bombardment the surprise was complete. Only when the main position was being stormed did the enemy machine-gun and mortar barrage come down around the base of the mountain, barely in time to catch the tail of the reserve company. The battalion quickly gained the crest and consolidated just as it was beginning to get light; then turned about and worked down the hill from the top, cleaning up the isolated machine-gun posts left behind in the first surge of the attack. Now there was desperate fighting, in and out of the thick scrub and thickets covering the slopes. But the Germans were bewildered by the speed and direction of the attacks and were no match for the victorious paratroops who overran their positions with great élan.

There were many individual acts of heroism, but one became almost a legend in the brigade and concerned Captain Mellor of 'T' Company. This officer was a well-known figure with his black patch over a blind eye and already had a great reputation for courage and incredible daring. During the assault his company was held up by three enemy machine-gun posts. At once he raced forward alone and destroyed them all, one by one, with grenades and a Schmeisser tommy-gun taken from a dead German. Soon afterwards his men saw him cut down by an anti-personnel mine.

'Don't stop, chaps!' he shouted in a matter of fact voice. 'Go on! I'm afraid I can't come with you! I've lost a leg!'

He would allow no one to stay with him, for any wavering in the final rush would have been fatal. When the stretcher-bearers found him after the position was won he was dead.

Meanwhile, one company had stormed the adjacent peak of El Alliliga. But the battalion was now too thin to consolidate the whole length of the ridge, and this company had to be withdrawn into a more compact perimeter on Djebel Mansour. The Germans reoccupied El Alliliga almost immediately and dug themselves in very strongly during the morning. The company of the Foreign Legion moved on to the western peak of Mansour and protected the 1st Battalion's left.

Work on the supply track had, however, suffered a disaster. An over-zealous carrier-driver had rushed ahead and plunged across the footbridge before it had been strengthened. The carriageway collapsed, and the heavily loaded carrier jammed fast, completely blocking the track. It could not be budged even by the lavish use of explosive, the only effect of which was to bring down the ravine walls. There was no possible alternative route, so it was decided to supply the troops on Mansour by mule train, a slower and more precarious operation altogether.

The second misfortune was the failure of the Guards' assault on the heavily defended slopes of El Alliliga. The Germans were by now strongly entrenched and very much on the alert, and the attack was held half-way up and could not be pushed home. They were also quick to exploit our difficulty in supply; a heavy mortar barrage was put down during the day and determined fighting patrols played havoc at night from ambush on the flanks. While our own troops were running short of ammunition, food and water, the Germans were being reinforced on El Alliliga with a Mountain Regiment, 105-mm mortars and 20-mm quick-firing cannon.

The next morning the enemy laid down a concentrated and accurate mortar barrage and counter-attacked at first light. As the 1st Battalion occupied an exposed face of the ridge they had been unable to dig new positions and were forced to occupy the German trenches. These were well known to the enemy mortarmen, and we suffered considerable casualties. Nevertheless the counter-attack was smashed almost at the point of the bayonet and the Germans were thrown back on to El Alliliga. In the afternoon there was another counter-attack, and a third the following morning, but all were held with the help of a 25-pounder battery which provided magnificent support throughout. Meanwhile, practically no supplies were getting through, water had run out, ammunition was very low and none of the men had eaten for more than twenty-four hours.

At mid-morning the Brigadier got through on the wireless to Colonel Pearson who reported that the battalion was in good heart and could deal with one more counter-attack with the little ammunition they had left. After that they had their bayonets. But the need for further sacrifice was past. The offensive could not go on while El Alliliga held; and the order was given to abandon the Djebel Mansour position. It had cost thirteen officers and nearly two hundred men.

It is a tradition of the Foreign Legion never to withdraw from any position previously won. Their commander gathered the remnants and gave the order to fix bayonets. Then, as the Germans closed in, they scrambled out of their holes and charged. Only eight men straggled back.

The remainder of the 1st Battalion withdrew, carrying all their wounded through a mortar and machine-gun barrage. It was during this withdrawal that Corporal Simpson of 'A' Troop earned the special award from General Eisenhower of the American Silver Star. A mortar bomb burst near him, seriously wounding two infantry comrades. Without hesitation he picked one up in his arms, put him over his head and across the top of his heavily loaded pack. This in itself was a considerable feat of strength, but after carrying him four hundred yards to safety he then returned through the barrage and repeated the performance with the second man.

After the Djebel Mansour battle the squadron passed some days in training among the rocks and heather round the camp.

One sunny morning my section and I were out practising field-craft, crawling about with muddied faces and festooned with foliage. Suddenly there was a slight rustle, and six horsemen with levelled carbines glided out of cover ten paces away. Their approach had been quite noiseless, and we were so surprised that we could only stare at the khaki-turbaned and sandy-cloaked Arab cavalrymen who ringed us round.

They were a patrol of the French 'Régiment Spahis Tunisiens'. Their officer, Lieutenant Frémond, explained that this was how they tracked down German patrols in no-man's-land, and as a precaution they had been stalking us for some time. His grey Arab ponies were unshod and picked their way through the undergrowth with the lightness of cats.

Frémond took us to his encampment in the bottom of a river valley about half a mile away, where his troopers had built igloo-like shelters into the hillside with turf and branches. These proved to be much warmer and drier than our own dugouts, and to us seemed the last word in comfort. But what really took our fancy were the sheepskins which covered their crude wooden saddles and at night formed luxurious couches!

Every evening afterwards Frémond brought his ponies up to our camp, and several of us went off for an hour or two's ride. The saddle, with its high pommel and cantle and large bucket stirrups, took a little getting used to, but our mounts were a joy to ride. They were soft-mouthed little thoroughbreds, tough and very keen and incredibly nimble at scrambling up and down the steep ravines.

The men had a lot of fun racing bareback round a large field, and at this Corporal Simpson, with long ranching experience in Australia, was quite at home. Perhaps his prowess made up for our lack of horsemanship in the Spahis' eyes.

'B' Troop was now ordered up to the 2nd Battalion, on the right flank of the brigade. All the battalions were holding very long frontages, with big gaps between company strong-points, and so the parachute engineers were being used as a reserve of infantry to be called on in emergency.

We found ourselves in a position called 'OP Farm' in the centre of the battalion front. This was on the reverse slope of a hog's-back ridge to the south of the Djebel Bou Arada and overlooked the German outpost line in front of Djebel Mansour and El Alliliga two thousand yards away.

No sooner had we moved into the line than it started to rain with a persistence which we had not experienced before – churning our farmyard into a sea of mud and making our supply track almost impassable. One night our ration truck containing 'compo' and ammunition for the next few days got bogged in the ford below us, now swollen into a chocolate flood, and it took forty men from eleven o'clock to dawn to salvage it.

Some of the infantry companies suffered far worse privations than ourselves. 'A' Company on the open farmland to our right had no cover whatsoever, while 'C' Company on a long spur to our left were under direct observation from the enemy and had to live in their slit trenches. They scratched burrows in the sides of gullies; but the rain found its way through their oilskins and seeped into dugouts, until they were plastered with clay and lived with the smell of mouldy clothing day in and day out.

Our discomforts had one item of compensation, for our infantry comrades discovered a large number of chickens running wild in a ruined farm half a mile out in front. We fed like kings for five days before the surviving birds became too wily and eluded the foraging party.

In the middle of February the Germans opened a surprise offensive in the south against the American 2nd Corps, captured Gafsa, Sbeitla and Kasserine and threatened to roll up the whole of our southern flank. The situation became critical, and a special armoured force was hastily scraped together and sent south with all speed to restore it. This force consisted of the 1st Guards Brigade, all the armour from 6th Armoured Division, and the greater proportion of our artillery, leaving a scratch force of the 38th Brigade and 1st Parachute Brigade to hold the Bou Arada sector. Meanwhile, the Germans moved the newly formed Hermann Goering Jäger Division (originally composed of airborne and parachute units flown over from Sicily) into the Goubellat–Bou Arada area, and by vigorous patrolling discovered how we had denuded this front to feed the Kasserine sector. On our side extra precautions were taken against a surprise attack, and we sat and waited for the inevitable. Less than a week after the failure of his Kasserine offensive Von Arnim struck again at our weakened front, using captured American transport to switch his forces rapidly from south to north.

The German offensive on 26th February was launched with a total of about three divisions in a series of rapid infantry thrusts. On the Goubellat sector the Germans poured round Banana Ridge, isolated units of the 1st Division who were holding it and penetrated as deeply as Sloughia, then being used as Divisional Headquarters. On the 38th Brigade sector parachutists of the Hermann Goering Division overran the outlying positions, advanced through the trackless wild country to the north of Bou Arada and were finally stopped at El Aroussa by our brigade rear echelon and a number of Churchill tanks. But the main positions of 38th Brigade were still intact and the Bou Arada bottle-neck remained firmly in our hands.

We ourselves had manned our trenches as usual half an hour before dawn. As the first streaks of light appeared there was a sudden flare-up of machine-gun fire about two thousand yards to our north. Red tracer flicked in graceful curves towards the dark mass of the Djebel Bou Arada and ricocheted skywards in fountains of golden rain. The display grew more intense as further guns opened up all over the hills, while far away to the north there was a flickering false dawn in the sky, and we heard the deep rumble of guns. Then we knew that we were in for trouble.

'We're standing-to until further notice,' David Westley announced when he came round our positions. 'Company Headquarters informs me that the enemy are attacking all along the front. The other two battalions are being heavily engaged.'

Apart from occasional shelling and vigorous retaliation by our own 25-pounders, nothing much happened on our own sector until midday. Then we received a report that large numbers of enemy infantry were moving down from Djebel Mansour and coming in our direction. About an hour later 'C' Company became embroiled with Austrian troops of a mountain regiment trying to move round their flank, and the 'B' Company forward positions were subjected to a heavy mortar barrage. Shortly afterwards the whole of our front was attacked by a horde of Italian infantry who emerged from the ravines and broken country and advanced towards us. A 25-pounder battery opened up rapid fire at point-blank range, while Vickers gunners on our hill further discomforted the attackers. As they disappeared into the ravines again the Support Company mortars had the time of their lives, firing all their normal stock of ammunition, their reserve, and a further replenishment which arrived by mule train during the battle. The luckless Italians were completely demoralized, and withdrew slowly through the broken country. When night came two strong fighting patrols swept the battle area from the north and from the south in a pincer movement. At about ten o'clock there was a sudden outburst of firing and considerable shouting, and an hour later the patrols came back with ninety very dispirited prisoners and a miscellaneous collection of rifles, machine-guns and other ironmongery of typical Italian design.

The following afternoon we stood down, and Major Stevens paid us a visit at tea time to tell us how the squadron had fared during the battle.

'Bad news, I'm afraid,' he told us. 'Ginger and two men were killed yesterday afternoon. But "A" Troop has done marvellously, and Paul has been put in for a decoration!'

We were very sad. 'A' Troop had had rotten luck ever since we landed in the country, and now we had lost poor Hamilton – our youngest and keenest soldier.

The main enemy effort on the Brigade sector – with Austrian mountain troops – had been directed against the 1st and 3rd Battalions holding the Djebel Bou Arada and had preceded the abortive attack by the Italian infantry against the 2nd Battalion.

The mountain regiment went about their attack in a thoroughly competent manner and began well with a stroke of luck. The 3rd Battalion maintained standing patrols during the day and listening posts by night on forward features which they could not cover. The standing patrols used to go out one hour before dawn to relieve the listening posts. The enemy advance began just as the changeover was taking place. The standing patrol was overrun before it realized what was afoot, and the German infantry followed the listening patrol in through our lines. Once inside they set to work furiously to dig in before daylight, setting up their heavy machine-guns and mortars on a low hill in our midst.

One of the platoon commanders, Lieutenant Street, saw figures moving about in the dark in the middle of his position and whispered hoarsely, 'Don't make such a row. There may be Germans about!'

The next instant he was overpowered and propelled at the muzzle of a Schmeisser before the enemy officer, who ordered him to lead the way to company headquarters. Instead, the parachutist led the Germans straight on to his own wire, set off the alarm devices and fell flat as our machine-guns opened up. The Germans scattered, but the British and German officers, to their mutual surprise, found themselves cowering in the same hole.

'Look out! Grenade!' shouted the Englishman, distracting the other's attention; and then hit the German with all his strength. A minute later the parachute officer rejoined his own men, bearing, in the spirit of tradition, the arms and equipment of the vanquished.

At first light the main German force tried to break into the battalion perimeter. Fierce fighting went on all day with attack and counter-attack, but there was no further penetration, and the enemy began to withdraw. Meanwhile, the 1st Battalion was also heavily engaged on its sector and could give it no help, so 'A' and 'C' Troops of the parachute engineers were sent up to the Djebel Bou Arada to lend a hand.

Immediately on arrival 'A' Troop were given the task of cleaning up an enemy platoon entrenched with two machine-guns on a hill in the 3rd Battalion position.

Under cover of a short bombardment by the 3rd Battalion mortars Paul Mason got the troop into position on the flank of the hill and then at a signal they charged upwards with bayonets fixed and Brens firing from the hip. At once they were met by heavy fire, but by great determination and skilful use of ground each section got within striking distance without serious casualties. Then one of the Spandaus jammed, and they were into the position with their bayonets, cheering like mad, with the Germans throwing their hands up all around. Twenty of the enemy and two machine-guns were accounted for, but poor Ginger had been shot dead in the moment of triumph.

In all, the 3rd Battalion took a hundred and fifty prisoners and accounted for over two hundred and fifty enemy dead.

When things returned to normal we settled down again to our routine of booby-trapping and mine-laying, using many devices to block the more obvious lines of approach. Ravines and gullies were filled with a maze of concertina wire, to which 'infernal machines' were attached. Trip wires and sudden death abounded everywhere, but the enemy did not attack again, and our total bag amounted to a couple of sheep. The infantry had too high a respect for our handiwork to salvage the corpses themselves, so *we* had mutton for dinner for a week on end.

At the beginning of March orders circulated company commanders for handing over our positions to American troops. The 1st Battalion was taken out of the line to a rest camp near Teboursouk, and our immediate future looked more cheerful.

Almost overnight an unusual flow of transport appeared on the roads as the new regiment moved into the line. This was an unprecedented sight, since the frequent German fighter-sweeps up and down the valley dictated a very cautious and limited movement during the day. So we watched this activity with anxiety. We soon discovered, however, that the Americans were quite capable of looking after themselves. Nearly every 3-ton truck had a half-inch machine-gun mounted on the driver's cab, providing an unwelcome surprise for intruders after the unarmed British vehicles. Down came half a dozen Focke-Wulf 190s, but the Americans stood their ground and replied with such a blizzard of heavy shot that the Germans sheered off and went in search of easier prey. How we envied the American armament which enabled them to hit back!

But our hopes of a rest were to be disappointed. On the 5th of March we learnt that it had been cancelled, and that we were being transferred to another sector of the front – not even the OC knew where.

We made the journey in two stages, driving all the first night until dawn and then stopping the following day in a transit area near Teboursouk. At dusk we moved off again, taking the road to Souk-el-Arba, then east through Béja and out on the winding hill road to Djebel Abiod.

At about four-thirty in the morning we tumbled out very cold and cramped into pale moonlight and dawn mist. We were on a tarmac road which ran across the foot of a valley coming in from the west. A river wound down the centre dividing the meadow land, and massive lumps of hills covered in dense scrub rose all around, looking very black and sinister in the darkness. To the north the road disappeared up a narrow gorge with a mountain torrent running in a deep ravine beside it, while to the south a railway crossed a gap in the hills by a huge steel and concrete viaduct, separating the valley from the open country beyond.

The trees on the ridge to our left were fully grown, and these woodlands and the lush meadow had a very English look.

We called it Happy Valley.

9
Happy Valley
March 1943

Earlier in the month the Germans had made a powerful attack on the northern coastal sector and had severely mauled the 139th Infantry Brigade of 46th Division which had been holding very thinly a large extent of front. Our men were forced to fall back about fifteen miles, abandoning the little village of Sedjenane and withdrawing rapidly to the cover of the rocky pass where the main road runs through the Tamera gorge.

This brigade had suffered heavily, losing a large proportion of its transport and stores, and was in no fit state to hold back the advancing enemy forces. Thus the 1st Parachute Brigade had had to forgo its much-needed rest and found itself, at dawn on 7th March, in Happy Valley, on the Djebel Abiod front.

The 1st and 3rd Battalions immediately took over positions astride the road and passed the day digging in painfully on rock-hard ground. The 1st Battalion had the most northerly position, on a long hump-backed hill named Death Ridge, in front of Tamera railway halt; the 3rd Battalion occupied a thickly wooded hill west of the gorge. The 2nd Battalion arrived late in the evening and moved up on to the crest of a high spur on the right flank. This was densely covered with dwarf cork trees and became known as Cork Wood. But already the Germans were on the move again, and at dawn on 8th March fell upon our positions in great strength.

As soon as it was light it was apparent that the enemy effort was in two thrusts; the main attack against the

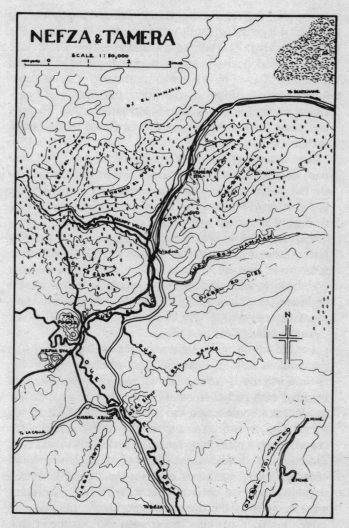

junction of the 1st and 2nd Battalions, and another along a bald ridge to our south in an attempt to outflank the Tamera gorge. The second was successfully held, thanks to a tremendous machine-gun duel engaged in by the 2nd Battalion assisted by the remnants of the Yorks and Lancs on the reverse slopes of the ridge; but the other penetrated deeply into Cork Wood, surrounded 'A' Company and curled round the rear of the 1st Battalion on Death Ridge.

An immediate counter-attack saved the day. 'A' Company of the 3rd Battalion crossed the road and charged up the hill, joining hands with a platoon of 'C' Company of the 2nd Battalion. Meanwhile a platoon of the beleaguered 'A' Company broke out and swept down the wooded slopes. These carried all before them, and the Germans fled leaving sixty prisoners in our hands. On the left the 1st Battalion stood firm, and by the end of the day the enemy was withdrawing, leaving all our front intact. As it grew dark a flight of Stukas dive-bombed Cork Wood and made enormous craters among 'A' Company's forward platoons, causing a number of casualties.

For the whole of the night and the next day the brigade dug without respite. Beneath a foot of peaty top soil the ground was mostly rock, and many hours would be spent working with picks, crowbars and sometimes explosives to remove a boulder and increase the depth of the trench by an inch or two. Apart from the rock the hills were covered with a forbidding tangle of undergrowth and cork shrubs, which deadened the sound of movement, reduced vision to a very maximum of twenty yards and lent itself to infiltration by a determined enemy. But the Germans were nervous of the danger lurking in the thickets and evidently afraid of this close country, so our men made friends with the woods, camouflaged themselves and their positions to be invisible even at the closest range, took in a lavish store of grenades – and waited.

In support of the parachutists were three battered battalions of 139th Infantry Brigade, of which the 2nd/5th Leicesters and the Sherwood Foresters figured most prominently in the ensuing battles. On our left was a formation of young Frenchmen, called the Corps Franc d'Afrique, who were very brave and had an able commander, Colonel Durand, but were poorly armed and undertrained. We could also call upon some artillery support from the medium and field regiments of 46th Division, of which four troops of 25-pounders were deployed round Happy Valley.

By this time the Germans were already in possession of the peak which dominated the whole battlefield. The rocky mass of the Djebel Bel Harch towered above all the other hills, and our 25-pounders were mostly under direct observation by the enemy. Consequently they were subjected to accurate counter-battery fire, but despite this they managed to escape serious punishment and gave sterling service.

We ourselves were given a reserve position near brigade headquarters in the woodlands on the southern side of Happy Valley and were required to provide a reserve of infantry whenever the need arose. After the attack of the previous day 'A' Troop were sent up to join 'A' Company of the 2nd Battalion, and Tony Miles went off with his batman to take over a platoon of 'S' Company of the 1st Battalion. He left us with a wry face – we knew that infantry subalterns did not last long in this jungle warfare.

Once again our wonderful 16th Parachute Field Ambulance were operating with their surgical teams right forward in the battle area and used the main dressing station at Tabarka as their base. Many times their operating tents were pierced by shell and mortar splinters, but they carried on undismayed. The knowledge of prompt surgical attention contributed enormously to our men's very high morale.

We now lived in a state of perpetual stand-to against a renewal of the offensive. The Germans shelled and mortared us continuously and were very active in the air.

Air attack was very unpleasant. Messerschmitt fighters would come skimming over the hills and down into the valley to shoot up any movement along the roads, or would rake the tops of Death Ridge and Cork Wood with cannon and machine-gun fire. Sometimes a flock of bomb-carrying Focke-Wulf fighters raced in, planted their bombs where they believed the 25-pounders to be, and whirled away before our own light ack-ack could get in an effective burst. There would be several seconds of appalling noise and concussion, clouds of dust and acrid smoke, but surprisingly little damage.

On one occasion brigade headquarters was attacked by Stukas, and *we* got the benefit of its bombs. We heard the usual sound of aircraft approaching, and a tight formation of Ju 87s appeared with their fighter escort weaving round them. Suddenly there was the deep moan of a Stuka beginning its dive, and I was horrified to see the plane standing on its nose vertically above me, apparently in the act of diving right into the bottom of my trench. The moaning whistle changed to a shriek.

'Get down,' I yelled. 'Here she comes!' And come it did. For a second everything went black with the concussion, and mud, branches and blackened clay came raining down around us.

There were no casualties, but it had scored a direct hit on our explosives store, and nearly a ton of ammonal, gun-cotton and plastic HE had gone up with the bomb. Small wonder that everyone was looking a little drunk.

On the 10th March we were aroused a little before dawn by racing bursts from belt-fed Solothurns and intense German gunfire. At once, tongues of flame stabbed the semi-darkness in the meadow below us, as our 25-pounders poured shells over Cork Wood into the dip at the foot of the Djebel Bel Harch. The noise of the battle intensified as it grew lighter – a sudden flare-up of machine-gun fire swelling in hideous crescendo, the crump and plumes of smoke from a cascade of 80-mm mortar bombs, and the almost incessant whip and crack of shells. Somewhere out in front our counter-barrage rumbled like thunder and gave us heart.

The Germans began their attack against the centre and northern positions of the 1st Battalion on Death Ridge. Then, at first light, lorried infantry were seen deploying at the level-crossing about half a mile to the north, and a heavy attack came in against the north-western end of the ridge, with another down the valley towards Tamera station. 'T' Company on the northern edge were at last surrounded and lost heavily during many hours of concentric attacks, but they held on stubbornly. Eventually the survivors were relieved in the late afternoon by a counter-attack led by Colonel Pearson himself with all immediate battalion reserves, clerks, wireless section, cooks and stretcher-bearers, who drove the Germans off the northern end of the ridge.

Another attack at midday against the southern end was held by the interlocking fire of the 1st and 2nd Battalions. The Germans tried to penetrate into Cork Wood, but were finally stopped on the northern and eastern slopes, and so heavy were their losses that they made no further attempt that day.

With the virtual loss of 'T' Company it was now impossible for the 1st Battalion to hold the whole of Death Ridge, particularly the exposed northern end, so it pulled back its line to the more densely wooded southern slopes and had to resign itself to the enemy occupying the slightly higher half.

In our counter-attacks separate groups could not keep touch in this dense jungle-like country, so we used to form up in an extended line, with three or four paces between each man. Then at a signal from the centre the force would move forward, beating the thickets as it went. Our camouflaged clothing and helmets were peculiarly suited to this type of country and practically invisible over a few yards. Invariably the German infantry had had no time to dig in, and as the noise of shouting and beating approached they usually slunk away through the undergrowth in twos and threes, firing wildly. Then, above the final bedlam of war-whoops and pot-shots, 'Ho – Mahomet!' the battle cry of the 1st Brigade, would ring out and echo round the wooded slopes, as the line closed and the Germans ran.

'Ho – Ma-homet!' was one of those inexplicable things which suddenly take root; within a few hours it was in common use throughout the whole brigade. Possibly it was derived from the long-drawn-out cry of the Arab muezzin from the hill-tops and mosques of Bou Arada, calling the Faithful to prayer – a sound which puzzled our men for a while, and which they used to mimic. For the Germans it was the knell of doom, heralding a determined counter-attack and thickets erupting green-clad men roaring to the charge. It was no idle reputation that the British paratroops won in the Tamera Valley.

'Well done, 1st Parachute Brigade!' Lieutenant-General Allfrey, commanding Fifth Corps, wrote later: 'I

—

knew that you would hold them!' Our three diminished battalions, with only the briefest period to prepare the defence, had indeed held a vastly superior German force flushed with victory. The credit was to the individual soldier, who held his ground and refused to be dislodged even when cut off.

There was, for instance, the sergeant of 'T' Company of the 1st Battalion, who became isolated with two companions but continued to fight on until relieved by the counter-attack in the afternoon. They found him sitting in his slit trench – his companions lay dead in the bottom. On the parapet were mounted a pair of Bren guns, with a pile of grenades ready to hand. In the undergrowth around were strewn about thirty dead Germans. 'Nobody gave me any orders to retire,' he explained, 'so we thought it best to stay here and fight it out.'

To an observer half a mile behind the front the battle had appeared strangely horrible in the way a pall of smoke hung like a shroud above our positions and the way German guns crackled above the din. There is always a tendency to over-estimate the power of an enemy attack; his machine-guns sound so much more powerful and terrible than your own, his mortar barrage quite over-whelming. The waves of Focke-Wulfs dropped their bombs along the ridge, then circled round to blast it with their guns. A fountain of white Very lights would go up as they swept in to bomb; this was to mark the limit of the German advance and show the pilots where to strafe. The Very lights had been coming closer and the crisis was approaching.

But it was not until the afternoon that we received the long-expected message. David came round the 'B' Troop dugouts and trenches and told us to get packed up quickly.

'We're going up to help the 2nd Battalion,' he told Roy and myself, who were occupying the same hole. 'The 1st Battalion's having a bad time, but the enemy hasn't broken through and the 3rd Bat's going to give them a hand. The 2nd Battalion's holding firm, but the Brigadier wants us to go up and protect their left flank – there has been quite a bit of enemy infiltration round the side of Cork Wood.'

Although the enemy had been shelling Happy Valley all the morning, to keep down our own artillery fire, there was a lull when 'B' Troop crossed the river and meadow in extended formation and moved rapidly into the cover of the wooded ground near the road. There were a few anxious moments as we passed the guns, but the enemy held his fire; the gunners smiled at us from the cover of their holes and wished us luck.

We met Colonel Frost of the 2nd Battalion outside his headquarters – an exceedingly damp dugout formed from a culvert under the railway lines. He explained the situation briefly. The battalion had not been forced to give up any ground, but the enemy had established a small foothold in the gap between 'B' and 'C' Companies and was being supplied with food and ammunition by air. (Even as he was speaking four Stukas came low over the top of Cork Wood and let go their supplies; the parachutes fluttered down and disappeared into the wood.) He proposed to deal with this pocket with a strong patrol during the night; a platoon would be withdrawn from 'C' Company for this purpose, and we were to take over its position. At the same time as 10 Platoon delivered its night attack, 'B' Troop would move down to the bottom of the slope on the north side of Cork Wood, to prevent reinforcement of the Germans in the pocket. The attack was timed for eight o'clock.

At dusk the Colonel called for his protective section and led the way to 'C' Company headquarters, where he disappeared into a hole in the ground with Major Ross, and a ground-sheet was pulled over the top; one caught the glimmer of a torch searching a map. All noise of battle had died down with darkness, and in the depth of the woods there was silence – except for the murmur of the voices and the drip of water on the sagging ground-sheet. In a few minutes a runner led us to our allotted position.

This was a small clearing on the northern edge of the wood. In front the ground fell away steeply, and our parapets were on the top of a rocky escarpment covered with cork bushes. It was the most western post of 'C' Company and guarded the long, wooded flank between the 2nd and 1st Battalions. As we approached, the post came to life as 10 Platoon crawled out of their trenches, stretched themselves and struggled into their packs. Alexander, the platoon commander, pointed out the various positions.

'We've got two German Solothurns,' he said in conclusion. 'One is out in that forward pit. I've got the other mounted on its tripod and firing on a fixed line across the front of the 1st Battalion. We've masses of ammunition and we'll let you have them as long as you're here.' These extra guns, with our four Brens, gave us considerable fire power.

As 10 Platoon filed off like shadows, through the wall of shrubs, we got our sections settled in and had a look round. The rocky clearing, dotted with occasional patches of bush, extended for about sixty yards. Beyond that, the cork woods closed in thickly, with a curtain of leaves which plunged the undergrowth into gloomy twilight even when the sun was out. To the east of us lay the left-hand platoon of 'C' Company, dug in beneath a covering of trees rather higher than the rest. To the west the land fell away gradually, and the undergrowth thinned a little for about two hundred yards, then sprang up again as the hill dropped to the railway line and the Tamera gorge. On the enemy side the cork thickets blanketed the front of the escarpment, making an approach from that quarter noisy and difficult.

There were sufficient trenches dug on the top of the clearing for Troop headquarters and one section only. The others had to dig in farther down the slope. The pits were very shallow, and the parapets had been built up with lumps of rock; so, with its stony walls and natural strength, we christened our position The Citadel.

At about seven-thirty we climbed silently down the escarpment through the interlacing hedge of thickets and went slowly through the wood towards the enemy's lines. We crept forward parting the branches carefully and stepping cautiously over the outcrops of rock. Each man kept a yard from his neighbour, and all orders were passed in whispers. Occasionally the moon peered through a rent in the rainclouds and cast ghostly shadows among the gnarled and grotesquely arm-like branches, then plunged us into a tomblike darkness again. Once or twice we passed a cluster of German corpses sprawled unnaturally among the ferns and rock. There was a horrible, eerie atmosphere down there; leaves wiped one's face, and branches plucked like fingers at weapons and equipment. At last came the whispered order to lie down.

With horrifying unexpectedness a German machine-gun opened up, it seemed, at our elbows. At once the woods came to life with confused shouts, breaking twigs, shots and flashes and then three thunderous cracks from bursting grenades, followed by a deathly silence for some seconds. Suddenly there was a blood-curdling scream.

'Oh – o – o – ow! Otto! Otto! Wo sind Sie? Oh! Otto! Ich kann nicht sehen! Otto! Wo sind Sie?' The gun hammered away again, hosing tracer in every direction. Several others took up the signal, and the combined noise filled the woods with a continuous roar.

Crash! Crash! Crash! Three more grenades exploded to our right, and the air moaned with fragments.

'Hände hoch! Hands up, Jerry! Hände hoch!' More shouts, a sudden rattle from a sub-machine-gun, another long, revving burst from the Solothurn, and again that piercing scream. Gradually the noise faded away.

After half an hour's vigil we were withdrawn and crept back to the Citadel. We heard that the attack had failed; the enemy were too strong and too well entrenched.

We had half the Troop standing-to all night. In every two-man pit, one remained alert while the other slept or dozed for a couple of hours. At an hour before dawn we stood-to in the normal way, straining our eyes to pierce the night's darkest hour and listening for the tell-tale rustle of the enemy approach. Everything remained still and ominous.

Thump! CRASH! Thump! CRASH! I had just time to dive to the bottom of my hole as four shells in quick succession from an enemy high-velocity gun shattered the woods below us. The dust cleared after a minute or two, and I put my head over the top.

'Everyone OK?' I asked. Other heads were appearing.

'Yes, we're OK, sir,' they shouted back. We joked about the rude awakening the Hun had expected to give us. Then someone came running up the hill. There was that rising mutter in the other sections which told of evil tidings.

That salvo had landed in our section position farthest down the slope. Roy was dead, killed instantly by the first shell, and three sappers seriously injured by the others as they went to give help. We buried him as deep as we could and marked his grave with his helmet on the top of a stake.

This dawn shelling became a feature of our stay in Cork Wood. Every morning at exactly six o'clock – typically Teuton – the same battery of 105-mm infantry guns would fire four shells. We became so accustomed to its regularity that we used to slide subconsciously to the bottom of the trench as the first gun fired. We were never caught again.

Just before we stood down, runners arrived with our water and rations – a blanketful of cold tins of stew and pudding and a packet of dry biscuits – also a warning from Major Ross that there should be no movement outside the trenches during the day. The Djebel Bel Harch looked down on us only half a mile away. We ate our greasy hash out of a slimy tin and rationed out the water at half a bottle per man. Then we endeavoured to scratch our holes a little deeper, feeling naked and uncomfortable as we looked across at the German positions.

Soon it began to rain. Each trench became a natural sump as a hundred rivulets snaked down the hill. The rain thundered through the cork leaves and poured in a transparent skin down the trunks and shoots. Landmarks faded, and even one's next-door neighbour grew dim and ghostly. It poured in a cascade off our helmets, through our water-laden clothing, and coursed down our bodies to find a reservoir between our toes.

In the afternoon it was still raining, having twice abated and poured again with undiminished vigour. At about two o'clock a long line of figures loomed out of the watery fog and picked their way slowly up the hill. Section after section of rain-sodden paratroopers passed us, their bayonets fixed and weapons cradled against the hip.

'What's up, chum?' my men asked. 'What mob are you?'

'Oh, us? We're the 3rd Bat!' replied a watery warrior. 'We're the lot what pick all the lousy jobs! Somebody wants us to go and sort out some Jerry machine-guns up here, or something! Couldn't have picked a nicer day, could they?' His expletives were lost in the thickets as he and his companions disappeared in the curtain of rain.

Five minutes passed before the first German machine-gun roared suddenly into life with a long startled burst. Red and white tracer flickered and crackled above our heads and curved away into the haze behind. Others joined in immediately and rippled out a rhythmic tattoo. (The Germans seemed to revel in these tuneful effects on the trigger – perhaps the noise was reassuring.) I found myself deliberating whether to jump into a trench filled with water or be killed decently and in comparative comfort above ground. In the end I huddled down behind a rock, watching the water splash from my helmet and listening to the bullets crack a few feet above my head. I laughed weakly and wondered whether the rain was watering-down the bullets, or bullets thickening-up the rain.

Grenades burst unexpectedly loudly. The machine-guns were suddenly silent as though stunned by the concussions.

'Hand up! Hands up, you bastards!' I was amazed how clearly the shouts drifted down to us. Then the firing broke out again, there were more wild shouts, orders and curses and finally the renewed roar of the machine-guns, drowning all other sound.

Two figures appeared out of the woods and staggered down the hill towards us. One was leading the other, who rolled drunkenly, a superficial wound in his forehead streaming blood, which the rain washed in a smear all over his face. The man was dazed and shaken, but otherwise not badly hurt.

'There's too many Jerries up there!' the unwounded man remarked as the pair tottered past. 'The whole place is stiff with machine-guns! We got one, but there's too many of them! We got pinned down! They're getting one of our platoons out now.'

A quarter of an hour later the company was withdrawn; the enemy still held a sizeable penetration area.

That night the whole of the troop was employed on carrying mortar ammunition up from the road. All the battalion mortars were being concentrated in the 'C' Company area for a massed barrage to cover a final assault on the enemy pocket. We ourselves had learnt how extremely unpleasant mortar bombardment in a thickly wooded area can be: the sensitive-fused bombs burst in the branches overhead with devastating effect, the fragments seeking out even well-dug-in troops.

At dawn the next morning a small patrol was sent out before the attack. They went forward cautiously, but they crawled on and on until at last they came upon the enemy pits, littered with dead, empty ammunition boxes, discarded weapons and equipment and all the rubbish of war, but no other sign of life. The fierce engagement of the previous afternoon had succeeded in alarming the Germans into withdrawal. We knew then that the immediate crisis had passed.

Our count of prisoners had by now risen to nearly three hundred. From the first they were dismayed to find such stubborn opposition.

'We were told there was nothing to stop us reaching Djebel Abiod,' they told the brigade intelligence officer. 'We had no idea that the englische Fallschirmjäger were on this front.'

The strength of the attack can be gauged from the number of German units represented amongst the prisoners. Some were parachutists like ourselves, in long dark-green overalls, from a parachute engineer battalion commanded by a Major Witzig, who had first gained fame for his drop and capture of the Belgian fort at Ebn-Emael in 1940, and his part in the attack on the Corinth Canal and in Crete. Witzig was a brave and experienced commander, so much so that, on the fall of Tunis, the Germans flew him out of Africa; but we were to hear more of him before that.

Others came from three motorized battalions of the 81st Panzer Grenadier Regiment of the 10th Panzer Division. They had been brought up from Bou Arada at about the same time as ourselves. Then there were a number from the three battalions of the Barentin Regiment, one of the few remaining regular formations in the German army, and who now wore the sandy-coloured overalls and palm-tree flash of the Afrika Korps. Some belonged to the battalions of the Tunis Regiment, a formation re-formed on African soil from the remnants of the original units flown in from Sicily. From the French on our left came Italians of a Bersaglieri regiment; this sector became known as the 'Second Eleven Match', but the Bersaglieri were the best formation the Italians had. The German commander on the northern sector, General von Manteuffel, had assembled an impressive display of first-class troops against us – ten German battalions concentrated for the most part against our three, each never more than three hundred men strong. But the

Tamera gorge position held firm, and the northern hinge to our line in Tunisia remained unbroken if a little insecure.

Every night from now onwards we gradually improved the strength of our position. Our first task was to get wired in, and every available man was put on to carrying up the rolls of concertina wire from the dump near the road. It was tedious work, and each man had to make four or five twenty-minute journeys a night, but at the end of four days we had hedged our positions about with such an impenetrable wall of wire in the already formidable undergrowth, that we felt very secure.

Yet, during daylight, we were exposed to a microscopic scrutiny by the Germans on the Djebel Bel, and the slightest movement would bring down a rain of mortar bombs. We could only crawl out at dusk to perform necessary duties, to eat our main meal and bring up rations and supplies. Throughout the entire day we crouched in our four-foot slits, and time weighed heavily on our hands.

The weather did its utmost to make our life unbearable. We did not mind the actual rain so much – we became quite used to the drenching flail which lashed us for hours on end. It was the everlasting contact with wet clothes, adhering clammily to one's skin, which was so unpleasant, and that pungent smell of dank and rotting cloth. Worst of all was the misery of trying to sleep huddled in a narrow pit, too small for any sort of comfort, with water seeping down the sides and collecting in puddles round your thighs – and many hours of darkness ahead before the first signs of daylight and warmth.

We came to live a very insular life up there in the woods. We never saw anything of company headquarters, which we only knew as existing a hundred yards away, deep in a wall of thickets. Very rarely did we get a visit from the commander of 9 Platoon, our right-hand neighbours, as remote as an atoll in the ocean – thirty yards away. Casual visits had their risks; for one could not hesitate long in distinguishing friend from foe, and there was at least one terrible mistake.

Our own artillery bombarding Djebel Bel Harch caused us more palpitations than did any surprises from the Germans. One particular troop of guns was sited near the Tamera Gorge directly behind us. Their target lay about two hundred yards on the other side of Cork Wood, but their shells only just cleared the hill, whizzing a mere six feet or so above our heads. It was quite terrifying – the thickets shook as though parted by a hurricane, and the air shrieked and throbbed with the torrent of shells. Every shot sounded exactly as though it was landing short and hurtling straight for us, and we felt almost as thankful when the bombardment ceased as the Germans at the receiving end. Afterwards, the silence seemed sweeter than music.

One attempt was made to drive the Germans off the Djebel Bel Harch, and so give us control of the battlefield. General Allfrey had visited Cork Wood on the 12th March; and on the 13th a battalion of the Sherwood Foresters passed through the 1st Battalion on Death Ridge and began to scale the almost precipitous slopes. We heard their Brens rattling away, getting nearer and nearer the summit. Finally there was a terrific flare-up of machine-gun fire, a burst of cheering, followed by silence. We thought the Djebel Bel was ours. But shortly afterwards our 25-pounders began to shell the peak. We learnt that the Panzer Grenadiers had counter-attacked and swept the Foresters away, and it was *their* shouts of success we had heard.

Immediately after this attack the Foresters re-formed under the lee of Death Ridge and that evening took over from the 1st Battalion, who were withdrawn to rest by the sea at Tabarka.

The 1st Battalion, during the last attack, had clung to their positions on Death Ridge by their fingernails. Although they were down to a mere handful of men they made up for lack of numbers by their tenacity and fire-power. Every workable automatic – captured German Solothurns from earlier engagements, Italian Bredas from Bou Arada, Besas out of our knocked-out tanks – everything was pressed into service.

But to show the state of complete mental and physical exhaustion to which a soldier can sink after a long period of battle strain it is necessary to tell how their few survivors came out of the line. The trucks arrived at Tabarka and drew up on the roadside, opposite a long line of tents about fifty yards away. There, hot food, clean dry clothes, blankets and warmth were waiting for them.

The bearded, ragged and filthy men tottered out of the trucks, collapsed on to the ground beside the road, and went fast asleep in the rain.

Immediately after our arrival in Cork Wood, brigade headquarters and our own squadron camp came in for very heavy shelling. The place was, of course, under observation from the Djebel Bel, and it was surprising that it had not happened before. Consequently they removed themselves to a less disturbed area behind Djebel Abiod, among the sand-dunes along the Tabarka road.

I had occasion to go back there one day – David wanted some special equipment and explosives sent up to us on Cork Wood. There had been changes since we had been away; 'A' Troop had been replaced by 'C' Troop in the line and were engaged in the more gentle occupation of improving a hill road for our brigade supplies, the main Djebel Abiod road being too exposed for traffic during daylight.

I found Tony at Squadron headquarters, taking a rest after a particularly unpleasant experience with the 1st Battalion. 'S' Company, reduced to fifty men and two other officers besides himself, had taken the brunt of the enemy attack and had suffered correspondingly. When they were withdrawn they numbered only an officer and twenty men, Tony and his batman having miraculously survived.

There had been a devastating artillery and mortar bombardment, supplemented by 20-mm pom-poms which blazed a scorching blizzard of tracer through the undergrowth. One 105-mm shell had landed on his parapet, filling the trench with blackened mud and rock and tossing his haversack and equipment into the branches of a nearby tree. He lay in a heap in the bottom of his pit, dazed, his mouth full of grit, ears roaring and a thousand lights dancing before his eyes. Everything was quiet again on top, and smoke hung in the air like a cloud.

'Here they come, sir!' his batman shouted. 'They're coming through!' Tony scrambled to his knees, to see the thickets swarming with men in field grey advancing in a horde. There was a confusion of rifle and Bren shots, grenades and bayonets: he saw the enemy fall and dive for cover, and then his automatic rifle was empty and he was fumbling for another clip.

At once they counter-attacked through the bushes in a cheering crescent, shooting suddenly at a running form, down the slope and up the other side. 'Wer-Ho – Mahomet!' they shouted as they reached the crest of the dunes to the north, and the Germans were suddenly gone.

Then Tony collected the remnants of the company and led them back.

They were now utterly exhausted, and many collapsed in their trenches. The next thing Tony knew was that he was lying face downwards in his and somebody was shovelling earth on top of him.

'What the hell's going on?' he enquired angrily, as he heaved himself up and shook the soil out of his hair – and then understood. A burial party under the battalion padre was going round filling in the trenches of the dead.

'I don't think I will be killed now,' Tony concluded. 'After all, whoever heard of a bloke being planted twice?'

On the 14th March the Germans came on again, this time making a wide outflanking movement to the right of the brigade sector. They had some initial success, but eventually outran their supplies and were forced to fall back. In the evening the Panzer Grenadier Regiment on the Djebel Bel flung itself against the north-east corner of Cork Wood, supported by a squadron of Stukas. Their forward troops put up their customary Very light signals, which were immediately copied by our men; and this so confused the pilots that they heavily bombed their own positions and completely broke up the attack. By nightfall all was quiet again.

The 15th was uneventful, except for bombing of the gun positions in Happy Valley; and that night the Leicesters replaced the 3rd Battalion, who were withdrawn to Tabarka.

After a further quiet day marked by great activity behind the enemy lines the Germans struck again on the 17th March. They switched the direction of their blow to the west of our area and attacked between the French and the Leicesters and Foresters astride the road. At first the

Germans were held, but they poured in relentlessly, thrusting particularly at the junction of the British and French formations. By the afternoon, messages of distress were coming from the French, who were eventually given permission to withdraw, while the Leicesters reported that they were almost completely surrounded.

By evening it looked as if the enemy was on the point of rolling up the whole of our positions, although Cork Wood had not yet been attacked. At once the 1st and 3rd Battalions – the 3rd had only arrived at Tabarka the day before – were ordered back into the line. At the same time it was decided to abandon the Tamera Gorge and withdraw to the hills covering Nefza.

During the night the Foresters withdrew from Death Ridge to a pre-arranged position in our rear and were followed by the Leicesters in the early hours of the morning. Meanwhile, the 1st and 3rd Battalions were due to arrive in the Tamera area just before dawn. The 3rd Battalion would move on to a series of low hills southeast of the viaduct. The 1st Battalion was to push up the Tamera Gorge and counter-attack the German penetration area, while the 2nd Battalion moved out of Cork Wood. It was just as well that we knew nothing about these movements until the next morning, or we might have passed a very anxious night.

On the 18th March we stood-to in The Citadel just before dawn as usual, especially apprehensive, perhaps, in expectation of the enemy's attack. Suddenly a terrific bombardment began; salvo after salvo of medium shells screeched over to land with geysers of black smoke and mud on Death Ridge. For half an hour the guns rumbled away behind Djebel Abiod, and the shells buried the wooded slopes four hundred yards away beneath a cloud of smoke and dust. Then the order came for us to pack up and get out.

As it started to get light we hurriedly booby-trapped our trenches with live grenades, then made our way down to the main road. We piled all our equipment and stores on to our Everest carriers, but a crate of Naafi beer defeated us. We drank what we could with hurried gulps, then smashed up the rest with our rifle butts. That was the first beer we had seen since Christmas.

David remained behind with a small party to blow up the culvert under the main road in the Tamera Gorge. Here the road takes a long bend, with the culvert at its middle point. On one side the cutting rises almost sheer for twenty feet, on the other side the river runs in a narrow gorge fifteen feet below – an awkward place to bridge and impossible to get round. The demolition party was very successful – the culvert went up just as a German armoured-carrier was coming round the corner. The driver jammed on his brakes too late, and the crew jumped clear and surrendered as the vehicle toppled over into the ravine.

As we withdrew down the road, under cover of the mass of Cork Wood on our left, the Germans got wind of our movement and began to shell the Gorge and valley with airburst and shrapnel shells. Black patches of smoke appeared in the low clouds with a succession of shattering cracks, and the fragments came pattering down. The 2nd Battalion were also moving out; there were long lines of them coming down from the woods, and we passed little groups of platoons sheltering in the ditch as they waited for the advance-guard to pass through. Those platoons were pathetically small, but I had to smile at their impressive display of weapons – each man with a long German machine-gun belt round his neck, and the majority burdened down with Solothurns on top of their other equipment.

When we reached the viaduct the columns divided, the 2nd Battalion going westwards to their new positions round Nefza, while the two engineer troops went on towards Djebel Abiod. We halted in the shelter of the giant stone columns and waited for 'C' Troop to catch up. The enemy shells were bursting three hundred yards away, and we wondered how long it would be before they started to search out us.

'C' Troop arrived, and we set off with fifty yards between sections, keeping out of observation as far as possible behind the embankment of the road. We had only covered half a mile when the Germans switched their attention to the viaduct – we had moved just in time. Heavy 155-mm shells were now landing all round the massive piers, and fountains of mud and water were thundering high in the air. The enemy had given up using airburst and had now re-fused for percussion – quite unsuitable here, for the shells lost all their effect in the mud.

A very large number failed to explode in the soft ground. We had noticed it time and again at Bou Arada and in Cork Wood, but this morning there seemed a larger proportion of duds than usual. One of the brigade's officers had composed a little ode to the Unhappy Dud, and this was running in my mind:

> Thud!
> In the mud!
> Another dud!!
> Thank God!!!

Too late, I heard the terrible warning shriek rushing down upon us. 'Look out!' I yelled. There was a blinding flash a few yards on our left, a dizzy blackness, and I felt myself cart-wheeling like a leaf in the breeze.

'This is the end,' I thought, but landed with a reassuring thump in the muddy slime of the ditch beside the road.

10
Victory at Tamera
April–May 1943

It was six weeks later when I rejoined our Rear Details in the farm at Boufarik after recovering from a peppering of shell splinters.

Nothing had altered much since we were here in January. The sun was shining, the hills behind Blida looked just as blue and the whole countryside smelt fresh and fragrant. It was the beginning of May, and the ground-mist of orange blossom which covered the plain was unbelievably beautiful. That certainly was something quite new, but when I saw the old familiar storks nesting on the barns I felt I was coming home.

I could hardly believe my eyes when I put my head in at an open window of the Officers' Mess and saw David Westley having lunch by himself.

'Where did you spring from?' he exclaimed. 'You're the last person I expected to see! Come on in and have some food!'

I swung my legs over the window-ledge and sat down at the trestle table. David bellowed for the mess orderly, and soon I was making up my leeway in all the news.

'What on earth are you doing here, David?' I enquired. 'You haven't been wounded too, have you?'

'Good gracious, no!' he replied. 'I brought a small advance party down yesterday, as the whole Brigade is arriving in a couple of days' time.'

Then my eye noticed the new crowns on his tunic, but David forestalled me.

'There have been quite a few changes since you've been

away,' he went on. 'Yes, I've been appointed OC of the 2nd Parachute Squadron and I am afraid I shall be leaving you all at the end of the week. I suppose you haven't heard that the whole of the 1st Airborne Division has arrived at Oran? Then, we have lost Henry Walker. He was never likely to jump again after his accident and he has gone to the SAS Battalion as adjutant. Jack Burroughs has been appointed second in command, George Irwin has taken over "B" Troop from me and Paddy has got "C" Troop.'

'And what news of the others?' I enquired.

'All well, I'm glad to say, except that two of our reinforcement officers, Ted Boyse and Gerald Sims, were wounded slightly. They came after you were hit. The other two, Tim Hollings and Joe Wallace, are with "B" Troop and Headquarters. Tom Slater did very well with the 2nd Battalion and even commanded a company for a short time during the big attack when we pushed the Bosche back to Sedjenane.'

'Sedjenane!' I exclaimed. 'But that was miles away!'

And so I had to hear the whole incredible story.

It had really started with the counter-attack of the 1st Battalion early on the 18th March. As we moved down out of Cork Wood we had seen them coming up the road in a long straggling column, fording the river just below the Tamera Gorge and then working up into the woods to the left; and we had greatly admired the carefree way they ambled up to what looked a desperate undertaking.

From all accounts they seem to have had a very good day. Their counter-attack plunged into the right flank of the German penetration just as the enemy was forming up for a further effort. The resulting skirmish in the dense undergrowth threw the enemy preparations into confusion, and that arm of the attack was broken up. The other arm came round the base of the Djebel Bel Harch and was aimed at cutting the main road below the viaduct. This was met and held by the 3rd Battalion waiting on the low hills to the east of the road. If both arms had swung together the enemy would undoubtedly have poured across Happy Valley and on to the next defensive position before we had been able to consolidate; but thanks to this timely action, our line was successfully re-established.

All three battalions of the brigade were now withdrawn to the Tabarka area, where they prepared defensive positions in the sand-dunes and made the most of a brief rest. But on the 20th the Germans renewed their attack very strongly, concentrating on the hill features covering the Nefza railway halt, two miles north of Djebel Abiod.

The Leicesters, who took the full force of it, were compelled to give up the main features, and there were reports that the enemy had broken through. The 3rd Battalion was immediately ordered up to Nefza and was in time to eject German patrols from the station and throw them back across the river, the Oued el Madene. That night, in order to delay the enemy, the 3rd Battalion sent out a strong fighting patrol on to the hill north of the river and found that it was held by two companies of the Panzer Grenadiers.

At Nefza the railway crosses the Oued el Madene by a bridge about a quarter of a mile north-east of the station. It is just by this bridge that the hill rises almost precipitously to form two massive domes. The nearer one was of solid rock and completely bald and was christened The Pimple; the other had a flattened top and was known as Bowler Hat. Both dominated Nefza and the flat plain to the south and supplied the open sesame to the Djebel Abiod position.

Accordingly, the 3rd Battalion planned a night attack. They crossed the river and worked their way round the base of The Pimple to assault from either flank. Then events took a very unexpected turn. We had reckoned without the initiative of Major Witzig; for on this very night a small party of his parachute engineers crept down to the river in the pitch dark and blew up the bridge behind the attackers. It would now have been impossible for us to supply and reinforce our troops, so the 3rd Battalion was ordered to return. Immediate and elaborate preparations were then made to deal with the new situation. The 1st Battalion was brought up from rest and was briefed for a new night attack to be carried out during the small hours of the 24th. The engineers were to play a prominent part in bridging the river under the lee of the hill and were also to help the infantry establish themselves on the rocky crest by blasting weapon pits to meet the inevitable counter-attack at dawn.

The late night attack caught the enemy very much by surprise; only an hour or two before, the Panzer Grenadiers had been relieved, and the new troops had barely settled into their positions. A brief but very heavy barrage from the divisional artillery was laid on the objective, during which the 1st Battalion marched up and across the river in column of threes right on to the start line before deploying. This was a daring move, but the night was very dark, and it was important that they should form up rapidly and silently without any confusion. The barrage lifted suddenly, and the battalion surged up the hill and over the defenders before they could resist effectively.

By daylight the position had been well fortified; but the enemy did not counter-attack, and The Pimple was once again firmly in our hands. Our men on the top were subjected to very heavy fire from batteries of rocket mortars – the 'Sobbing Sisters' – both by day and night, but the German thrust had spent itself, and the recapture of The Pimple marked the turning-point of the Tamera battle.

For three days neither side made a move except to shell and mortar each other incessantly. But meanwhile our counter-offensive was being organized, and there was a new feeling of optimism in the air. The 139th Brigade were to attack on the right of the main road, the 1st Parachute Brigade and a formation of Moroccan Goums on the left, and support was to be given by all the corps artillery. The first objective of the parachute brigade was the ridge of large cork trees on the south side of Happy Valley, which was the main defence line of the 81st Panzer Grenadier Regiment and Witzig's paratroops.

Owing to the success of the earlier night assault the preliminary attack was prepared for the night of the 27th/ 28th March. In order to get the attacking troops on to their marks white tapes were laid over no-man's-land by compass-bearing as soon as it was dark on the 27th.

By nine-thirty the troops were lined up, with the 1st Battalion on the left, the 2nd on the right and the 3rd following in reserve. At ten o'clock the plain behind Djebel Abiod suddenly exploded into a volcano of fire, and a torrent of shells cascaded on to the ridge in one uninterrupted roar. Far away the night rippled with the gun flashes, and the arch of the starlit sky shrieked and rustled to the avalanche of high explosive. Ahead, the earth shook and trembled as sulphurous smoke gathered above the enemy positions.

The paratroops advanced slowly into the valley following the tapes, then up into the cavernous woods, where a black fog hung in the branches excluding any suggestion of light. They shouted to each other to keep contact and let the enemy machine-guns guide them to their objective. One by one the enemy pockets were hunted down, pounced on and winkled out.

The 1st Battalion on the left had singular success, and the Italian Bersaglieri in front of them surrendered en masse. But the 2nd had stiffer opposition, and dawn found them consolidating a false crest short of their objective. Suddenly a deluge of mortar bombs descended without warning on a two-hundred-yard front, so that it seemed the woods cracked open with flame and destruction. Then Major Witzig's parachutists poured in behind the barrage and pressed deeply into the battalion. Just when it seemed the enemy must break through the attack crumpled under our concentrated artillery and mortar fire, combined with an enveloping movement by 'B' Company and part of the 1st Battalion. With this defeat the Germans went reeling back and never attacked again on the northern front.

While the 1st and 2nd Battalions dug in on the ridge, the 3rd Battalion passed through in pursuit of the enemy. They forded the river at first light on the 29th March, crossed the open meadow in the dawn mist and gained the farther ridge of woods without any serious opposition. The enemy was pulling out fast, leaving pockets of a few desperate men armed with a machine-gun to delay us. By ten o'clock in the morning the 3rd Battalion had gained the second ridge of hills, and the only signs of the enemy were the herds of bewildered prisoners who were passing continually towards the rear. Altogether, over eight hundred German and Italian prisoners were accounted for – more than the present strength of the brigade – apart from a great number of dead.

* * *

The next day our patrols re-entered Cork Wood and our old positions on Death Ridge. One party of our men went up on to the top of Djebel Bel Harch and reported it clear of the enemy. It must have given them considerable satisfaction when they entered the timbered and shell-proof observation post and looked back on what they had overcome.

After our withdrawal on the 18th March the Germans had kept to the road and more established tracks, leaving Cork Wood very much as when we vacated it twelve days before. Their dead mingled with the bodies of our men, still unburied among the thickets. If the cork jungle had been an eerie place before, it was now a gruesome mortuary. The men were unusually silent, I was told, on their return from a sweep to clear it; even the more hardened souvenir-hunters avoided it like the plague.

The primary task of the Parachute Brigade in the offensive was now at an end. The infantry brigade on our right was temporarily held up to the south-east of the Djebel Bel, but they burst through, and the following day the village of Sedjenane was cleared of the last enemy resistance. Then on the morning of 3rd April the 1st Brigade was moved by lorry to a position near Green Hill, and after a week of vigorous patrolling completed their assignment by clearing the last German outpost from the area.

As the Goum Regiment alongside us had no medical service of its own, one of the surgical teams of the 16th Parachute Field Ambulance was attached to it during this period. This brought the Brigade into close and friendly contact with these fierce warriors from the Atlas mountains and gave us an insight into their ways and methods.

As mountain troops they had few equals. They were hardy and born to fighting among the wilder places of the earth; they required little elaborate equipment and their hooded woollen robe was ideal for the North African climate; their mules gave them great mobility, even over the steepest terrain; and their wives who accompanied them on campaign provided what comforts they desired.

They certainly established a tremendous reputation for patrolling. Story had it that their nominal pay of a few sous a day was supplemented by a bonus of five hundred francs for every prisoner or enemy head brought back – a grisly but no doubt effective system. The claimant had, however, to prove beyond all reasonable doubt that his trophy came from enemy shoulders and was not just any old head he happened upon!

The Germans covered their withdrawal on to Green Hill by intensive air activity against our lines of communication. Stukas attacked our dumps and repair parks, and there were daily fighter sweeps up and down the main road. Focke-Wulf 190s raced across the Sedjenane plain, shooting up anything unlucky enough to be caught on the road at the time. Owing to the lie of the land these attacks were so sudden that drivers could do little but leap for the ditch and hope for the best. Only urgent transport moved during daylight, and then with air sentries standing in every vehicle scanning the sky. Many burnt-out wrecks lined the Sedjenane road as a warning to the unwary.

In spite of the present lull in the battle the men of the brigade were in desperate need of a rest after weeks of fighting and the heavy drain of casualties; and so the news that they were at last to be relieved caused some excitement. The usual crop of rumours went about, but what actually happened took everyone by surprise. At the beginning of the third week of April the American 2nd Corps moved into the area after a remarkable cross-country journey behind the rear of the whole British Army, from Sfax to the northern sector. What had been a brigade area became a corps front overnight!

Convoy after convoy poured along the main road for the best part of a day, and remembering Bou Arada, our men watched for the Focke-Wulfs expectantly. At about midday a flock of 190s came over; three were shot down by the heavy anti-aircraft machine-guns, and the others fled and were not seen again while the brigade was there.

And so it was that the 1st Parachute Brigade was withdrawn from active participation in the campaign, after nearly five months' continuous service in the line. The fear of the unknown and of sudden death was lifted for the time being, and there was a feeling that better things lay ahead. Even the rain clouds rolled away at the end of April, and our return to Boufarik marked the end of an unpleasant chapter.

But first we were to say good-bye to our brigade commander, Brigadier Flavell, who had conducted our operations with such distinction. His first-hand knowledge of battle experience in Tunisia now had to be passed on to the new formations at home, and he left to become the Commander of Airborne Establishments at the War Office. The appointment of Brigadier Lathbury as his successor was, however, universally welcomed; he had raised the 3rd Battalion in 1941 and so was already well known to many of the veterans.

Before we finally left North Africa the engineers erected a small memorial to those of our number who fell during the Tunisian campaign. Our casualties had been heavy and totalled approximately two thousand officers and men, killed, wounded and missing – a very grievous loss, equalling the full strength of the brigade.

We chose Happy Valley for the site as it was here that we had suffered most, and the Tamera battlefield seemed to be the most representative of all the stubborn actions. And so a concrete obelisk now stands just below Cork Wood on the right-hand side of the road as you go up towards the Gorge, in front of what used to be 2nd Battalion headquarters. It attracts your eye immediately, a column of unnatural whiteness among the trees.

I believe they have built a cemetery for our dead in the wide green meadows of Happy Valley, which fittingly claims the land for our own. New grass has grown over the shell and mortar scars, and the valley is once more quiet and peaceful.

I very foolishly went back there at the end of June. We drove up the road from Djebel Abiod and across the Bailey bridge: all looked the same as before. The only difference was that there was a heat-haze over the hills, instead of the veiling wall of rain. It still had the look of the battlefield – the abandoned junk, the twisted bits of iron, the blackened patch marking the end of a burnt-out tank, and that air of loneliness and desolation which only shell-swept country can acquire.

I got out of the car in Happy Valley and then walked up the road towards the Gorge. Suddenly my heart was filled with despair, as though a chilling shadow drifted over the ground. Thick red dust from the passing traffic hung in the air and tinted the withering cork leaves. Where once had been the penetrating mud that seeped through every garment, this drifting powder covered everything, giving the place the appearance of a disused and haunted room. Blasted stumps of trees stood stark and bare in the blazing sun, like gaunt skeletons in a russet shroud.

Then my eye fell upon a group of wooden crosses each bearing a battered parachute helmet and surrounded by an enclosure of whitewashed lumps of rock gleaming in the sun. That was too much, and I turned away.

PART THREE

Sicily and Italy

May–December 1943

SICILY & ITALY

Scale in Miles

75   50   25   0   50   100   150

11

Preparation on the Mascara Plateau
May–June 1943

A red dawn was breaking when I awoke and began to take in our new surroundings.

We had bivouacked on a gentle slope of a ridge overlooking a flat open plain. The early morning haze lay over the ground, but here and there islands of trees and groups of farm buildings poked their tops above the white sea. Far away to the north rose another ridge of hills, and an African town sprawled like a fungus patch on the slate-grey wall of rock. So that was Mascara, the metropolis of our world for the next two months.

Just below us lay the long earth runway of a newly constructed airfield; and the little cluster of black pyramidal tents signified that the American airfield staff, like ourselves, had only just arrived. Farther off to the left a small group of Dakota aircraft were parked in the lee of the hill, the forerunners of a great fleet yet to come.

An American 6-wheeled truck crawled like a beetle across the red table of the airfield, leaving a plume of dust hanging in the air. Bumping down on to a sandy track, it drove off towards a village which peered between the ranks of cypress trees; this, we discovered, was Matemore, a half-French and half-Arab hamlet around which the 1st Parachute Brigade was to be concentrated.

We had arrived in the small hours of the 3rd May, having been deposited on this empty hillside where we had lain until the morning. It was a depressing sight that greeted our awakening – a wilderness of scorched, red earth with an occasional patch of sharp-pointed spear-

grass and two small marquees sagging limply a little
distance off. The lizards were the only other sign of life.

Our uprooting from Boufarik had been very sudden.
The brigade had barely been back from Tunisia a week
and had just made plans for local leave, when we heard
that we were to rejoin the 1st Airborne Division at once.
So the engineer squadron, skilled in constructing the
necessaries of life for a- tented camp, was sent off to
Mascara at a day's notice to prepare sites for the whole
brigade.

We had been given the task of providing each unit with
a water supply, grease pits, washing facilities and latrines,
and had to erect tentage for the advance parties. Relishing
the chance to use their crafts at last our carpenters and
joiners tackled the structures with enthusiastic vigour; but
not so the less fortunate pioneers who had to undertake
the plumbing. All camp works had to be dug in the rock-
hard soil to a depth of as much as ten feet, and when
multiplied by the number of units in the brigade this
amounted to an excavation of staggering dimensions. Our
few bodies armed with picks and shovels viewed the work
ahead with despondency.

But the problem was solved by accident. The sight of
our men digging stripped to the waist always attracted an
interested throng of Arabs who used to come and watch
by the hour. The time came when one of them offered to
take a hand with a pick. In exchange he was given a
cigarette. From that moment we never looked back. The
hitherto inactive crowd was galvanized into violent activity; picks and shovels changed hands, and the bottom of
our holes descended with measurable speed. The news
spread quickly among the local population, who turned
out in force on following days, and by arranging a simple

cigarette pool for services rendered our work progressed apace.

We had the sites in reasonable shape by the time the brigade arrived five days later. Then a canvas town sprang up, with white-painted petrol cans marking the tracks and roadways through the camps, and our barren hillside was suddenly transformed into a busy hive of humanity stretching in a half-mile crescent above the plain. But there was not one leaf of shade, and the interiors of the tents – which had no flysheets – became unbearable during the day. Very soon the earth turned to a loose carpet of dust, which stirred in the breeze and drove continually through the camps on the hot Sahara wind, finding its way into our food and water, collecting in our clothes, caking our hair and forming a red sweaty paste upon our backs. With these conditions of heat and sand we might have been encamped in the desert.

We were told that we had to train and get fit after our life of trench warfare. We started off energetically with route-marches and other hardening exercises, but the weather soon forced us to adopt a less exhausting programme. So we began our day at four-thirty, when it was quite chilly after the sultry heat of the night. Breakfast at six was our best meal: it was really the only time that we could endure the mess tents or work up any enthusiasm for food. Thereafter we trained until lunch at twelve o'clock. Those hours seemed never-ending in the hot, drowsy morning, but then the day's work was virtually over and we looked forward to a siesta, tea and the cooler hours of the evening devoted to football and other games.

Our discomforts often had their amusing side. The desert 'Dust Devil' was a frequent visitor, usually hatching out on the airfield beneath our camp. The dust cloud

raised by an aircraft would beget a spinning spiral, small
at first but growing as it sucked up the sand to form a
towering column several hundred feet high and thirty
yards across at the base, and gaining speed rapidly it
would stalk across the plain like a hungry giant. It usually
happened during the siesta period when we were lying on
our beds stripped to a pair of shorts or less. Suddenly we
would feel the hot warning gust and see the column
bearing down upon us. The walls of our tents would
billow and flap wildly under the rush of air, the ground
would writhe and a shadow fall as we were overwhelmed.
Shirts and underpants drying on the guy-ropes, towels
and blankets airing in the sun, newspapers and writing-
pads, all would be snatched up and carried aloft. Then
there would be angry shouts and a general stampede of
semi-naked humans chasing their property over the hill,
to the accompaniment of cheers and much laughter.

Worst of all, however, was the plague of flies. We tried
everything to keep them down; we sprayed the garbage
dumps and fly-proofed the mess-tents, but it seemed to
have little effect. Every night the mosquito curtains over
the tent-flaps were closed, and we went to work with
swatters. At the end of half an hour we could eat the
evening meal in peace, but a few hours later a new
seething host would have materialized and covered the
walls.

In the hot, breathless evenings, boredom was the chief
complaint. There was little in the way of entertainment,
except perhaps for a weekly cinema show on the American airfield at Thiersville. For reading matter we
depended entirely upon books and magazines sent from
home in the mail, and these, of course, did not go far.
Even the red Mascara wine failed to induce much gaiety
into our life, and our portable gramophone merely got on

our nerves. We sat and sweated and became irritable at the slightest cause, while depression hung heavily on our shoulders. After a hard campaign this arid plain was purgatory to battle-weary men, and all our thoughts were of a cool, green land a thousand miles away.

They gave us two days' leave in Oran at the end of May so that we should start the exacting parachute training in a happier frame of mind. During the past weeks, the airfields round Mascara, at Matemore, Froha and Thiersville had filled up with aircraft and were now chock-a-block with Dakota transports, Albemarle glider-tugs and Horsa and Waco gliders.

Many of us had not been in the air since the operations the previous November and we were very earthbound from living so long in holes in the ground. Now we had to think in terms of being parachutists again.

So our first jump was to be a 'guinea-pig' drop – a descent under ideal conditions, wearing no equipment and without any accompanying tactical exercise on the ground. For getting the maximum enjoyment out of parachuting, a guinea-pig drop into the warm atmosphere of an African morning is as good a way as any. After a brief twenty minutes' flight we were above the dropping zone and then were cascading out into the brilliant sunshine and shimmering air.

To a person on the ground a mass parachute descent is an intensely gripping spectacle, especially when the coloured container-parachutes, distinguishing the arms and equipment of the different units, blossom like flowers among the drab and green ones of the men. But on this occasion we held our breath in horror as we saw a container plummet through an open personnel parachute, and then the orange parachute of another entwine itself

around the same man's rigging-lines. The flapping mass
plunged earthwards with sickening speed, slowly untwist-
ing. Instinctively we began to run. When a bare fifty feet
above the ground the parachutes parted, and by a miracle
the khaki one snatched open an instant before touching
down.

We found the man was Tim Hollings, quite unhurt but
very shaken. Waves of orange silk had broken all about
him, he told us; and his arm had been burnt by the rigging
lines of the container which fell through. And there under
his arm was its pilot-parachute! Tim was quite undaunted
by this terrifying experience and insisted on doing another
jump after lunch to prove to himself that his nerve was
unbroken.

The rest of us made perfect landings on the feather-bed
surface of a well-ploughed field. Owing to the heat upcurrents played curious tricks and made the afternoon's
drop very amusing to watch. Under normal conditions
number one touches ground just as the last man is leaving
the plane, but now very erratic things occurred. Some
men, caught in a hot up-draught, remained indefinitely
aloft, others not so fortunate came down unpleasantly fast
in a shaft of relatively cool air, and not infrequently
number fifteen arrived before number one. We thought
one very small man was never going to come down. He
was still hovering about two hundred feet up long after
the rest of his stick had landed, and remained there for
over three minutes – somebody timed him! All sorts of
ribaldry and wisecracks floated up from the spectators,
replied to by much abuse from above. This went on for a
minute or so, then eventually boiled down to a conversation between air and ground something like this:

Voice high above the earth: 'Oi! Help me down! I'm
stuck!'

Wag on the ground: 'You've got your sky-hook caught, Charlie! Try jumping up and down; you might shake it off!'

'Throw us a rope, can't you? And stop making silly remarks. Get me down out of here; I'll miss my dinner!'

'Don't worry about that, Charlie! We'll keep it for you! Or would you like it sent up to you nice and hot?'

'Hurray! I'm moving!'

'Like hell you are! You're going up now instead of down! Tenth floor, going up! Stand clear of the doors, please!'

''Elp! Save me! What shall I do?'

'Make your will and say good-bye!'

Fortunately he got into a down-draught almost immediately, and the rest of the conversation was lost in the wave of cheers which greeted his rapid descent.

A few days later we began parachute exercises in earnest with the rest of the brigade, and started training in night jumping. Our first exercise, Cactus I, involved no more than landing, forming up on containers and then 'rendezvousing' under the relatively difficult conditions of darkness. To most of us, who had not jumped at night before, this was to be quite a new experience.

We ourselves were flying in Albemarles of the RAF 38 Wing. Dusk was falling as the engines of our aircraft burst into life, and the black ribbon of the oiled runway was marked by a lane of twinkling stars.

The plane took off and climbed rapidly into the night sky. It cruised so steadily as to seem motionless while the earth slid beneath us like a darkening blanket. After a minute or two I crawled along into the tail and settled down on the kapok matting, surrounded by perspex windows.

Time stood still as we rose into the heavens. It became

lighter, until at last the glow of sunset appeared again in the western sky. When we finally flattened out at three thousand feet I was able to witness the fall of night as it really is, and not as I had hitherto conceived it. Night does not fall, but wells up like a flood from the ground.

I watched the world go to sleep, and it was as though a black mist gushed out of the ground like a spring and filled every hollow and gully, then covered the lesser hills and mounds until only the tops of the highest ground showed above the inky pool. Upwards and upwards it rose until the little lumps of light sank beneath the waters of darkness, and night was upon the whole earth. Above, the stars stood out in contrast with unusual brilliance.

The moon came up at last and breathed new life into the scene. A glow appeared behind the hills and grew rapidly, until the Mascara ridge was crowned with a silver crest. Then an enormous golden orb floated into the heavens, and the cold hand of death melted from the plain.

Once again I could make out the features of the landscape. There were the white ribbon of the main Thiersville road and the river glinting in the moonlight, and then the olive groves, vineyards and Arab farms and gardens plotted out by cactus hedges.

'Five minutes to go! Action stations!' The shout came back no louder than a whisper above the noise of the engines, and for the first time I realized I was numb and icy cold.

We opened the two elliptical doors in the floor and fastened them back against the walls of the fuselage. Cold air rushed up through the six-foot aperture, and a silvery panorama glided slowly past my feet. I gripped the doors tightly and leant out over space, waiting for the jumping lights. The others crowded up behind.

I saw the edge of the dropping zone a moment later; the ground was covered with an unnatural rash of blotches – parachutes!

Red light! The baleful eye glowed in the roof above the hole. I stiffened involuntarily and glued my eyes on the signals, watching for the red to change to green and unconsciously counting the seconds.

. . . Four . . . five . . . six . . . green, and the fuselage disappeared as I plunged downwards through a gale-strength wind. Spirit fingers plucked at my back, there was a ghostly rustling of billowing silk, and I was pulled up like a marionette on the end of a string. My legs swung upwards and splayed apart in a grotesque uncontrollable posture. Then I swung down again like a pendulum, and there was a silence all about me, three hundred feet above the ground.

The whole dropping zone was picked out beneath my feet in black and white relief. I could make out every detail of a large cornfield beside the white road, with the corn in orderly stooks and a Waco glider lying where it had landed on the edge. I found myself drifting towards the road with great oscillating sweeps, so seized the forward lift-webs and tried to damp the movement but only made it worse. Then a sudden gust caught me and spun me round. I was descending rapidly in the cold night air, and this plunging oscillation was carrying me towards a dark patch with rows of hedgelike shrubs. That was a vineyard, and for the brief moment before I touched down I conjured up visions of being impaled on one of the tall iron posts. I covered my face with my forearms, braced my legs together and hoped for the best.

There was a crash as I tore through a vine but luckily landed between the rows, sending up a cloud of dust from the tilled ground as I bowled over and skated on my backside to a stop. I saw the rest of the stick landing farther away, so scrambled out of the harness and set off across the field to join them.

We found our containers about four hundred yards off where they had fallen in the middle of the stick. The blue marking lights were working well, and we had no difficulty in locating them in the half-light. We assembled the two collapsible trolleys, loaded on the Warsop petrol-driven rock-drill, the explosive packs and mine-clearing equipment and made for the rendezvous. The dropping zone was now alive with similar parties moving in a southerly direction; and then there was the winking blue light of the rendezvous signal directly ahead.

The next week we went through the same performance but included a small tactical scheme. On the first exercise many planes, Dakotas and Albemarles alike, had dropped their men miles wide of the target area. So on Cactus II a special Pathfinder team from brigade headquarters jumped a quarter of an hour before the others and marked the dropping zone with distinctive lights. This was a big step forward, as under the best conditions the pilot only gets about ten seconds in which to decide whether or not he is over the right place, and these ground signals were the greatest assistance during the run in. They could not, however, remedy faulty navigation. In battle one cannot advertise a parachutists' landing zone to the extent where planes, right off the map, are drawn to the area like moths to a candle.

The Cactus exercises gradually assumed a definite form. We were always attacking a railway bridge, a viaduct or some equally distinctive landmark, and the same tactics were rehearsed on each occasion. An assault force from the 1st Battalion with a party of engineers dropped half an hour ahead of the main force, and secured the objective before it could be destroyed. Then the rest of the brigade flew in on three separate dropping zones, set up road-blocks, destroyed enemy strong-points and, finally, converged on the objective to consolidate its defence.

Our brigade had now been strengthened by a glider element of 6-pounder anti-tank guns from the 1st Air Landing Anti-tank Battery, and, profiting from experience in Tunisia, the parachute battalions were re-equipped with heavier weapons for defence. The problems of weight were no longer of such primary importance now that the glider-borne jeeps and trailers were allocated to the brigade, and each battalion possessed a Vickers machine-gun platoon, a 3-inch mortar platoon – no longer forced to carry all their guns and ammunition on their backs – and an anti-tank platoon armed with the Piat projector, a small weapon of considerable punch. We could now take on objectives of much greater importance and hold them with every chance of success until relieved by ground forces.

By the middle of June we had repeated Exercise Cactus in various forms something like half a dozen times, obtaining better results with each. Then, at the beginning of the third week, we had orders to prepare for a move. We knew now that there would be no more rehearsals and that the curtain was going up.

12

Base Camp at Sousse

'All ranks are now confined to camp until further notice,'
Major Stevens announced after a morning parade at the
beginning of July. The men exchanged glances, and some
smiled grimly. We all knew what this meant: the anticipated operations were already upon us.

Only a few days ago the entire division had moved from
Mascara to Sousse by air and rail and was now concen-
trated in a tented city among the olive groves near
M'Saken, an Arab town on the road from Sousse to
Kairouan. We had also been joined here by the 4th
Parachute Brigade from the Middle East; so with the 1st
and 2nd Parachute Brigades and the 1st Air Landing
Brigade we constituted a very powerful airborne force.

That morning we learnt that Sicily was shortly to be
invaded by the American Seventh and the British Eighth
Armies, and it was the task of the American 82nd
Airborne Division and ourselves to cover the seaborne
landings, then to seize important objectives inland to get
the ground forces forward as fast as possible.

The 1st Airborne Division was mounting three operations ahead of the Eighth Army with the object of
accelerating its progress from the beach-head up the coast
road towards the Straits of Messina, thus cutting off the
German divisions in the centre of the island from their
Italian bases. The 1st Air Landing Brigade was to start
off several hours before zero by seizing the Ponte Grande,
a road bridge near Syracuse; the 2nd Parachute Brigade
would follow on the next night by capturing a bridge near

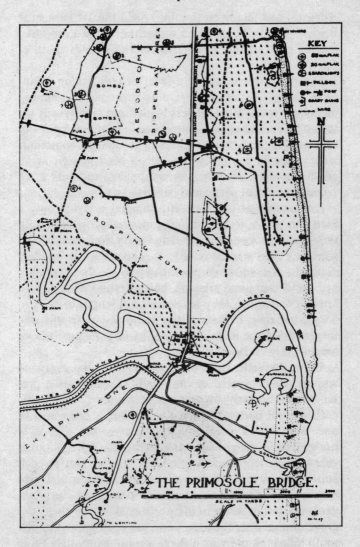

THE PRIMOSOLE BRIDGE.

Augusta; and finally on the third night the 1st Parachute
Brigade was to be dropped round the Ponte Primosole,
the big bridge over the Simeto river, six miles south of
Catania.

The camps were now in a fever of preparation. Maps
were issued to study at leisure and commit to memory,
parachutes were fitted, gliders loaded and made ready for
the air, arms and equipment packed in containers prior to
bombing-up. As we were jumping at night all containers
were specially painted white with a black design as an
additional aid to identification on the DZ; and ours was a
zig-zag pattern of particularly liverish aspect.

Parachutists at this time still jumped carrying only a
Sten gun and a couple of magazines for protection until
they could retrieve their normal weapon from a container,
when the Sten was discarded, or collected at the rendezvous as a reserve for defence. But now the 2nd Battalion
had decided to jump carrying their rifles and Bren guns in
felt sleeves, which they let down on a length of cord to
hang from their harness during the descent. In this way
they avoided the initial vulnerability of parachute troops
immediately on landing.

When we finally came to use the briefing hut everyone
was greatly impressed by the wealth of information presented, particularly by two enormous air photographs,
each six foot by four, which covered nearly the whole of
one wall. These were of our objective, the Plimosole
bridge, to the scale of fifty yards to the inch. The pillboxes
guarding the approaches stood out clearly, two at each
end. There were the barbed-wire fences, the fortified farm
buildings, the block-houses and the road-blocks, the vineyards which ran down to the north bank of the river, the
grove of poplar trees by the farm, the open ground on the
south side broken by high flood-banks – every detail was

picked out and framed by the noonday shadow so as to be unforgettable. It was obvious that in this operation nothing was to be left to chance.

'B' Troop grouped themselves round the big sand table, and George Irwin proceeded with the briefing. The plan was very cut-and-dried and followed the pattern of the Cactus exercises at Mascara.

The river Simeto came down from the north-west in a series of loops across the Catania plain and flowed beneath the Primosole bridge at a point where it was both wide and tidal. It was joined five hundred yards above the bridge by another river, the Gornalunga, which came in from the south-west and had an embanked road running along its southern side. The plain itself was absolutely flat, but was chequered by numerous irrigation dykes and ditches. Five miles to the north of the bridge, up the dead-straight highway, lay the strongly defended area of Catania airfield; southwards the ground rose after a mile to a ridge of hills which overlooked the bridge and plain and constituted the key points of the whole position.

There were extensive fortifications. The coast was dotted with pillboxes and obstacles; blockhouses and heavily wired entrenchments guarded the crest of the ridge at the point where the road descended into the plain, and numerous gun emplacements and flak batteries covered the area. It was decidedly a very tough nut.

The coup de main party of one company of the 1st Battalion was to land on DZs, north and south river, half an hour before the main force, and rush the bridge at once. With them would be one section from 'A' Troop, under Gerald Sims, who were to remove all the demolition charges.

Then at eleven o'clock the remainder of the brigade would begin dropping on four DZs – the 1st and 3rd

Battalions on the north side of the river; the 2nd Battalion, brigade headquarters, the engineer squadron and the field ambulance to the south. Immediately on landing the 3rd Battalion was to neutralize a battery of 88-mm guns within a mile of the bridge, and the 2nd was to deal with another battery and then capture the blockhouse on the ridge. Two hours later the anti-tank battery would land from Horsas with their sixteen guns and move into the brigade defence area.

With their initial tasks complete the 3rd Battalion would take up a position astride the main road a mile north of the bridge, the 2nd on the crest of the ridge to the south, while the 1st would form a hard core round the bridge itself. The 1st Parachute Squadron, Royal Engineers – consisting of a skeleton headquarters with Major Stevens and Joe Wallace, and 'B' and 'C' Troops – were to assist in the defence by laying minefields, making a ford over the river for the guns in the event of the bridge being blown, and if necessary preparing alternative Bailey bridge sites; and generally, of course, by providing a defence reserve. The field ambulance picked a likely looking farm about half a mile to the south of the bridge, where they could deal with casualties from all round the perimeter.

'The air plan is quite simple,' George concluded, 'so there should be little chance of our missing landmarks and being dropped wide. Seventy bombers have been laid on to paste Catania airfield before we jump, so that'll be well alight. That should keep the flak quiet as well.

'Our aircraft will fly in elements of three up the east coast, keeping some miles out to sea until we reach the Simeto estuary. There the planes turn in, fly up the river, over the bridge and put you out on your DZs. You will be flying in practically west-south-west, and by the time you drop the moon will be very nearly full and south. After landing, keep walking with the moon on your right side and you'll join up OK round your containers.

'Our Squadron rendezvous will be with brigade head-quarters at this large farm under the embanked road, about a mile from the bridge. It may be occupied by the enemy, so don't wander in until it has been flushed by the brigade defence platoon. The pass-word for the first night is as follows: challenge – "Desert Rats"; reply – "Kill Italians". I suppose some bloodthirsty Eighth Army bloke thought that one up!

'Finally, the relieving troops are expected to reach us within twelve hours of the drop. If all goes well we shall be out of the wood by the following midday.'

On the afternoon of the 9th July a hot wind was blowing across the Sousse plain at almost gale strength. For the first time since our arrival the branches of the olive trees stirred, while little whorls of dust whipped round the thorn bushes and clumps of cactus beyond the groves. We shut ourselves up in our tents to get out of the flying sand.

At about six o'clock a plane roared low overhead: there was an outburst of cheering through the camps, so Tony and I dashed out to look. An Albemarle was just disappearing in the direction of Sousse, and behind it a heavily laden Horsa pranced and bucked all over the sky in the teeth of the wind. For a glider to be up in that gale could only mean one thing. The invasion of Sicily was on.

As a second tug and glider appeared, and then a third, we cheered too. This was quite a landmark in history; the largest use of airborne troops yet attempted. From then onwards it was a continuous procession of Albemarles and Horsas, Dakotas and Wacos heading out to sea for half an hour. When finally the cavalcade had passed and the last one was out of sight we wished them Godspeed, feeling thankful that it was not ourselves who were up there yawing in the gale. It is bad enough being airsick at any time without having to tackle an invasion as well.

The glider landings on Sicily were a terrible disappointment, due principally to the extraordinary weather conditions. Some of the pilots under-estimated the power of the head wind and cast off too soon, with the result that their wards failed to make land and pancaked in the sea. The wooden Horsas fortunately stayed afloat for several hours, and many of the crews were rescued, but the more lightly built Wacos cracked up quickly in the waves, and some of the air-landing units suffered heavy losses, three hundred or more being drowned. Our divisional commander, Major-General Hopkinson, who flew to Sicily in the leading glider, came down in the sea himself but managed to swim ashore, making, like Julius Caesar, a less dignified landing than intended.

Those gliders that reached their destination crash-landed heavily on the cliff tops, and nearly all cracked-up on hitting high stone walls and anti-invasion obstacles. Nevertheless the men poured out and went into action against any enemy who appeared. One glider load, for example, containing our CRE, Lieutenant-Colonel Henniker, and other senior divisional headquarter officers with their batmen attacked and captured a coastal battery as the troops allocated to it had not arrived.

Owing to the scattered landing of the gliders only a small proportion of the brigade reached the objective. These few overran the Italian garrison, removed the explosive charges under fire, then put up a very gallant defence against strong enemy reinforcements for over fourteen hours. When all ammunition was expended and every fighting man left alive round the bridge was wounded, the survivors were overwhelmed, but luckily were rescued in time by British armoured cars. Thanks to the successful defence of the bridge the Eighth Army entered Syracuse on the evening of the 10th.

The rough sea, however, caused difficulty at first in getting the heavy transport ashore. This led to a slight delay in the battle schedule and to the army being somewhat behind the line proposed for the second night. So the next operation against the bridge at Augusta was postponed for twenty-four hours.

Back at Sousse we were very surprised to see all the 2nd Brigade return to camp at about six o'clock in the evening. This meant that our own operation in its turn would be put back a day – another day of grace, but also one more of suspense.

The next morning the Eighth Army got under way again and made rapid progress northwards against negligible opposition. By the early afternoon they had overrun the 2nd Parachute Brigade's objective at Augusta and pressed on towards Lentini. That parachute operation was, therefore, cancelled altogether, and the brigade once again returned to camp looking very dejected. It was a cruel outcome to their weeks of preparation.

There was now considerable speculation as to whether the 1st Brigade would get away the following night. Information seemed to indicate that we should. The forward troops were reported in Lentini early the following morning, and the Italian divisions in the neighbourhood were offering little resistance to our rapid advance. But the Germans had evidently realized their mistake in being lured away to the west by the American landings and were now hurrying back to the Catania plain. Units of a

Panzer division were already in action near Lentini, and more were on the way.

We ourselves completed our last-minute preparations. Then, after a final meal before take-off, we loaded our lorries at about three o'clock and set off for one of the eight airstrips near El Djem, twenty miles to the south.

There is something very peculiar about that last truck ride out to the airfield before a parachute operation. From the moment you get in, buried under a heap of jumping accessories, you are like a casual observer from outside. This activity around you means nothing, you are already living in the future. Another six hours to go, you tell yourself, no need to worry yet! As the airfield is approached your mind snatches at another straw – another two hours to take-off, and then a three-hour flight ahead. And when, finally, the engines rev-up, and the plane strains at the chocks before the taxi to the runway you feel calm and completely resigned to fate. Nothing can alter the swift onrush of events now.

At our airstrip near El Djem there was a huge Roman amphitheatre standing beside the main road, the sole survivor on this barren plain of a forgotten civilization. The French had partially restored the balconies and galleries on the west side so that the stone looked new and golden.

The walls tower out of a sprawling clump of cactus and are visible from a distance of ten to fifteen miles. When I first saw it on that drive to the airfield in the warm afternoon sun it looked just like a gleaming crown standing at the end of the long white ribbon of road – the reward at the end of the journey of life. With the prospect of battle just round the corner one lives in a strange realm of fancy.

When we reached the airfield there were C47 Dakotas

parked in the dispersal areas, but none on the grass runway ready for a massed take-off. This was strange.

Several minutes passed and nothing happened, so we clambered down from our cramped positions and stretched our legs. Half an hour went by, and still there was no move. The men were getting restless, and conflicting reports and rumours began to circulate up and down the line of trucks.

At last an air liaison officer walked down the parked convoy and spoke briefly to the senior officer of each unit.

'Operation postponed twenty-four hours. Return to camp.'

On the following day, the 13th July, events took almost exactly the same course, minute for minute, until we arrived once again on Airstrip F at five o'clock in the afternoon.

But this time there were American aircrew representatives to meet us, and standing on the running-boards of the vehicles they directed us to our aircraft, the numbers of which were already chalked on our trucks. When we drew up alongside ours we jumped off and admired the plane which was to deposit us on the Primosole bridge.

I read the inscription on her eager aquiline nose and winced; 'Miss Carriage'.

The fuselage had been peppered with flak and the holes had only recently been hastily patched. Black marks smeared the undersides of the wing behind the exhaust manifold. Her paint was chipped and dingy from long service in the African theatre.

The American crew chief joined me and smiled. 'Yeah, we've seen plenty of service in this crate,' he said, 'and this little business won't worry us any! Don't get this baby wrong! I guess she could fly you there and all the way back by herself!' We laughed as I explained I was interested in a single ticket only.

We spent the next hour fitting our six containers into the bomb racks, checking the electrical release mechanism and getting our equipment aboard. Then at seven o'clock our squadron 3-tonner came round with containers of tea, after which we lay about beside the plane to enjoy the last moments of the day. We had brought a large thermos flask with us filled with a strong mixture of tea and rum, to drink in the plane about half an hour before the jump. There are very few things which had been overlooked on this operation. How different from before Depienne!

At seven-thirty we emplaned. A messenger brought the latest situation report from the Sicily front, and I read it aloud to the stick, feeling very hollow inside. It gave the names of places reached, all of them unfamiliar, and a long list of enemy units identified in the battle. I handed the message back and then realized I could not remember a word.

In the middle of all this the aircrew arrived, and I was introduced to the First Pilot of the ship. He was a young North American with a keen face and a confident eye, and we got straight down to business, checking over the details of our respective briefings.

'I am the lead ship of our element of three aircraft,' he said. 'We've got the navigator, so we shouldn't go far wrong. I guess the enemy will be shooting when we cross the coastline, so I am flying in low – at deck level where those 88s can't get us. Now, this kite may be bucking all over the sky as we go in, so I want your boys to hang on tight. Get a good handful of the side of the ship; she won't break! Then we fly in at zee-ro feet, hop the coast, over the bridge and on to the drop zone. Now I pull the stick way back, and up we go to five hundred feet. Hold on all you've got, because I'll have to climb pretty steep. Then we flatten out, throttle back, green light and out you go. And I want you guys to make it snappy, because I'm a sitting duck while you're jumping and I want to get out of it before I'm drilled like a colander. OK boys, and good luck.'

We took off just as the sun was going down and circled the airfield until our two wing planes joined us. Looking out of the open doorway I was in time to see the third plane leave the runway and soar up to meet us with a speed that amazed me. It banked gracefully and climbed neatly into formation above and behind our tail.

We turned east and headed for the coast, gliding easily over the plain, a brown and yellow carpet thickly splashed with green. We crossed a series of shallow salt lakes, each one a blue lagoon, divided from the more ruffled sea by a narrow strip of sand. Surf was breaking like flecks of cream against the sea-wall, evidence of the heavy swell from the recent gale. Then we headed out to sea, and our carpet changed to a sheet of grey and blue streaked with shadows and thin silver paths. Except for the grain of ripples the sea looked as solid as a sheet of glass.

Two and a half hours of flight in darkness lay ahead, so we settled down to snatch a little rest.

We edged closer to the surface as it grew dark, and the moon came out of the sea to meet us. Moonbeams shone in through the windows, providing an eerie light and sending wavering patches of gold creeping backwards and forwards over the fuselage walls and bodies slumped in sleep.

13

The Parachute Assault on the Primosole Bridge

13–15 *July* 1943

I

'We are going in now!'

The crew chief was bending over me with his mouth close to my ear. The chief members of the stick were rousing themselves, making a final check of their jumping equipment and sitting forward expectantly on the edge of the bucket seats, taut and apprehensive of the ordeal ahead. There was a grotesqueness about their shapeless bodies, distended by a heavy load of equipment, harness and bulky statichutes: they looked like the rubber Michelin man, in the darkness of the cabin, weird and unearthly and quite in keeping with the present tense situation.

'Stand up!'

My voice sounded very weak and far away amid the roar of the plane. We lined up facing the jumping door, and the crew chief took up his station alongside it. Holding the corners of the door firmly I took a look out.

The sea was racing beneath our wings, only a score of feet below. At first there was nothing but an expanse of rolling waves heaving like a pulse; then the plane banked steeply and altered course, and I saw the coast – an ominous shadow between sea and sky.

Suddenly we heard the guns ahead – the furious crackle from the quick-firing pom-poms and the deeper intermittent crack of the heavier barrage. At once terror gripped me as I braced myself to meet the inverted red-hot rain. I had had no experience of flak, and those fountains of red and orange tracer looked quite appalling. There is something especially disturbing about being shot at from below – one's body seems so much more vital when attacked from that direction.

The searchlights caught us for an instant when we were about three miles out. The cabin was suddenly filled with a blinding light but this dimmed almost immediately and we were back in the twilight of the moon. Two swords of light were probing out to sea, but our plane eluded them and rushed on towards the shore. The beams were now off our line and searching for the next flight coming in.

Little blobs of light were reflected on the inside of the fuselage and slowly passed diagonally upwards towards the tail. The aircraft swerved violently, and immediately there was the high-pitched crackle of the 20-mm cannonade. A bewildering flicker of tracer sizzled past us. I saw what seemed to be a galaxy of coloured globes floating leisurely above the land. They peeled away from a dark mass, which I took to be a hill, and danced towards us like a swarm of angry bees rising from an upturned hive. They curved over, coming faster every second, then they were flaming comets roaring and crackling about the plane in streaks of light. We were running through the curtain of light flak – an interlocking apron of tracer shells flicking up in intricate patterns of gold, red and white.

The plane suddenly rocked and quivered as though the Titans were slamming the metal sides. Crash! Crash! Tiny particles of shell pattered against the fuselage. Two 88-mm shells had burst above and behind our tail.

Wham! Our world suddenly turned upside down and then blew up with a roar, opening a yawning chasm beneath our feet. Everything was momentarily black . . .

revolving planets . . . plunging meteors . . . the sound of tinkling glass . . . the acrid smell of high explosive. Then my vision cleared, and we were lying together in a heap on the matted floor.

We scrambled to our feet very dazed and shaken and seized with a wild desire for self-preservation. We calmed down a little in a second and sorted ourselves out. The overhead anchor cable – mercifully not in use – was cut and trailing in the centre of the fuselage. All the windows on the starboard side were broken, and moonbeams peered through a dozen ugly gashes above our heads.

Then we were across the coast, and there was land beneath our feet, so close that we seemed to brush the tops of the olive trees as we swept inland. The heavy flak ceased abruptly, and even the rain of 20-mm died down a little. We rose to clear a slight fold in the ground and dropped into the trough beyond. We hopped over an embanked road and swerved to avoid a large obstacle in our path. Then the floor of the fuselage tilted abruptly to an alarming angle, so that we had to hang on tight to avoid being flung into the well of the tail; and the tune of our engines changed to a high-pitched shriek as airscrews clawed frantically at the sky. The plane bucked suddenly as we flattened out.

Green light! and my batman hit me on the thigh as the signal to jump. The next moment I was dazzled by the blast of the slipstream and plunged downwards with the air buffeting my face.

After the inferno of flak and the pandemonium inside the aircraft I was overwhelmed by the unexpected stillness. My parachute had pulled me up with a jerk, and now there was no sound except for the wind rustling in the dark, silken shadow above my head. I felt afraid my floating body might provide an individual target for the enemy gunners, but my confidence grew as I sank lower towards the shadows and the comparative safety of the ground.

I glanced quickly about me to get my bearings. For some reason I could not see the river and I remembered to look for the fires from the bombing of Catania airfield. Then for the first time my brain took in the burning landscape; the whole area was a confusion of twinkling fires and tongues of flame. Haystacks were blazing and patches of dried-up grass were roaring fiercely, while over all hung a thick haze of smoke.

Before I was fully conscious of what was happening I landed heavily on my back in a gully ten feet deep, having struck its wall with a force that knocked all the breath out of my body and left me gasping among the reeds. For some seconds I lay and sobbed for air, incapable of unravelling myself from the silken cords.

Something warm was pouring down my leg, and my fingers encountered a wet patch. I must have been hit, I thought. Then I found that the water bottle beneath my smock had burst and been flattened by the impact.

I crawled to the lip of the gully, then grabbed my pack and Sten and set off up the dropping zone with the moon on my right, to look for our six containers. I had only gone fifty yards when I found three lying among the stubble of a freshly cut cornfield, the marking lights giving out a ghostly blue glow. Clarkson joined me a moment later, and we hoisted one on high, so that the rest might rendezvous at the light. The whole plain was silent except for the crackling fires, so I gave the rendezvous sign with my torch down the dropping zone. After a minute or two the men began to collect until finally the stick was complete.

While the others hunted around for the two remaining

containers and our collapsible trolley, the sergeant, my batman and I had a look to see where we had landed. I climbed an embankment cautiously and found an unmetalled road on the top. Then I saw the winding ribbon of water peeping through a deep screen of rushes and knew that this was the Gornalunga and that we had landed in the right place. It was now comparatively easy to find the brigade rendezvous.

But the men returned with bad news: not a sign of the missing containers. We could only assume that they had been dislodged from the bomb racks by the blast of the shell burst and had fallen in the sea. One of them had half the section's arms, and we were a Bren and several rifles deficient, as well as a quantity of ammunition. The loss of the trolley was not so serious, but it meant that we should have to leave the heavy stores to be collected by the brigade salvage party. We distributed our spare Sten magazines amongst those who had no other weapon and set off westwards for the rendezvous.

The flak started up again before we had gone far, so we went to ground in a ditch to get the layout. Another aircraft flew in from the sea, dodged under the sweeping searchlight beams and ran the gauntlet of the 20-mm tracer. Streams of red and orange balls hosepiped up to meet it and curled away towards the horizon like a string of coloured beads. Then the sky cracked open with a blinding thunderclap as the heavy battery fumbled for the range, and the night shook with the roar. The plane forged through the hail, throttled back and began vomiting parachutists above our heads. The tracers followed the plane while the black canopies sank towards the earth. A few seconds later these shadows had gone, and the men had disappeared into the ground.

When everything was quiet again I was suddenly struck

with a terrible thought: since we had landed, only one plane had followed us in, whereas there should have been scores. The dropping zone should now have been filled with a swarm of men, but except for the odd dozen whom we had just seen, the plain was empty and apparently quite deserted. We were so obviously alone that it seemed as though we were the only living beings within miles, and deep in a heavily fortified enemy country at that. Doubt began to creep into my mind. What had happened to all the other aircraft, and why were the dropping zones so completely empty of life? It is not easy to feel confident when a thousand and one fears race through one's brain.

A minute or two later my anxiety was increased. About fifteen shadowy figures loomed out of the flickering half-light and came towards us across the stubble in open order. We remained under cover and challenged them at twenty yards.

'Halt! Who goes there? . . . Desert Rats!' Our Bren gunner covered them from the shadows of a haystack. The advancing group halted at once.

'Kill Italians!' The leader returned the counter-sign and was ordered to approach and identify himself.

'What unit are you?' he enquired when he reached our position. I replied that we were a section of the parachute engineers.

'We're 1st Battalion. I knew I was on the wrong DZ, and I've lost half my platoon. There's been an almighty muck-up somewhere!'

'Good heavens!' I replied. 'You should be on the north bank. What about the rest of your battalion and the assault force? Has the bridge been cleared yet?'

'Goodness knows! You're the first party I've seen so far, and I have been down half an hour. I'm on my way to the bridge now, but I don't know whether anybody's had a crack at it yet; there's a light flak gun which opens up periodically from that direction.'

'Well, you will find out for certain pretty soon. I'm making for briagde headquarters – if I can find anybody there.'

'OK. I had better crawl up close and have a look. I might meet some more of our blokes who'll be able to tell me what's happened. Otherwise I suppose I'll have to get across the river and try to contact the rest of the battalion.'

With that the infantry got to their feet and moved off quickly in the darkness. I saw three of their number slide over the top of the road; then they were gone.

We set off in the opposite direction to find the rendez-vous, following the muddy bottom of a ditch. After about a quarter of a mile we saw the dark shadow of the farm standing out against the sky. We approached with fingers on the trigger, ready to throw ourselves flat if a machine-gun opened up.

I took half the party forward, leaving the Bren and some riflemen to cover us in. We searched the sheds and outbuildings and went cautiously round the whole circuit of the farm. The main building was barred and boarded up, clearly long unoccupied. Of the brigade staff, the field ambulance and the rest of the sapper sticks there was not a sign. I wondered what had happened to Tony and George who had flown in the aircraft on my port and starboard wing.

I flashed the code signal in every direction and strained my eyes for an answering point of light. There was nothing save the fires winking on the plain.

Then the brigade major arrived.

'Have you seen any of my signal section?' he enquired. 'Or any stragglers of the defence platoon?'

'No, sir,' I replied. 'Only half a platoon of the 1st Battalion, and they went on towards the bridge.'

'Hell! We've lost about half brigade headquarters, and now I can't find the Brigadier to tell him I can't find any of our wireless containers.' Then he went off again.

Little by little a small force of men collected: two sections of the defence platoon under the platoon commander, then several stragglers from the 1st and 3rd Battalions, and finally the Brigadier and about thirty men. He immediately held a short conference and decided on an emergency plan. It was quite obvious by now that something had gone very seriously wrong with the parachute landing, and only a minute proportion of the brigade had arrived on the Catania plain. The bridge, our vital objective, was still in enemy hands, with all chance of surprise gone, and we had no communication with the two battalions on the north side of the river. The operation could not have gone worse.

Brigadier Lathbury made arrangements for getting in contact with the 1st Battalion and reorganized our small force rapidly into four parties. The engineer section was to form a rearguard to brigade headquarters, and my Bren gunner and his mate were loaned to the defence platoon who were to lead. If the bridge had not been taken earlier we should have to have a go at it ourselves.

There had been a certain amount of traffic on the main road, in spite of our drop, and convoys of headlights passed occasionally in either direction. Presumably the garrison had to remove road blocks to let the trucks go through. The Brigadier's plan was for the assault parties to wriggle up to the side of the road under cover of darkness, wait for a convoy to go through, then rush in behind with grenades and automatics. From the absence of enemy offensive patrols against the dropping zones it looked as though the garrison had shut themselves up inside their pillboxes in the hope that we would go elsewhere.

While we were waiting to move on, our glider element flew in from the sea. The flak opened up with great savagery, but the Albemarles came on quite unperturbed, and the gliders cast off directly above our heads. The golden rain poured up to the planes, coned them and then followed them along. One of the Horsas dived in steeply, made a good landing about half a mile away but then caught fire and blazed like a torch. Five minutes later it blew up with a roar. Another circled slowly, looking for its landing zone. It appeared quite impossible for this 'snail' to escape the thundering fury of tracer, but she sailed on, sank earthwards and landed out of sight on the other side of the river. Two more Albemarles passed over, trailing tow-ropes, and escaped without mishap. When all was quiet again we set off in single file towards the bridge.

We had a second rendezvous at a culvert beneath the embanked road about half a mile from the bridge. When we reached it and were taking up a rough defensive position we were met by Jock Gammon, the intelligence officer of the 1st Battalion, from across the river. He informed the Brigadier that the 1st and 3rd Battalions only mustered about two hundred men altogether, about a company each; and, worst of all, they had lost most of their mortars, Vickers machine-guns and wireless, as well as Piat anti-tank projectors and much ammunition. The dropping of our heavier weapons and stores in containers from the bomb-racks had been an abysmal failure. Only the 2nd Battalion, who had jumped with their rifles and Brens attached to them, were in rather better shape.

Brigadier Lathbury received the intelligence officer's

news without a word. He was now faced with pulling off a very hazardous operation with only one-fifth of his original force, and a large part of that armed only with Sten guns – little more than pistols. We waited for several tense seconds while he considered the situation, his tall figure dwarfing those about him.

Then he issued his orders. He sent Lieutenant Gammon back to tell the 1st and 3rd Battalions to concentrate on the immediate bridge area, while we would move on it from the south.

The 2nd Battalion now arrived, with Colonel Frost hobbling on a stick from a damaged knee on landing. After a few minutes' conversation with the Brigadier under the culvert he led his column off to the south, to capture the fortified ridge and secure it against counter-attack. In point of numbers, too, they had been luckier than the rest of the brigade and were about two hundred and fifty strong. The battalion filed by noiselessly as shadows and passed out of our immediate world.

Then we formed up for the attack and moved off under the culvert and along a deep ditch filled with reeds. The moon had waned long ago. It was about four o'clock in the morning, and the air damp and chilly, with a mist hanging over the plain. I began to shiver violently, and my jaws ached from trying to prevent my teeth from chattering.

We swung to the right on reaching the Simeto. After the magnificent illusion presented by the air photos the appearance of this sluggish, stagnant dyke was most unexpected. The muddy banks were covered with a forest of reeds and bulrushes, from which croaked innumerable frogs. Everything seemed fantastic and unreal – except the grenade in my hand.

Dawn was just breaking as we moved away from the

river towards a plantation of young fir trees which took shape to the right. There was the sound of an axe and splintering timber, so we fanned out and went towards it rapidly.

A Horsa glider was lying on its side at the edge of the plantation. One wing was crumpled into matchwood, while the other pointed at the sky; the nose was crushed and ribs of the fuselage gaped through long rents in the fabric. A swarm of men were cutting and wrenching at the tail unit to get their gun and jeep out.

Then there was the southern end of the Primosole bridge, an enormous box of criss-cross girders looming as large as a skeleton house out of the haze.

Our leading sections had gone through unopposed, but there was a sudden skirmish at the north end. Rifles cracked, and there were the crumps of grenades; then suddenly a great puff of flame and smoke writhed in and out of the tunnel of latticed steel. Tiny figures could be seen flitting past whitewashed walls lit by the glow. Then it was all over, and only the crackling of the fire broke into the grey stillness. Our men were crawling over the approaches, dragging the machine-guns out of the pill-boxes and clearing the wire and other obstacles.

The 1st Battalion had captured the bridge some time before our arrival and were now engaged in organizing its defence. What we had just seen was the destruction of four German trucks which had unwittingly tried to cross the bridge after we were in possession.

I shall not forget my first view of the Primosole bridge as we scrambled over the trampled wire and up a high embankment on to the road.

The tall hexagonal pillboxes, one on a floodbank across the road, the other on the river bank fifty yards to the left, were vividly painted in streaks of brown and yellow and draped with tattered nets interlaced with straw. Raffia matting hung down over the entrances which had small fir trees planted on either side.

On the roadway there were staggered concrete blocks, a movable heavy-rail barrier and, beyond, the barbed wire knife-rests closing the wire entanglement.

The road took an S-bend before running on to the bridge, and here and there was a further blockhouse with a guardhouse alongside it. The blockhouse had a 50-mm anti-tank gun trained down the road. Both concrete buildings were decorated with bead curtains, and the guardhouse displayed two whitewashed window-boxes of bright flowers.

The next moment we were on the bridge itself, and began stripping the explosive charges and leads from the girders. There was no sign of Gerald Sims and his party, nor for that matter of any others of the squadron. We had borrowed pliers, wire-cutters and machetes – heavy two-foot slashing knives – from the infantry and gunners, and we worked from both ends at once.

Broken telegraph wires trailed down from overhead. The carriageway was blocked by an abandoned German lorry, its windscreen starred by bullets, its doors hanging open. A 75-mm anti-tank gun lay where someone had unhitched it from the towing-hook. Another truck was blazing at the far end of the bridge where it had received an anti-tank grenade, and black smoke writhed in and out of the girders.

I came on the Brigadier standing with his trousers fallen round his ankles. His batman was applying field dressings to splinter wounds in his back and thighs. He stopped me as I hurried by.

'How long will it take you to get all this stuff off the bridge?' he enquired, indicating the demolition charges.

'Only about a quarter of an hour, I think, sir.'

'OK. Get a move on, then. It must be finished by daylight.' Then, as an afterthought: 'How long would it take the Bosche to put it all back?'

'Not less than four hours for a bridge this size, I should say, sir. They would have to start again from scratch with new explosive and packing and new leads and connections. It would take a good four hours.'

Brigadier Lathbury was no doubt thinking how long we should have to hold the bridge with our tiny force in order to ensure the success of the operation.

He had just been over to the battalions on the north bank and had got involved in the scrap with the enemy trucks. The German drivers had jumped for their lives throwing 'potato-mashers' left and right; and it was fragments from one of these that had wounded him.

Preparations for the bridge's demolition had been thorough, though fortunately not put into final readiness. The cutting charges on the girders were contained in special clip-on metal boxes, but the detonators had not been inserted and were dangling from their electrical cables or instantaneous fuse.

On examining the two stone piers we found that the bridge had been constructed, like many other continental ones, with an eye to war. Each pier contained three covered chambers, about two feet square, sloping downwards for about five feet into the heart of the masonry. We pulled five 20-pound sacks of a granular explosive out of each of the six chambers, enough to blow the stone to powder.

Meanwhile the sappers were hacking away up above. The bridge was festooned with field telephone wires and heavily insulated lighting cable mixed up with the fuse and firing leads; and as we had no time to distinguish them, all had to come down. The boxes of explosives had come away easily, but the tendrils of wire proved much more troublesome until we attacked savagely with the machetes. We dumped the lot in the river, where the explosive could do no further harm.

The guardhouse contained a large stack of German Tellermines and fuses, and these we spared as they were invaluable for our anti-tank defences. We spent the rest of the time before daylight carrying fused mines to the infantry positions.

II

When the sun came up out of the sea we got our first real view of the Sicilian landscape; and our spirits improved as the warmth dispelled the mists and the plain came to life. Everything was still and peaceful, as though nothing had happened a few hours before to disturb the night.

From the top of the embankment I looked over the countryside which was to become the battlefield later in the day. Northwards across the river the ground was thickly screened with vineyards, from which poplars and cypresses rose around the farm buildings to the left of the road. In the distance the purple cone of Etna could be seen faintly against the sky, with a wisp of smoke curling lazily above it. To the south the country was flat and marshy, with many dykes and embankments, until it began to rise up to the ridge which was covered with olive groves and terraced vineyards.

Our defences were now nearly complete. The 3rd

Battalion and the bulk of the 1st Battalion effectives formed a perimeter of pillboxes or shallow weapon pits round the northern end of the bridge, while the rest of the 1st Battalion and the brigade troops held the southern bank. A liaison officer from the 2nd Battalion arrived on an Italian motor cycle and told the Brigadier that they had cleared the blockhouses commanding the road and were well established on the ridge. The brigade major had used a German truck to tour the dropping zones of the previous night and had managed to salvage many missing containers and their weapons. Another cheering factor was that the pillboxes and blockhouses had been well armed with Breda heavy machine-guns and a good stock of ammunition which we could now turn to good account. About half a dozen anti-tank guns had reached us, with a reasonable amount of armour-piercing shot; and these were supplemented by the German 75-mm and the two Italian 50-mm guns in the blockhouses firing on a limited traverse. Moreover, Italian prisoners were streaming in, often with their arms and ammunition. Things began to look slightly better.

The capture of the bridge had been absurdly easy, in spite of the strength of its defences and the ample warning given. The Italians were badly scared during the parachute drop, but the glider landing proved the last straw. The Horsa which had come down by the fir plantation had actually cannoned off the top of the bridge, ripping away its undercarriage and crash-landing with all the accompanying sound effects. Another had swooped down like a black shadow, with air whistling in its struts, collided with the embankment and slithered to a stop about a hundred yards away. When the 1st Battalion rushed the bridge the majority of the garrison was either cowering in cellars or had fled to hide in the vineyards. There was very little resistance.

An extraordinary collection of prisoners was rounded up during the first few hours of daylight. Most were from coastal fortress battalions, but others were coastguards in white yachting caps, air force personnel on leave with suitcases ready packed and an assortment of militia and carabinieri whose one idea was to finish the war in peace. They were all duly locked in the cellars of the farmhouse on the northern end of the bridge, where they spent a very uncomfortable time during the later battle.

The brigade major had assigned my section a position on the south-eastern edge of the perimeter (see battle sketch). Here, an unmetalled road with a three-foot ditch alongside it ran from the bridge towards the coast along the top of an eight-foot floodbank. On the northern side the embankment fell away to the river in an easy slope covered with thickets and brambles. The river banks at this point were about six feet high and the water was very shallow, with a sand and shingle bottom. The south-eastern pillbox stood on the embankment near the junction with the main road; and covering it a barbed-wire double-apron fence came up from the river, over the secondary road and ditch, down the steep embankment and then round over the main road to the river again on the other side of the bridge. Our position was just inside the perimeter wire east of the pillbox, using the ditch as a trench. We cut ourselves niches in the sides so as to cover the flank and rear. Then, having nothing better to do, we got out our rations and had something to eat while we could.

We now waited for the Germans to make some effort to eject us, but nothing happened until about ten o'clock. Some of us were dozing after our sleepless night when we were awakened by the sound of aircraft overhead and saw a couple of Focke-Wulf 190 fighters circling the bridge. The leader dipped his wing and came streaking down, and we hastily shrank into the cover of our holes. A long crackling burst ploughed into the farm buildings opposite; then the other plane followed in, and the first came round again, and so on, for about half a dozen runs. Sometimes they dived and concentrated on the farm, at others they came racing up the river bank, plastering the vineyards and approaches to the bridge. A thick cloud of dust rose and hung motionless in the air. A haystack caught fire and crackled merrily. When the aircraft had flown off in the direction of Catania life went back to normal, and the drowsiness of the morning returned upon us all.

The sun was now well up in a cloudless sky and beat down unmercifully. We stripped off our Airborne smocks, and later our sweat-soaked shirts, and laid them out to dry; perspiration poured from our padded steel helmets. Thirst was very trying for a while, until one of the sappers found a German 5-gallon jerrican. It was punctured by a bullet, but we plugged the hole with chewing-gum and then got water from the farm across the bridge.

It was a strange and uneasy situation. We knew the enemy would and must attack us, but he made no move, nor was there any sound of unusual activity in the area. We put on our sun goggles against the glare from the whitewashed buildings and searched the vineyards and olive groves to the east with binoculars, but there was nothing to arouse suspicion. Yet I felt like a cornered rabbit. This pregnant inactivity preyed on the nerves; an enemy attack would at least furnish the relief of action.

Meanwhile we sought for any vestige of shade. We squirmed beneath clumps of undergrowth and edged into the ruts, but as the sun mounted higher and higher it

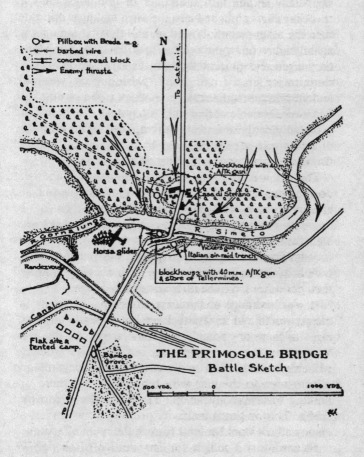

O⌐	Pillbox with Breda m.g.
ᶦᵢᶦᵢ	barbed wire
⊢⊣	concrete road block
⟶	Enemy thrusts

N

To Catania

blockhouse with 40 m.m.
A/Tk gun

Casa di Stefano

R. Gornalunga

R. Simeto

Horsa glider

Vickers gun

Italian air-raid trench

Rendezvous

blockhouse with 40 m.m. A/Tk gun
& store of Tellermines.

Canal

Flak site a
tented camp.

Bamboo
Grove

THE PRIMOSOLE BRIDGE
Battle Sketch

500 YDS.   0   1000 YDS.

To Lentini

found us out in our meagre cover and glared down unblinkingly from above. So we lay and endured, straining our ears for the first indications of the attack.

Like the first murmurs of an impending storm we heard the beginning of the German thrusts against the 2nd Battalion to the south. There was a single shot, then a fusillade followed by the tapping of a Bren, which swelled and thickened until the hills echoed to the roar of battle. Intermittent bursts from racing German machine-guns, insistent rifle shots, the crash of mortar bombs and thump of grenades ebbed and flowed in discordant riot.

Suddenly, without warning, the drowsy air burst about our heads with a paralysing crash, flattening our bodies involuntarily into the earth. The air hummed with shrapnel which thudded into the sunbaked ground.

A mushroom puff of blue smoke was hanging fifty feet above the bridge. 88-airburst I thought, and swore under my breath as I dug with the entrenching tool to make my hole a little deeper.

Crang! Crang! Two more shattering bursts right above us. A lump of jagged metal whirred down and dropped spent beside me. I picked it up and burnt my fingers badly. Two red puffs of smoke were hanging in the air, a little nearer this time. The gunners were bracketing the range and were using coloured bursts for better observation.

'Hi! Mr Terrick! Mr Terrick, sir!' Someone was shouting from a few yards along the ditch.

'Hullo, has anybody been hit?' I enquired, twisting round without raising myself.

'No, sir,' the man shouted back. 'We've found a good trench here, sir! You'll be much better off down here while the shelling is on!'

The rest of the section were installed in a deep Italian

air-raid trench near the pillbox. It was in the ditch and, being itself over six feet deep in places, was proof against anything but an airburst directly overhead. I carried my equipment down and settled myself in a corner. Apart from its protection the great thing was that the bottom was in the shade and was delightfully cool after the fierce heat outside.

A moment later the barrage came down on us in earnest. Every flak gun around Catania airfield opened fire, and the air over our heads boiled, shrieked and roared. The incessant crash of shells and roar of guns intermingled, so that sound had no further meaning; the noise pulsated, swelled and erupted and then fell back to the roll of a thousand drums before building up to another sickening peak, tearing the world apart. We sat huddled and dazed. Wisps of pungent yellow smoke seeped into the trench. Somebody coughed and relieved the tension. Then, suddenly as it had come, the barrage lifted.

For a moment my numbed brain could not comprehend the sudden silence. One had got so used to the raging thunder of noise that this new emptiness almost hurt. A rifle shot and then a burst of Bren brought me to my senses.

'They're coming through!' I found myself shouting. 'Back to your positions. Bren gunners come with me!'

We swarmed out of the trench, scrambled down the ditch and found our old holes. I pulled my two grenades out of my pouch and laid them beside me – just in case.

Battle was joined on the opposite side of the river, but it remained invisible behind the thick screen of vineyards except for the occasional tracer ricochet. The Bren gun rattled out three more short bursts, and then a German machine-gun roared into life unexpectedly close. Rifle shots were cracking away all round our bridgehead. A

Vickers gun started up and chattered out a long five-second burst, very comforting to hear. Then the noise of the battle became too confused to distinguish individual sounds, and rippled in waves round the northern perimeter. Tracer flickered through the vines and threw up long welts of dust.

My section passed their Bren magazines up to the gunner. He held the gun into his shoulder and peered intently at the undergrowth downstream.

Gradually the fire slackened and then died away into another lull. We strained our ears and listened anxiously, wondering what it might mean. Suddenly the barrage came down again. As there was no point in remaining on top we crawled back to the shelter of our trench and waited for the lift.

In my dazed state I became fascinated by the different sound effects produced by the rain of shrapnel. Some uttered an almost human cry, a plaintive wail like a child. Others sobbed and howled, curdling the blood. Some whirred like a partridge, a heavy, ugly sound. Some droned and buzzed like bees. The air throbbed as red-hot slivers of steel flew in every direction; and, as a finale, the telegraph wires parted with a twang, and the copper wire rustled down with a hushed singing noise.

To supplement the barrage of airburst from the massed 88-mm flak-guns two large-calibre coastal guns of the 14-inch variety joined in and pounded away at the bridge. The shells came whining over, the noise changing pitch with terrifying speed. Fortunately, every one passed overhead to land with heavy concussions from two to four hundred yards away. The gunners never succeeded in getting the range; probably they had no direct observation and could not bracket for fear of hitting their own positions. But they were sufficiently close to rock the walls of our trench. Chunks of earth flaked off, and soil trickled down our backs.

After a quarter of an hour the barrage lifted again and fighting flared up, growing in intensity as before. After another unsuccessful attack the enemy desisted, and the storm of shells came down again. They employed quite a novel signal to request the renewal of the barrage – a stream of red tracer fired nearly vertically into the air. When we learned what this meant we dived for our trench as soon as it was spotted.

The day passed slowly. Sometimes the enemy held off to draw breath, giving us a respite of an hour or so before battle opened once more. But they always came on again as fiercely as before, crawling down the avenues of grapevines and working closer and closer towards the bridge. As the afternoon wore on their attacks gained weight as reinforcements arrived and heavier and heavier support-weapons were brought into play.

Once, a squadron of Spitfires came over, flying in extended formation, weaving graceful wavelike patterns in the cloudless sky. We fired a yellow recognition flare to show our position. The time was four o'clock and there was still no sign of the relieving column, now long overdue. The cloud of brilliant chrome-yellow smoke pillared into the hot air and hung there for several minutes, but the squadron passed over and disappeared towards Catania without acknowledging our signal or giving us other cause for hope.

The position of our dwindling forces on the northern bank was now critical, as their ammunition was almost exhausted. So the Brigadier gave the order to withdraw from the north bank and to deny the bridge to the enemy by holding the southern end. The noise of battle in the hills to the south had died away an hour ago, and there was no further communication with the 2nd Battalion. We could only hope that they had beaten off the enemy, but it looked ominously as if they had been overrun.

The brigade signals officer had, however, been able to get in contact with part of the relieving force, a tank unit of the 50th Division. He had managed to convert one of the inter-company wireless sets for extra range and eventually cut in on English voices. The code message was passed that the bridge was still in our possession, and we now felt that the ground forces, although some distance away, would do all in their power to break through.

Meanwhile our men were coming back over the river – a little company about a hundred strong. They waded through the mud and shallow water beneath the roadway of the bridge and were directed to new positions on the southern bank. A Vickers gun team moved out to our right, and the brigade major ordered me to take my own Bren gun and two or three men to give them protection and additional fire-power.

We crawled up the ditch, under the wire and then on for about thirty yards until we came to a thick mass of undergrowth. We found the Vickers team squatting in the ditch with their gun mounted so that the heavy water-cooled barrel just cleared the road. We took up a position in the undergrowth on the flank, and waited for events.

After half an hour the enemy resumed his attack with a short but heavy bombardment from his 88-mm guns, while his infantry moved into the vacated northern perimeter. Our Vickers crew spotted something down the river and swung their gun, blasting the bank with a long, satisfying burst. Then the gun jammed and the gunners swore. Feverishly they cleared the obstruction and soon let fly at another target. The number two fitted a new belt of ammunition and searched the opposite bank with his binoculars for further movement.

Gradually the Germans worked their way up to the bridge. Suddenly a 20-mm quick-firing cannon opened up at close range with a shattering roar. They were searching for the Vickers gun; a stream of tracer shells passed across our front and ploughed into the embankment on our right. Half a dozen Tellermines which we had laid on the track exploded with a tremendous crash. We pressed our faces into the bank and crushed our bodies into the earth.

A captured Breda machine-gun was now firing spasmodically from the pillbox behind us, sounding very hollow and resonant from the interior. It made us jump each time the bullets cracked over our heads but it gave us a new feeling of confidence – so badly shaken by the enemy gun. The Breda swept the northern bank and flattened the German guns into silence.

As the sun dipped lower and the shadows crept out I saw that it was after eight o'clock. There is little twilight in the Mediterranean and it would soon be dark. There was a further lull, and we wondered if the enemy was waiting for dusk to launch his final attack.

It was upon us sooner than we thought, and the air rippled once more to the airburst cannonade, supplemented now by a thundering cascade of heavy mortar bombs. We cowered down, stupefied by noise and concussion. 20-mm cannons roared on the opposite bank, flicking streams of tracer across at the two pillboxes. Flakes of concrete flew from the walls under a bombardment of armour-piercing shot, exposing the skeleton of steel reinforcement. Loopholes crumbled into dust, leaving a gaping socket in place of the oblong slit. The Breda spoke no more.

Our ammunition was now virtually finished and our

guns had fallen silent one by one as their limited stock ran out. Rifle ammunition had gone to feed the Brens, and very few of the men had any left. Our own Vickers was on its last belt and only occasionally rattled out a round or two, just sufficient to check any movement down the bank. We chose our targets with care, firing only when we could observe the result. The sun went down, and in the gathering dusk, shadows cast by the vines looked like moving men.

I was startled by a rustle in the ditch behind me. Turning, I saw the brigade major crawling up through the undergrowth.

'The Brigadier has given the order to abandon the bridge,' he said rapidly, on reaching us. 'Collect as many men as you can and make your way back to our own forces over the hills to the south. Our tanks can't be very far away now. Clear out of here and go like hell before the enemy comes through!'

The two men on the Vickers needed no bidding for a last chance to hit back, and let drive with a more exalted burst, swinging the gun in a flaming arc like men possessed. Another burst, and then another, ending up by holding on the trigger until the belt had run through. Quickly they removed the firing mechanism and flung it into the river. Then they picked up the gun, tripod and all, and heaved it into the brambles. Without looking back we squirmed through the undergrowth, down the embankment and went like the wind.

III

We lay in the middle of a dense bamboo plantation about three quarters of a mile from the bridge. Where we had forced our way in the shoots had sprung back behind us. We lay very quiet in the spongy grass, scarcely daring to breathe in case German patrols were out looking for stragglers. We hoped that when the general commotion, caused by our rather dramatic exit from the bridge, had died down it would be easier to slip away unnoticed.

Our withdrawal had caught me without any plan. I did not fancy the idea of plunging straight into the hills, which might be full of enemy troops, without having first considered what was the best thing to do. Everybody was pouring out of their positions, rolling over the embankment and racing for the cover of the rough ground a quarter of a mile to the south. By the time we had reached it and comparative safety I had collected a party of about twenty, half of them infantry who had lost their own units and attached themselves to me. Then I saw the bamboo grove and decided to lie up until it was dark enough for a body of men to move without risk of ambush. It was a very large plantation covering several acres, and we plunged in and fought our way through the tangled shoots until I judged we had gone far enough. As we lay and waited I thought out a plan.

It was impossible to tell who occupied the hills astride the road, so we would take no chances and make a big loop to the west to skirt the danger area. To clear the flak positions below the hills meant going due west until we struck the embanked road near the Gornalunga. Then we would change course and head south-west across the open country for six or seven miles. From there we would turn southwards into the hills, move over a thinly populated farming area and rejoin the main road somewhere behind our own lines near Lentini.

It was a great temptation to move directly it was dark, but I decided to give the night half an hour's grace for the countryside to settle down. At ten o'clock everything was silent except for the thunderous croaking of frogs, so we stole out noiselessly, keeping in the shadow and avoiding the bright patches of moonlight.

We moved through some olive groves and soon reached the main road. There was a pillbox about a hundred yards down the road; in the other direction a red hurricane lamp was standing by an open gateway, throwing a pool of light on the tarmac. We chose a spot about half-way between the two and nipped over one at a time.

As we crossed a meadow a dark shadow loomed up on the left. We were on it before I recognized it as one of the sand-bagged emplacements of the 88-mm flak site which I had meant to avoid. However, it was deserted. The gun was gone, but stacks of shells stood all around, and empty cases were still lying where they had been ejected from the breech. The German gun-crews seemed to have moved out in a hurry. We passed four emplacements in all, each in the same state as the first; and a little farther on the tented sleeping-quarters of the crews, with the mosquito nets hanging up inside.

Half a mile beyond we reached an irrigation canal, and pushing through the high reeds waded across the twenty yards of oily water. The bottom was deep mud, so that we went in up to our waists before gaining the other bank.

We dried out quickly as we walked on, and felt better for our wetting. Then we had another stroke of luck which revived us considerably after the strain of the battle. We were crossing a vast field of low plants when something squashed under my foot. They were tomatoes – acres of them. We ate our way across and then filled our helmets and camouflaged face-veils with as many more as we could carry.

We came to the embanked road, then turned south-west and walked over the two southern dropping zones of the previous night. The discarded parachutes lay everywhere, and here and there, the dazzle-painted containers, lying open and abandoned and amid rigging-lines and coloured silk – rich booty no doubt for the Sicilian peasants.

Beyond the western limit of the 2nd Battalion dropping zone we found ourselves walking through further clumps of parachutes. I examined one and saw that it was of a coarser texture than our own, with thicker rigging-lines. Then we stumbled across two square-sided containers, painted white but quite unlike any British type. One lay open and had a tubular steel towing-handle and two rubber-tyred wheels. That struck a familiar note! I turned it over and read 'V Fallschirmjäger Regt' in black gothic lettering. So they were German after all! After that we fanned out in crescent formation with weapons at the alert and moved cautiously, scanning the shadowy landscape before making the next move.

I learnt later that two battalions of a German parachute regiment had been landed on very nearly the same dropping zones as ourselves on the night before our own drop. They had moved up into the hills immediately, as reinforcements to the German rearguard fighting near Lentini. Strangely enough a further German battalion was flown in and dropped only a few hours after we had left the spot – other observers in the hills saw them come down – but by that time we were some miles away.

We marched for six hours that night and covered about ten miles, which was good progress considering our frequent halts and careful reconnaissance. We crossed an embanked railway line but afterwards moved across open farmland gridded with irrigation channels. Once we heard a German machine-gun rattle away on the slopes of the black hills on our left, but for the most part we plodded on for hour after hour without hearing any other sound. Two large fires were burning like beacons on the crest, but otherwise the country seemed devoid of life.

At about four o'clock in the morning we turned south and headed for the hills. It was now too late to hope to get through to Lentini before dawn so we had to find a place where we could lie up for the day before moving on the next night.

Here again we were very lucky. As we neared the foothills we heard the sound of running water and headed in that direction. We found the stream and following it up the hill came to the spring – a strong jet of water gushing out of a pipe driven into the rock. Close at hand was a dense thicket which would suit us admirably. We all had a long drink and filled our water bottles before working our way deep into the undergrowth. After removing all trace of our entry those not on watch lay down among the roots – taking good care not to disturb the bush above our heads – and immediately fell asleep.

We passed the whole of the next day in rest, sleeping most of the time, so that the hours passed quickly in a drowsy twilight with short snatches of dazzling sun and glowing warmth. We agreed that there should be no talking or smoking and the minimum of movement; for even the peasants were liable to betray us. We finished the last of our rations so as to be fortified for the night march over rough country. We had to get through to our lines that night. Every successive day one is forced to spend behind the enemy's lines increases the danger of discovery – one gets over-confident and careless. From the map Lentini was not more than ten miles away, and it was probable that our lines were much closer. We could start directly it was dark and slip through the hill barrier – where the Germans were likely to have their line – before the moon was up.

That evening there was a most glorious sunset – a good omen for a clear night and successful march. Etna rose majestically in the north-east, just distinguishable against the gathering blues and violet of the night. A Sicilian peasant, singing a gay operatic air in an unusually fine voice, drove his herd of cows down to the stream and then to bed.

We crept out of our hiding-place in the gathering darkness and began the ascent. At first the going was easy, over terraced vineyards and olive groves, but after recrossing the railway we hit the main wall and had to climb in earnest. We scaled a cliff which rose steeply for about three hundred feet, then up a rugged slope to the crest, and dropped down the other side into a rocky wilderness intersected by deep sandy ravines. We crawled up another slope to the road leading westwards to Gerbini and then came to the highest ridge of the hill mass. As we cleared the top the moon appeared, so we had to make all speed down the southern slopes to gain the protection of the more-broken country below. We reached the olive groves and vineyards at last after two hours' rough going at a breakneck pace, and the worst of our journey was behind us.

We were now very blown and tired, so I called a halt in

the middle of a vineyard. We lay down and drew in deep breaths of the cool night air. Then, with the light of the moon to guide us, we moved on again and made good progress.

We turned south-east towards the Catania–Lentini road and we seemed to hear the sound of traffic ahead. Occasionally there was spasmodic machine-gun fire and we saw the red tracer curve into the air. We must be approaching our outposts, so I advised everyone to exercise the greatest caution. I had no desire to be shot-up by our own men now that we were so nearly safe.

As we were moving up a shallow valley a machine-gun burst into life very close at hand, sending a stream of tracer over the rise in front. Another gun answered and chattered away at a rather slower rate: I could have sworn it was a Bren. We thought we heard someone shout, 'Did ye get them, Jock?'

There was a nice flavour of Scotland about the voice, but we could not be sure. Not wishing to become embroiled in a patrol clash we lay still and listened. The countryside remained maddeningly silent, so we crept on again.

We crossed a cornfield with stooks in irregular rows, then passed down the hedge-like lanes of a vineyard. We paused at the edge before going out on to a rocky downward slope, to allow the rear of our party to close up. The moon was now shining as bright as day, throwing up the white outline of a large farm a hundred yards away. I cautioned everyone to remain stock-still if challenged, then we deliberately walked down the slope in a large body in the full light of the moon.

'Halt! Who goes there?'

A clear voice rang out in the night air.

We had arrived at Lentini.

14
Aftermath

The Sicilian countryside sparkled in the morning sunshine as we made our way back to Syracuse, where we heard the 1st Parachute Brigade was collecting. We sang and whistled as the trucks bounced over the dusty road and felt in a gay mood after the recent strain.

We got a lift on a returning petrol convoy at Lentini as far as Augusta, and then picked up another carrying German and Italian prisoners to the rear. Our trucks, which belonged to the 50th Division, had come all the way from Alamein and had passed their prime of life, so that many made heavy work of the steeper grades. On one long hill near Syracuse some failed altogether and had to be towed and pushed up. The prisoners were highly amused at being pushed by their guards and cheered as each foot was gained.

It was at this moment that General Montgomery passed, standing up in the front of his jeep. All the men gave him a terrific cheer as he came down the line of trucks, and he waved in return. On seeing our green Airborne smocks and sprinkling of red berets he stopped in the middle of the convoy and enquired whether the men were short of cigarettes. Hearing that many had not had a smoke for two days he handed out largesse.

'Well done!' he told us all as we gathered round. 'You have saved me a week. That week will make all the difference later on!'

As he drove off in the direction of Lentini we felt that

we really had done a good job of work, even if everything had been against us.

We arrived on the quay at Syracuse and joined the dense crowd of paratroops waiting to embark. An avenue of trees lined the road along the waterfront, on the far side of which was a row of dingy shops and tenements. It was siesta time, and there were only a few urchins running in bare feet from group to group selling oranges.

A huge tank-landing ship lay nose in to the quay with doors agape. Two assault craft were moored alongside and rose and fell rhythmically with the swell. Out in the harbour a long flat-bottomed lighter plied lazily to and from a heavily laden cargo vessel. Our own men sprawled on the pavement or sat with their backs to the tree-trunks, and only their equipment and weapons laid out in rows suggested the orderliness of their units. The air was drowsy with the heavy smell of seaweed and salt, the droning murmur of low voices, the creak of mooring lines and tackle, the distant cry of seagulls skimming the oily water and the far-off shouts and thumps as the stores and packing cases were unloaded. Many men were already asleep, with boots and socks off and toes turned up to the sun. It was the aftermath of battle, when the exhausted warrior forgets his fear and troubles in blessed oblivion.

At last we were aroused by shouted words of command to get our 'kit on and get fell in', and the quayside shook itself awake. In a moment we were a disciplined parade again, and stood drawn up in ranks waiting to embark.

Assault landing-craft came alongside, took on thirty men apiece, then backed out and headed for the bay. Here there was a mass of shipping – hospital ships gleaming white in the sun, Liberty ships in rusty grey paint and war craft of every size and description. We made for a tank-landing ship riding high at anchor, swung round to the bows and made fast alongside the lowered ramp lying level with the water. The open doors gave on to a cavernous interior. We clambered aboard and picked our way over bodies lying about the dimly lighted hall.

At once we were greeting old friends. First there were Major Stevens and Joe Wallace on the companionway: squadron headquarters had been dropped near Lentini, and apart from rounding up a large number of Italian prisoners with two platoons of the 1st Battalion, they had seen little of the battle. Then there was the bulk of 'C' Troop clustered on the transport deck, with Paddy Roorke, Martin Brush and Tom Slater. Their three aircraft had put them out on the wrong side of the hills before the Primosole bridge, and they had found their way almost to the objective only to meet its defenders coming back. Of the two other 'B' Troop plane-loads with George and Tony, and the assault stick from 'A' Troop led by Gerald Sims, there was no sign. There was a report, however, that many planes, failing to find the dropping zones, had returned to Africa with their men still on board.

The battalions had fared no better than ourselves. One survivor of the 2nd Battalion told how his section had been dropped across Catania airfield, and only he had managed to avoid capture and slip back to our lines. Another officer had landed on the lava slopes of Etna; the majority of his stick failed to link up in the rough ground, and only a few had returned. The most common error had been to mistake for the Simeto estuary a small river valley ten miles to the south, and a large proportion of the force had been dropped there. After our weeks of training and rehearsals on the Mascara plateau, the results were heartbreaking.

We gathered that our aircrews were insufficiently

practised in carrying paratroops to a battle area, and were more used to cargo-carrying flights over well-established air routes, when they went about in large formations relying upon the leading aircraft to plot the course; for only the minimum of navigators could be spared for non-combat duties in Transport Command. On our operation there had been only one navigator to three aircraft, the two wing-planes hugging the leader by screened green lights on the upper surface of the wings. When the aircraft were forced to take evading action in the flak the wing planes became detached and were not seen again.

The flak proved a major factor which had hardly been taken into consideration. To us the anti-aircraft fire seemed terrifying, and the curtain of tracer to constitute a barrier through which it looked impossible to fly unscathed. To the pilot it must have appeared suicidal. This was the first time that many of our aircrews had been under fire, and they had indeed had a gruelling baptism. Our own particular aircraft had done a superb piece of navigation and flying, dead on the mark and schedule.

As we compared our experiences the fog of the war which had so completely enveloped us at the bridge was now gradually lifted. The 2nd Battalion on the ridge behind us had not been overrun but had fought off attack after attack from German parachutists, who had surrounded them and occupied the farm at the foot of the hills where the field ambulance had established their dressing station. The last attack at six o'clock was very formidable, but was broken by heavy fire from a British 6-inch-gun cruiser lying off-shore. After that fighting died down, but it was not till dusk that they discovered that the Germans had withdrawn westwards and had released our medical staff on leaving.

The tragedy of it was that advanced elements of the

relieving force, after battling with a fanatical German parachute regiment, had actually reached the ridge on the evening of the 14th, and tanks and reconnaissance units got down to the bridge early the next morning – just eight hours after we had been forced to evacuate. The Germans had blown a large hole in the carriageway with Teller-mines, but the bridge was structurally undamaged and five tanks crossed immediately. These were, however, at once engaged by 88-mm guns which knocked out two of them, and the rest withdrew to the southern bank. Later in the morning Colonel Pearson of the 1st Battalion led a company of Durhams across, but they were confined to a narrow bridgehead in the vineyards round the farm.

The expansion of this bridgehead took a further week of bitter fighting before the Army broke through to the Catania plain. An infantry officer who was there at the time later paid tribute to the execution done by our 1st and 3rd Battalions. There were, he said, about five hundred enemy dead round the perimeter which had been defended by a couple of hundred men.

Our ship did not sail that night, for another party came into Syracuse at the last minute and delayed our depar-ture. The crew were uneasy; they had been bombed in the harbour the previous night and did not relish spending another there. They were right. The air-raid warning sounded soon after dark, and a few minutes later the bombers were overhead.

Being bombed on board ship is, I firmly believe, one of the most unpleasant experiences in this life. You know that the enemy is singling out your ship for individual attention, and the thin steel walls seem to offer no more protection than an eggshell.

There were fifteen hundred troops on board, and every

inch of deck space was packed. Nevertheless when the shrapnel from the heavy guns around the town began to patter down everybody was moved below, overcrowding the lower deck to the point of suffocation. The officers crammed into the tiny wardroom. It avoided casualties but induced a feeling of being trapped if the ship were hit. To add to our mental discomfort the captain ordered a smoke-screen to be laid to mask our silhouette from the raiders above. A poisonous cloud of thick, oily, pungent fumes seeped down the companionways, until it was literally impossible to see one's hand in front of one's face.

'Mr Quartermaster, make more smoke!' the captain bellowed every time the fog got thinner and we hoped for a respite. 'More smoke, Mr Quartermaster! Get those candles alight! Guns starboard, here comes another!'

The ship had an anti-aircraft armament of half a dozen 20-mm Oerlikon cannon and one 3-inch gun mounted in the stern. Every now and again the heavy gun would rock the ship, but the Oerlikons kept up an almost continuous barrage to keep the planes high.

Most of the bombs fell harmlessly in the water, the concussions thudding below the water line with a dull booming. Once a bomber roared low over the ship and let us have its whole stick right across our length. Then there was indescribable pandemonium and what with the frantic thunder and crash of the guns and the thump of bombs bursting close, I thought we had well and truly 'had it'. But the noise died down eventually, and even the choking smoke cleared sufficiently for us to see across the room. When all was quiet we went up on deck again and spent the rest of the night in peace.

The next morning we left Syracuse behind in the flattering veil of distance and the glow of the early sun. It was a perfect day with a calm sea. The troops were in exceptionally good spirits and passed the time sunbathing on deck as though they had not a care in the world. Now that our operation was behind us, successfully accomplished, we felt pretty good, the elation of danger past.

The reaction came when we reached Sousse the following afternoon. After the easy freedom of Sicily following the parachute operation, I felt resentful at the return to boredom, to the wretched conditions of camp life under a broiling sun, the everlasting routine and inevitable 'Come here' and 'Go there' when all I wanted was to get somewhere alone and rest. As if in confirmation of my fears, there on the quay was the reception committee of staff officers ablaze in blanco and brass, so completely in contrast to all of us back from the battle who stood and watched them from the deck. But already the ship had nosed into the dock and made fast; the two bow doors swung open, and we all went pouring out like a tide. That moment concluded the Sicilian operation.

The next minute we were forming up in units with the old bustle and efficiency, giving parade ground words of command and boarding the convoy of trucks waiting to take us back to camp. And there were George and Tony to greet us on arrival, tea was ready, and life went on very much as though we had never been away.

However, they sent us away for seven days by the sea at Hammamet to restore us to a less irritable frame of mind. It was very pleasant in the bivouac camp among the olive groves and sand dunes right on the sea edge, and we took things extremely easy with the minimum of parades. The troops did PT on the sands, bathed and played football, spent most of the day in nothing but a pair of shorts and wandered down to the local estaminet in the evenings for a glass of wine. There were opportunities for the men to visit Tunis, but many preferred just to stay basking on the beach. When we returned again to Sousse we all felt better than we had ever been before in Africa, and once more mentally fit for the society of man.

Yet things were not quite the same as they were before the Primosole operation. Gerald Sims and his party had completely disappeared and his plane had not returned. We missed other familiar faces – Major Ross of the 2nd Battalion, whom we had known so well, Colonel Pearson of the 1st, who had been invalided home with malaria, and many other people who had seemed to be such an integral part of the brigade. When the establishments were at last made up with reinforcements from England it was sometimes difficult to recognize the units that we had known before.

15

The Taranto Expedition

September–December 1943

We had been away rock climbing on the Djebel Zaghouan, so missed the excitement which culminated in the
surrender of Italy. On our hurried return we found the
division preparing for another operation, this time by sea.

We were clearly in for something unusual. We were
allowed a minimum of baggage and equipment, and were
warned that on landing we would have to operate without
transport and quite on our own for at least a week.
Moreover we were off at once: the 2nd and 4th Parachute
Brigades had already left, and we and the Air Landing
Brigade followed three days later, on the 10th September.

That night found us at Bizerta in the port transit camp,
which with the pack of troops collected there looked like
Epsom Downs on Derby Day. We were allotted a pitch
fifty yards square, where we slung our mosquito nets from
bayoneted rifles spiked into the ground and whiled away
the scorching hours of the 11th playing poker beneath the
chassis of our 3-ton truck, which proved to be the coolest
place. Then at dusk we humped our loads of kit and
stores down to the docks and stripped to the waist toiled
till midnight under the arc lights loading the *Princess
Beatrix*, in better times a Channel steamer. It was very
hot, and we welcomed the breeze and open sea when we
sailed in the small hours.

When the sun rose on a golden pathway before our
bows Bizerta was a dim shadow on the horizon astern,
and our last view of Africa was of the headland of Cap
Bon, with the dark mass of the Djebel Grombalia in the

background. Then on the morning of the 13th, as we sailed up the coast of Calabria, we were told that we were bound for Taranto.

The landing of our division at Taranto had many features of an airborne operation, even if we were going by sea. All priority in warships and transports had been given to the Fifth Army at Salerno, so the Eighth Army had made their initial landings on the 'toe' of Italy by way of the Straits of Messina, where light landing craft could be ferried backwards and forwards under cover of field artillery on the Sicilian shore. But once the difficult mountain positions in Calabria had been turned by a landing in the rear, the Army would push rapidly into the eastern plain of Apulia with its valuable airfield area of Foggia and the seaports of Taranto, Brindisi and Bari. With our special light equipment and natural self-sufficiency we were well suited for this task, and only six light cruisers and two landing ships were required to convey the whole division and stores in two waves.

We arrived off Taranto in the afternoon and, passing through the anti-submarine boom and steaming slowly down the swept channel, dropped anchor in the outer harbour. Dusk fell as we made the journey to the shore in the long cavalcade of the ship's assault boats and nosed into the deserted quay. Only an officer from divisional headquarters was there to meet us, and the town was silent as we bivouacked for the night among the railway wagons and warehouses.

All had not been so peaceful when the 2nd and 4th Brigades had landed two days earlier. The cruiser *Abdiel* carrying the 6th Battalion had been blown in two by an acoustic mine on entering the harbour, and half the battalion with their commanding officer had been trapped below and perished.

The two brigades had, however, advanced up the main roads running north-west and north, meeting only slight resistance from the German 1st Parachute Division which was pulling back. They had entered Massafra and Castellaneta, two important road junctions ten and fifteen miles north-west of the city, and now controlled a huge area to the east as well, including the port of Brindisi. Then another blow had fallen. Our divisional commander, Major-General Hopkinson, who was always to be found well up with the forward troops, had been killed by a stray bullet while watching an attack on a road-block outside Castellaneta. His death was felt keenly by the whole division for he was much respected.

The immediate plan of campaign was for the 2nd and 4th Brigades to continue to drive the enemy back by local thrusts and long-range patrols, while the 1st Brigade and the Air Landing Brigade consolidated a firm perimeter round Taranto, to await the arrival of the 5th Corps.

So on the morning after our arrival we moved out to the defence perimeter, where our three battalions held positions astride the Appian Way. The engineers had to assist them in excavating weapon pits in the rock with explosives and were also responsible for a sector on the extreme left of the brigade line. Here the ground fell steeply to the railway line running along the coast beside the mirror-like water of Taranto Bay. Near by stood a fifty-foot water tower of white sandstone, and on the whitewashed walls of an outbuilding an enormous Fascist slogan was emblazoned in letters two feet high:

'VIVERE PERICOLOSAMENTE!'
(Live Dangerously!)

The men laughed when it was translated to them; they could hardly imagine the local peasants living other than the quietest of lives!

Beyond lay the whole panorama of the bay, with a carpet of olive groves stretching away to the distant hills, a streak of violet against the sky. Drenched in the glow of a September afternoon nothing could have been less convincing background to the writing on the wall.

We were allowed an afternoon in Taranto, and this gave us an opportunity to see how the armistice had affected Italian life and the attitude of the people to the occupying troops. It was very different from what we had expected.

The civil population did not view themselves in the light of a conquered race but rather as if they had been liberated from a power which everyone disliked, and could now take their place among the allied nations. This was incomprehensible to us at first; we had been fighting them only a few weeks before. But our men in khaki-drill strolled unarmed down the wide boulevards and rubbed shoulders with Italian sailors and blue-uniformed coastal troops.

There was plenty to be bought in the shops – if you had Italian money; but the shopkeepers would not look at the Allied paper currency with which we had been issued, and preferred their paper lire which were virtually worthless with the Germans holding the Bank of Rome. It caused considerable difficulty until the matter was straightened out.

Local government had broken down with the disappearance of the Nazi and Fascist administration, and there followed a very noticeable apathy; for anyone who pushed himself to the fore and tried to create some order was liable to be dubbed a Fascist and courted an untimely end. So the Italians just left everything to us. Our 9th Field Company and divisional RASC performed a herculean task in clearing bomb debris, establishing water points, operating the docks and providing transport, but their resources were extremely limited.

After a week we moved up to the front to relieve the 2nd Brigade, who were then to take our place in the perimeter. The railway was still intact as far as Castellaneta, so for our journey the Italians were induced to get the trains going again. Our departure produced something of a pantomime among the railway staff, who had no desire to become involved in the war. But we got away at last and on arrival at Castellaneta went at once to take over positions on high ground astride the Laterza road.

Castellaneta was now a strong island base from which deep mobile patrols went out to test the enemy defences. Our small numbers could only be offset by great mobility, and we had secured a number of Italian lorries and 15-cwt trucks. The latter, with large wheels and balloon tyres, made excellent cross-country vehicles, and we armed them formidably with Vickers machine-guns and Italian Bredas.

The Germans had a similar base at Altamura, about fifty miles to the north-west, with a series of fortified outposts to cover it – from Ginosa, Laterza and Matera in the west to Gioja and its airfield in the north. In between was a no-man's-land in which every bridge had been destroyed and every road and track mined, and wherein German parachutist and British airborne soldier fought each other vigorously in gentlemanly engagements of a company a side.

So successful was our patrolling that the Germans gradually withdrew on our front in step with the advance of the Eighth Army on our left. Laterza withstood two night attacks and was then abandoned; Ginosa and Matera fell without a fight. The Air Landing Brigade

caputed Gioja and its fighter airstrip and went on to find
Bari free of enemy troops. Then at the end of September
we learnt that the Germans were pulling out of Altamura
itself, and determined to hasten their departure. Sufficient
transport had arrived from Africa for the whole brigade
to be carried in one lift, and we rolled forward late in the
afternoon armed for battle.

But the night went off quite peacefully. Just before
sunset Ted Boyse and an engineer patrol from Laterza
penetrated into Altamura and found the Germans gone.
The inhabitants, intent upon bringing the grape harvest
into town in their horse-drawn tumbrils, had cleared all
the mines from the roads. As the patrol were the first
Allied troops the people had seen they were fêted and
wined by a very enthusiastic crowd. It was as well they
had wirelessed back their report before they entered the
town; the evening was warm and the wine strong.

Altamura, on its hilltop, had the air of a fairy castle – a
glimpse into another age and veiled in mystery.

The centre of the town, the old walled city, was quite
fascinating with its magnificent cathedral and curious
rabbit-warren of cobbled streets, old-world shops and
balconied buildings nearly meeting overhead. This was
the world of Hans Andersen. The more modern part of
town oozed out beyond the walls and was quite another
matter. The streets were in an appalling state of disrepair,
the houses were squalid, the drains stank and chickens
scratched among the filth and refuse which choked the
gutters. This plastered and whitewashed abortion was like
the scum left by the waves breaking against the immortal
cliffs.

We set up our encampment in the olive groves alongside the Matera road, with its avenue of trees stretching away to the south. At first we had little need for our tents, for the days were hot and cloudless and the nights warm. But the autumn rains were already long overdue, and one day a torrential downpour turned the camp into a sea of mud. It was the first rain since the deluge in the Tunisian hills six months before. The indications were that we should be staying in Altamura for some time, so we moved into a large country mansion on the outskirts of the town. It was strange to live in a house again and to change from the easy carefree life out of doors to the more rigid etiquette of civilization.

The enemy had gone right back on our front, leaving a large tract of country to be surveyed by engineer reconnaissance parties. It fell to my lot to do the last of these patrols, a sweep of about sixty miles towards the Ofanto River, where it was thought the Germans might make a stand.

After an early start we passed through Gravina before the sun was up and took the bypass northwards round the two demolished bridges on the Spinazzola road where 'A' Troop were working on the diversion.

Then we were out in the no-man's-land. It was just that; the thoroughness of the German destruction staggered us. Road bridges were blackened rubble at the bottom of ravines; railway viaducts and multi-span steel bridges lay in a twisted mass on the river beds; lines had been torn up; even wells were blocked with concrete or fouled with a dead mule. In their military demolitions the enemy had gone out of their way to leave a lingering memory behind, and it was small wonder that the peasants welcomed us as liberators.

I shall not forget our reception at Mineravino, about twenty miles on. There had been cheers and 'vivas'

before, but as we cautiously entered the narrow streets –
wary of a possible German armoured-car patrol lying in
wait up a side street – we saw the throng lining the road.
The next instant we were brought to a standstill and
engulfed. My arms were seized and worked up and down
until they ached, people clambered over the bonnet and
sides and clung on wherever they could find a hold. All
was a medley of arms, legs and laughing faces, and our
horn was drowned by the babble of tongues. Baskets of
fruit were emptied into our laps, and dark girls smothered
us in kisses. Our driver got the jeep going again at last
and edged it forward, parting the crowd gently.

Never have I seen so much fruit at one time. It kept
pouring in until we were sitting up to our thighs in grapes
and nuts, while almonds and walnuts rained from the
balconies above. When we emerged on the other side of
the town we were exhausted and deaf from the tempes-
tuous hubbub.

Ten miles beyond Mineravino we were overtaken by
three armoured cars of the 1st Canadian Division, the
spearhead of the Eighth Army advancing from Calabria,
and made good speed for the next twenty miles under
their protection, slowing down again as we got near the
Ofanto. We were making for the town of Canosa on its
banks, near the ancient battle site of Cannae, and here
we felt sure the enemy would have a bridgehead.

Three miles out of Canosa the road joins the main Bari–
Foggia highway, and as we approached the road junction
we suddenly came upon hitherto undreamed-of military
activity. We had been travelling north in a backwater and
instead of being as we thought the vanguard of the army
we had missed the main axis of advance and were only
now joining the army on the march. The 5th Corps had
arrived, having landed at Bari the previous week.

We passed troops bivouacked among the vineyards, tank battalions resting beneath camouflage netting and a new swarm of vehicles parked under cover beside the road. The Bari road itself was packed with a double column crawling down the hill towards Canosa. There were Sherman tanks two abreast, artillery Quads and 25-pounders, long-barrelled 17-pounder anti-tank guns and the red berets of the Air Landing Brigade in a stream of TCVs.

We managed to dodge in and out of the tanks until we came into the crowd-lined streets of Canosa. The people here were tired of cheering and just gazed in awe at the cavalcade of armour. They had been up since daybreak, having gone to bed with the German rearguard in the town and awoke to find British troops in occupation.

On the far side of the town the column was jammed tight down to the river's edge. The long concrete bridge was no more than a shattered switchback, while near by was the wreck of the old stone bridge, with a blackened gap in its graceful gothic arches. A file of vehicles was fording the hundred yards of shallow water as engineers prepared a second ford, sweeping the shingle beach for mines and pegging out a lane. Until they had a two-way system there was only confusion in mid-stream – a gang of sappers pushing a roaring truck in a scurry of foam, a motor-cyclist with his engine hissing and, in front, a stalled jeep holding up the rest. The waiting convoy laughed and shouted encouragement, so that it was more of an entertainment than a serious military operation with a war up the road.

I saw that my task was done, so disengaging ourselves, we sped for home to hand in our report before it was quite out of date. Foggia fell next day, and with it the all-weather airfields which would bring every part of Hitler's Europe under fire.

November – and the coming of the first breath of the Mediterranean winter. Black banks of thundery cumulus piled up, shutting out the sun, and there were frequent fierce showers of rain. Leaves fell, turbulent streams appeared in the ravines, tracks and footpaths became a squelching quagmire, and everywhere a cold biting wind whistled over the landscape. Italy is a land of sunshine, and fares badly when the rain begins to fall.

The army had passed on, and now we were relegated to the reserve, to duties on the lines of communication and to training.

In Altamura strange things were happening. Whenever we went into the town we were greeted by knowing smiles, by expressions of regret at our imminent departure for the front and the hope that we would soon come back again. We would laugh and tell our Italian informants not to be fools.

Then, curiously enough, the rumours were confirmed. The 1st Parachute Brigade received orders direct from 5th Corps to prepare for a secret operation, and once again we were back in the old routine of going to war.

We moved to Barletta, a small seaport to the north of Bari, and began amphibious training in several landing-craft sent specially from Brindisi. We used to parade with our battalions in full battle equipment, and march down to the docks in column through the town. No doubt we made an imposing sight in our camouflaged helmets and green smocks, with our Everest carriers and array of support weapons and trundling our trolleys over the cobbles, for the crowd shouted vivas loud and long.

Our practice beach was a small isolated cove fifteen

–

miles up the coast, and with high hills all around should have been secure from prying eyes. But in Barletta our every movement was known, and it was even hinted that our destination was the German-held port of Pescara. To us, who had been used to rigid security before a parachute operation, all this was extremely disturbing.

Eventually came the night for a dress rehearsal. By now a small fleet of infantry landing-craft had collected, together with three long flat-bottomed tank-landing vessels for the brigade's jeeps and battery of anti-tank guns. This time we gave a really impressive display, and our procession to the ships was in the nature of a Roman triumph. The town turned out in force and cheered and wept alternately at what they took to be our final departure.

But the exercise was a complete fiasco at first. When we embarked we viewed with some relief the low clouds and squally rain which blotted out the moon: German planes had been over the harbour on most fine nights, and after our experience at Syracuse we preferred to take our air-raids on land. Soon a strong wind blew up from across the Adriatic, and everyone became prostrate as we tossed like corks on the heaving green mountains. Our convoy was scattered, and as we lay off our cove at first light, ready for the assault, we found that we were alone. When the others arrived at last, and we made a belated attack, it was without our guns; for the tank-landing craft, which were none too seaworthy owing to long service, never left port at all.

We returned to Barletta depressed and perturbed. That evening Major Stevens called us into the office and closed the door.

'You can all sleep with an easy mind tonight,' he said. 'This operation is a hoax.'

When the uproar had subsided he went on:

'Some time ago our intelligence people unearthed a spy system behind our lines, and it was decided to turn it to our advantage before pulling it in.

'German reinforcements have been moving down the Adriatic coast from northern Italy, and the Army Commander wanted these delayed while he attacked across the Sangro. So hints were dropped that we were going to Barletta to prepare for a seaborne assault against enemy communications. Sure enough, this information duly went to the Germans, so we persevered and the ruse worked. A Bosche infantry division on the way to the front had been switched to coast defence at Pescara, and is waiting there for us now. They will not be entirely disappointed, for the Navy is going to shell them well tonight.'

Relief was written boldly on every face, and this changed to excitement when he concluded:

'You will have to put up with one more sea journey. We are going home. The division is packing up, and we are sailing for England in a few days' time!'

PART FOUR

Arnhem: Journey's End

September 1944

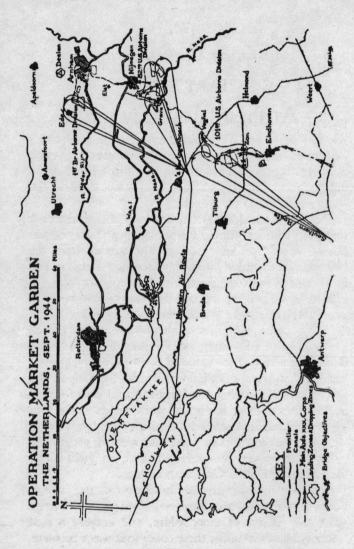

16
Operation Market Garden
September 1944

By the time we finally took off for Arnhem every man was chafing to go. We had had too many false alarms – loading aircraft and gliders, adjusting parachutes, keying ourselves up for the ordeal ahead, going to bed on so many nights wondering whether it really was to be the last – and we longed to get it over.

For 'Operation Market Garden' was the seventeenth time we had been warned for battle since D-Day on the 6th of June. We had followed the armies from the Normandy beachhead, across France and Belgium and into Holland with frequent briefings, only to have our landing zones overrun on each occasion before we could get into the air. Some of our ventures promised well, like 'Transfiguration' ten miles south of Paris, which had all the makings of a liberating spree; others like 'Wild Oats' during the agony of the battle of Caen were a nightmare, with our battle maps flecked with Panzer formations. But all had come to nothing; the Germans went back too fast, and there was more important work for us to do. Our great potentialities could not be used up lightly, for once we were put into the air, and our mass of gliders and airborne equipment committed to battle we could not be used again until all this had been replaced.

Since our return from Italy in December the 1st Airborne Division had been dispersed throughout the townships and villages of Lincolnshire, and keeping a rigid 'security blackout' under these conditions was a problem. Our squadron was billeted in Donington, and everyone had become assimilated into the village life. Many of the men were courting girls, and others had wives and families in the vicinity. The best we could do was to confine all ranks to billets during the stand-to periods, to double our sentries and to erect barbed wire round the squadron offices and the inner sanctum of the briefing hut. Much credit is due to the local people, who saw most of our preparations and last-minute activity yet went about their business as if nothing was in the wind. It was only when we came back from the airfields after another cancellation with our tails between our legs, that their welcoming smiles seemed to say, 'What, you back *again*!'

Arnhem first came into the picture with 'Operation Comet', for which the division was briefed at the beginning of September. At the time, the chances of the war being over in 1944 were very good indeed; for, even if the Germans succeeded in halting the allied armies on the Siegfried Line, the route through Holland gave access to the open tank country of the North German plain and would have turned the readily defended areas of the Rhineland and the Ruhr. Three river lines lay between the Second Army and the realization of this hope. They were the Maas, the Waal and the Neder Rijn.

As usual we stood-to, loaded aircraft and gliders and were briefed in considerable detail. And once more we got a new currency. It had become quite a pastime, and our pockets jingled and rustled with odd coinage and notes. Now the section's money had to be converted into Dutch guilders at the awkward exchange rate of sixteen to thirty shillings, and again I seemed down on the transaction.

The plan was an ambitious one, with each of the three brigades of the division being responsible for one of the river crossings. But when the Second Army attacked

—

across the Albert Canal very heavy resistance was encountered, and 'Comet' went into the melting-pot. General Montgomery decided that more time would be required to build up his bridgeheads and that a far greater airborne force was necessary to carry the river lines. So, for Operation Market Garden on the 17th of September, three airborne divisions were committed – two American and one British – the 101st Division to create an intermediate stepping-stone north of Eindhoven, the 82nd Division to land between the Maas and Waal and secure the Grave and Nijmegen bridges, while the lion's share, the spearhead and the big road bridge at Arnhem, fell to the 1st Airborne Division.

We had little to do in the way of packing containers, for these had been left in readiness after 'Comet'. Additions to our usual equipment were such items as flame throwers and folding reconnaissance boats; while, as a development of the 2nd Battalion's idea at Primosole, we now had the leg-kitbag for personal weapons and stores, which was lowered on a twenty-foot rope during the descent. We also had more transport. One bomb-rack on each plane was carrying a light motor-cycle in a protective steel cradle to be parachuted down with the containers, and each troop's jeep and trailer were coming with the brigade glider train.

The 1st Brigade was flying from two aerodromes of American Transport Command near Grantham – the 2nd and 3rd Battalions from Saltby, and the 1st Battalion, brigade headquarters, the 16th Parachute Field Ambulance and ourselves from Barkston Heath. Both these airfields assembled an incredible display of Dakotas and Horsa gliders, all painted with the broad black-and-white invasion stripes. Take-off was to be shortly before midday on the 17th, a Sunday, and when we went across for loading on Friday morning the planes were already marshalled on the perimeter track. There were about eighty, drawn up in two adjacent rows facing in opposite directions, and so closely packed that from a little distance they looked a solid mass.

We went over our individual aircraft with the crew chief, checking container-parachutes and release switches, seeing that anchor cables and strops were properly secured and that projections and sharp edges on the jumping door were masked with adhesive tape.

We were briefed on Saturday. The OC gave the squadron a general talk before each troop took its turn in the briefing-room.

The landing of each of the three divisions was to begin the following afternoon, but it was to be spread over three days as there were insufficient aircraft to carry them all in one lift. At the same time the ground forces, led by the armour of the 30th Corps, were to establish a corridor through to Arnhem via the American 'islands' at Eindhoven, Grave and Nijmegen. The success of the whole venture depended on our securing the crossing over the Neder Rijn for the final offensive into Germany, so our division was being strengthened by the Polish Parachute Brigade; and the 52nd Mountain Division was to be brought over later in Dakotas to land within the bridgehead as soon as runways could be prepared.

At Arnhem the 1st Air Landing Brigade, the 1st Parachute Brigade and part of divisional headquarters were flying in on the first day; the 4th Parachute Brigade, the Light Regiment, RA, and other divisional troops on the second, and the Polish Parachute Brigade on the third.

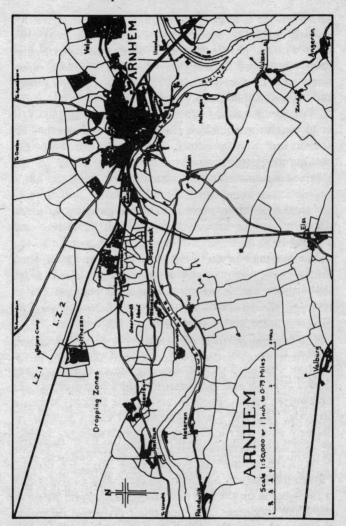

George Irwin gave 'B' Troop further details when we came to the briefing-room. On this occasion, unlike the previous rush operations, Joe Wallace's section had had time to present the excellent intelligence in great clarity. There were recent stereoscopic photos of the road bridge and its surroundings, and a nine-inch-to-the-mile town plan of Arnhem with German-occupied buildings marked in blue. The maps which papered one wall covered an area from the eastern outskirts of the city to the neighbourhood of Utrecht and the Zuider Zee.

Arnhem lies on the north bank of the river and has a population of about one hundred thousand, with a built-up area over three miles across and nearly two miles deep. It was an important centre for the enemy and contained the underground telephone exchange for all the German armies in the west. Apart from the main-road bridge there were a railway bridge about three miles lower down and a partially dismantled pontoon bridge between the two. All were strongly defended by flak batteries in the area within the loop of the river.

The German garrison was apparently only a small one, but there were fair-sized Gestapo and Luftwaffe head-quarters – Deelen airfield was only eight miles away to the north – and these, together with an artillery school and another for SS leaders, could all produce troops and arms of a sort at short notice.

We were having an escort during the fly-in of nearly two thousand fighters, of which several hundred were detailed for ground 'strafing'. Deelen airfield was being heavily bombed while we dropped, as well as all the local flak positions.

But in view of the concentration of flak near the bridges our landing and dropping zones were about seven miles west of the city near Wolfhezen, to the north and south of the railway line running to Utrecht.

The operations on the morrow were being opened by the independent parachute company of divisional headquarters, who were to drop from Pathfinder aircraft to mark the dropping and landing zones. Twenty minutes later the first gliders were coming down to the north of the railway line. These would contain the divisional reconnaissance squadron and their jeeps, whose task it was to make an immediate dash for Arnhem bridge. They would be followed shortly by our own glider-borne transport and the Air Landing Brigade.

The 1st Parachute Brigade was timed to begin dropping at 14.00 hours on the dropping zone to the south of the railway, near the village of Heelsum. The 3rd Battalion was leading and would protect the dropping zone until we had all landed. The 2nd and 1st Battalions were following at five-minute intervals, brigade headquarters, the field ambulance and the engineer squadron coming in with the last battalion in the third wave.

There were two main tasks on the first day. The Air Landing Brigade was to consolidate the landing area; the 1st Parachute Brigade was responsible for the bridgehead in the town. For the attack on Arnhem the 3rd Battalion was coming in on the Utrecht road and the 2nd Battalion was taking the lower road nearer the Rhine. The 1st Battalion was in reserve. The one object was to reach the bridge quickly, and opposition was to be by-passed wherever possible.

As for our own part in the proceedings the three troops were going with their respective battalions. My own job was to take a small party with 'C' Company, who were leading the 2nd Battalion. This company would peel off at the suburbs of Oosterbeek to go and deal with the railway bridge.

Other details were that the field ambulance were setting up the main dressing station in the St Elizabeth hospital in Arnhem, and that the RAF would be dropping supplies from Wednesday onwards if all went well.

'One more thing,' George Irwin concluded, 'the direction of the fly-in. We cross the Dutch coast by this island, Schouwen, and fly east to Hertogen's bosch. Here we turn northwards over the three rivers and drop half a minute after crossing the last, the Neder Rijn. It's about two-and-a-half-hours' flight altogether, two over the sea and half an hour across Holland.'

We turned in early that night. We had rehearsed the last-minute procedure so often that it was now an unhurried routine. Our belongings had been sent home days ago and our battle clothes were laid out on our bedside chairs. By the dressing-table lay my parachute with harness already adjusted, and haversack containing rations and personal kit. Near by was my 'walkie-talkie' wireless set, Mae West life jacket, and map case with those sheets first required folded under the talc. From the chair hung compass, binoculars and web equipment with Sten magazines in the pouches; while over the back the mottled Airborne smock was draped like a weighted sack, pockets stuffed with grenades ready primed, fuse igniters, emergency chocolate, field and shell dressings, morphia syrettes and the section's benzedrine tablets. Then, to complete this paraphernalia, my garnished parachute helmet and Sten gun were hanging on the wall, ready to be grabbed in the morning.

We were called at five. It was perfect weather, cloudless and slightly misty, and the early sun was just warming up the village square. So 'Market Garden' was on, and this was the day of days.

Everyone was unusually calm as we met in the bathroom over shaving. All doubts and worries were things of the past: our minds were swept clean of what had gone before, now we were eager for what was to come. We dressed quickly but carefully, then made a hearty last breakfast, rounded off with beer to finish up a spare crate before our departure.

None of the village was up to see our long line of lorries slide away over the railway bridge and down the Grantham road. On arrival at Barkston Heath we loaded our kitbags and other equipment into the plane and then lay about in the sun alongside. There were three hours yet. A tea-wagon came round at about ten. Then our aircrew turned up with a large tin of spam, for which they seemed to have lost their appetite, and offered it to us. Chepstowe, my new batman, stowed it away in his kitbag, along with the two loaves he was taking with characteristic foresight.

Chepstowe was a remarkable man in many ways. He was not always popular with the sergeant-major but as a bodyguard and batman in the field he was quite unequalled – producing a mug of tea when you needed it most and having a meal ready and a dry place for you to sleep on return from duty. A vital part of Chepstowe's battle equipment consisted of his Primus stove which he carried everywhere in his pack. He was only a small man, and now his bulging kitbag weighed almost as much as himself.

That crowded perimeter track was a sight never to be forgotten. First the serried aircraft, then the thousands of green-smocked paratroopers taking the sun, and beyond, the lorries waiting in rows on either side to see us finally away. Here on this narrow strip was a complete fighting formation which would be at war four hundred miles away within a matter of hours. At half-past ten the sleeping groups came to life as we dressed ourselves, wrestled with our harness, then, one by one, bundled each other into the plane.

The crew chief came back into our compartment to see that we had all we wanted, and remarked on our cheerfulness and self-possession. This was not bravado – every man was genuinely thankful to be off.

Soon after eleven, the peace of the Sunday morning was tossed to the four winds as each plane started up its engines and revved them at full throttle. Our aircraft quivered and strained, while the grass trembled in the gale. Slowly the long lines moved forward and marshalled themselves at the end of the runway. They formed up in flights of three, nose to tail and wing-tip to wing-tip. Engines ticked over smoothly, and we awaited the order to go.

At eleven-thirty the first flight was airborne, followed at fifteen-second intervals by the others, until there was a continuous stream of planes roaring into the air three abreast. Now we ourselves were bounding down the tarmac and the ground had dropped away. We circled Barkston Heath several times until the formation was complete, and then the flat fields of Lincolnshire slid away beneath us and were gone.

17
Arnhem Bridge
17–21 *September*, 1944

The shadows of our huge fleet moved in perfect formation across the surface of the glassy water as though it were another flock of aircraft below us and not just the image of ourselves.

Then at length the sand-dunes and sea wall of Schouwen Island appeared ahead, with white foam breaking on the shore. We tightened the chinstraps of our helmets and hooked up.

We passed over a patchwork quilt of farmland. A Horsa glider was down in a field, the skid-marks showing up like a weal through the long grass, and a group of tiny figures were fussing round the tail. The island seemed otherwise deserted.

The patchwork changed to sand-dunes again, and immediately we were out over the Waal estuary. The wedge of water narrowed as we flew on. Some puffs of white smoke appeared in the sky half a mile away, and we heard the cracks of bursting shells.

'See that?' exclaimed the crew chief. He was kneeling by the door taking pictures with a Leica. 'As long as it stays right there that's okay by me.'

We could see the flashes of the guns firing on the edge of the water to the north. The shells tracked our course well out of range. Now we were over land again.

Then the sky was full of aircraft – fighters, hundreds of them, diving, twisting and turning, racing backwards and forwards beneath us like greyhounds after a hare. A light flak pom-pom gave us a short burst, but two Typhoons were on to him at once. We passed a column of smoke rising from a burning farm – another flak position until the rockets had found it. Spitfires and Mustangs flew up and down searching out the batteries, while above us and on either side – forming a tunnel down which we flew unmolested – other squadrons roared by in echelon, on the look-out for the Focke-Wulfs and Messerschmitts. We watched with awe and wonder and very thankful hearts.

'Ten minutes to go,' the crew chief warned and wished us luck. Just then we turned north. We pulled the folding bicycle forward and lined up. The crew chief stood back, forward of the door, to manipulate the container switches and jabbed his finger at the jump indicator as the red light snapped on. Four minutes now! I put my head out into the slipstream.

Suddenly the Rhine was below us, a broad snake with timber breakwaters jutting out into the stream. A few more fields, a copse, a village (Heelsum) with windows glinting in the sun, then the ground covered thickly with hundreds of coloured parachutes. Chepstowe thumped me vigorously. I heaved out the bicycle and followed.

I landed softly in a patch of mustard. Everything was quiet as on an exercise in England, with men swarming across the dropping zone towards their several rendez-vous. Blue smoke was going up half a mile away from the corner of a copse.

I hurried back, found our containers and assembled two trolleys. One of the sappers uncrated the motor-cycle and chugged off steadily over the rough plough. Then Tony Miles arrived, sweating and very red in the face from making speed across the soft ground. 'This is too much of a guinea-pig drop for my liking!' he said, mopping out his helmet and helping me load one of the trolleys. 'No enemy and everything going like clockwork. Depienne started like this!'

'Yes, but we weren't putting down the whole division then.'

'Well, I hope you're right!'

We dragged our trolley towards the rendezvous while two sappers took the other. Just then the bombs went down on Deelen airfield. The earth shook as clouds of purple smoke and dust rose behind the woods to the north, and an ugly rumbling went on for several minutes.

One of the 2nd Battalion's carriers, landed by Hamilcar glider, clattered across piled high with men and stores. Dutch civilians were bringing out their horses and carts and helping the RASC to salvage containers. We passed groups of the 3rd Battalion occupying covering positions and here and there a knot of Luftwaffe prisoners sitting, sullen and dispirited, under guard. I tried my walkie-talkie and came up on Joe's net.

'OK, Baker two!' he said. 'The 2nd Battalion are moving off in a minute, so step on it!'

At the rendezvous we found the rest of the squadron assembling and taking up temporary positions in the undergrowth. I handed the walkie-talkie over to my section sergeant and chased off through the trees with my four men.

Apart from Chepstowe I had chosen Corporal Dory, Clarkson, now my best Bren gunner, and Stewart for my party. These three had jumped with me at Depienne and all were battle-hardened veterans on whom I knew I could rely to the end.

'C' Company had already gone when we reported to Colonel Frost, and we set off helter-skelter up the column to catch them. The battalion was going at a great pace and was spaced out under cover of the roadside trees.

Two passing jeeps gave us a lift until we reached our company headquarters, when we dropped off to join them on the march.

There had been little sign of any resistance hitherto, and it seemed as though it was going to be just a Sunday afternoon picnic. Then we came upon the wreckage of a convoy of German staff cars. They were riddled with bullet holes, doors hung open, and the untidy bodies of the occupants sprawled across the pavé amidst the debris of a disrupted vehicle and splintered glass. The place was a shambles.

This scene, we heard later, had repeated itself several times as German officers, surprised by the airborne landings and trying to escape eastwards, had run into ambushes. The South Staffs of the Air Landing Brigade killed SS Major-General Kussin and two of his staff in this way.

As we progressed firing broke out ahead and hammered away on the flanks. The column halted and went to ground in defence positions. Long bursts of Spandau machine-gun fire were rippling out to the north – the 3rd Battalion on the Utrecht road were running into trouble. The head of our column reported that they were held up by an armoured car. A party was working round through the woods to get within Piat range. Some strays from the skirmishing on the Utrecht road crackled over our heads. I began to feel uncomfortable as we lay and waited; we could see nothing, and all the while the noise of battle was mounting steadily on every side.

In five minutes the column was moving again, and we pressed on up the road now clear of the enemy. A paratrooper was lying in the ditch with a bullet through his leg, smoking unconcernedly while a medical orderly applied a field dressing. He smiled as we chaffed him on his luck; he would, we supposed, be back in England very shortly with a perfect 'blighty'.

We passed through the outskirts of a small residential estate, with fine, graceful houses standing in large wooded gardens. Here the Dutch thronged the pavements to greet us, and seized our hands and arms until they were nearly pumped out of the sockets. Everyone wore an orange flower in his buttonhole; all the windows displayed orange tablecloths, stair-carpets, quilts, anything with the national colour. One old man came out of a house and trotted along beside me.

'How many of you are there?' he asked anxiously.

'Very many,' I replied. 'Many thousands, and the British Army is on the way.'

'That is good! Very, very good!' he went on. 'We have waited so long for this day, and now our troubles are over. Thank you so much for coming.'

We were now going at a steadier pace, pausing at times, since the leading platoons were moving with some caution. We came down the long slope into Oosterbeek, and the people met us with baskets of apples and pears. We filled up our smocks as they kept pressing them on us and pouring them into the men's helmets. Others brought us jugs of water and beer, while one farmer was dipping out milk from a churn.

Those Dutch men and women, in their overwhelming enthusiasm, showed complete disregard for danger. Every now and again a sniper's rifle would crack quite alarmingly near and be answered by the clatter of a vigilant Bren, but no one paid the least attention. There was heavy firing to the north, but to them it was merely the prelude to peace.

We munched apples down the quiet suburban avenues but kept a wary eye open as we pushed on with all speed.

The railway bridge came in sight at the bottom of the slopes where the road turned east to skirt the meadows bordering the Rhine. Here we left it and took a cart track across the fields. The point platoon was followed by company headquarters and ourselves, with the two other platoons bringing up the rear. Everything was normal, and only the intermittent automatic fire in the distance disturbed the warm autumn evening. We passed a 40-mm flak-gun camouflaged by branches in a gateway. Two rifles stood propped against it, and a box of potato-masher grenades lay open on the ground. The crew had bolted.

Our lane ended in a large disused brick-kiln near the river, and we were now about two hundred yards from the high railway embankment and bridge. On our right a flood-bank rose about five feet above the level of the meadows. Across the river another flood-bank, with a road running along it, screened all the country beyond; but we could just see the upper floors of a farm building on the far side and a couple of small houses by the bridge.

The leading platoon had now gained the fifteen-foot railway embankment and was scrambling up the steep grass sides. We picked our way through the havoc caused by rocket-firing Typhoons on the flak battery which guarded the bridge. Four-barrelled pom-poms waved tentacle-like arms at the sky, the pieces twisted and blasted out of recognition. The sandbagged pits were ripped and tossed around like bags of flour. The ground was pitted with the shallow craters of graze-fuse bombs, and German dead lay about in horrible abandon. Two cows, blood pouring from shrapnel wounds, grazed quietly beside the dead, making no sound. A third lay on its back kicking and mooing pitifully.

The forward platoon was now on the bridge and well down the first of the three spans while our party was nearing the embankment. Suddenly a series of rifle shots cracked out from the buildings opposite, and two of our infantry dropped. The rest fell flat and wormed for cover. Then the bridge blew up with a shattering explosion. A great red-and-orange flame stabbed the girders on the third span, which was then covered by a pall of smoke. The explosion and blast-wave reached us on the instant, and we fell involuntarily to the ground.

The company deployed quickly along the bank, and immediately Brens were returning the fire. The infantry on the bridge withdrew under this cover bringing their two wounded comrades with them. The third span of the bridge sagged drunkenly in the river.

We ceased fire after a minute or two. Ten minutes went by and then two German trucks came along the embanked road, towing a couple of small guns. At once our automatics opened up again. The two trucks caught fire under a hurricane of tracer and careered out of control down the bank and out of sight. Sparks and billows of smoke rose from the wrecks.

Dusk fell at about eight o'clock. There had been a certain amount of sniping at long range from Oosterbeek way but it caused us little inconvenience. Meanwhile, the rest of the 2nd Battalion had passed on and were fighting their way into Arnhem. Every so often there would be the crump of grenades, a spirited outburst of machine-gun fire and a fountain of tracer ricochets in the evening sky. The battalion appeared to be a long way down the road.

Fighting was now flaring up to the west of us as well. There was rifle and machine-gun fire in the direction of Renkum and Heelsum, and once the agonized wail of the German rocket mortars – the 'Sobbing Sisters' of Africa, terrifying and satanic.

Just as it was getting dark 'C' Company received the order by wireless to leave the bridge and follow after the rest of the battalion as fast as possible. We got to our feet and moved noiselessly away.

We had only gone half a mile when the company commander sent for me.

'I've had another message to send you back to the railway bridge,' he said. 'They want to make certain that there is no more explosive on the two remaining spans and that it can't be damaged further. Search it well and then come on behind. There don't seem to be any Bosche there, so you should be all right.'

I turned my four men round and marched back along the road, then through a garden and down a bank out on to the empty, silent meadows. We felt as though German eyes were peering at us from every house and wall. The farmhouse on the other side of the Rhine was burning fiercely now, and an eerie red flicker danced among the willow trees and meadow dykes.

We reached the bridge by about ten o'clock, very weary from the excitement and exertion of the afternoon. I tore my trousers badly in climbing over barbed wire fences, and the night air chilled my naked thighs, but I was too tired to care. We removed our haversacks and left them at the bottom of the embankment, then crept on to the bridge with our Bren and Stens at the ready. Leaving the Bren gunners to cover us I went forward with Dory and Chepstowe, feeling my way cautiously over the sleepers. After fifteen minutes the railway lines rose into the air and then plunged down into the water. The current swirled and sucked round the fallen girders, drowning any noise we might have made. We listened intently for some time, then turned about and crawled back searching the bridge as we went.

The night was now very dark, and it took us far longer than we anticipated to search the structure thoroughly. We crawled about on our hands and knees, lay on our stomachs and reached for the girders underneath the track and clambered like monkeys over the piers. Corporal Dory found a box of workman's tools, and Clarkson a Sten dropped by one of the wounded men, but that was the sum total of two-and-a-half hours' labour. By twelve-thirty we had satisfied ourselves that the bridge was clear, and set off across the fields and dykes for Oosterbeek.

By the time we reached the main road it was one-thirty, and everyone was dog-tired. The streets were deserted and deceptively quiet. About two miles farther on sudden bursts of firing shattered the night at periodic intervals, and all around there was the suggestion of furtive movement. We were now enclosed by houses on either side, and the clatter of our boots on the pavement decided me to call a three-hour halt until dawn. Our small party was inviting ambush along this well-defined route in darkness.

We found a shed and took it in turns to keep watch while the others dozed. We dared not sleep heavily, so got little rest and only painfully stiff, and we were almost thankful when the dawn appeared over Arnhem and we could get on the move again. We swung our heavy haversacks on to aching backs and plodded rather dejectedly out of the lair. The air was cold, and we shivered violently.

As we were moving off four more paratroopers came out of a house and joined us. They were a corporal and two privates of the 2nd Battalion who had become separated from the others in a clash the night before and a medical orderly who had remained behind with the wounded. We all went on together.

We passed underneath the railway arch near Oosterbeek station in the half light and slipped into the cover of an avenue of trees on the other side. Here we were lucky, for a German company occupied the position immediately afterwards and must at that moment have been moving down the railway line towards us. RASC supply jeeps had run into German fighting patrols at this spot during the night.

We now came on the gruesome evidence of another skirmish – one of our own dead lying face downwards in the road, and a little farther on a number of German corpses in the ditch. We gave the dead one look and pushed on faster.

We entered the outskirts of Arnhem at about six o'clock and covered each other up the street in quick 'bounds' of about a hundred yards. Then we passed two burning houses on which a group of the city fire brigade were playing their hoses.

It was now fully light, and the city was beginning to stir. There were definite sounds of troops moving in adjoining streets, and a heavy motor vehicle, suspiciously like an armoured car, was heard a little to our north.

As the city shook itself awake the battle flared up ahead with terrible ferocity. Rifle shots rang out, then a fusillade, a snarl from a Spandau, several bursts of Bren, and finally the awful paean of machine-gun fire as every automatic let go at once. Then all the flak on the southern bank of the Rhine blazed forth together. There was the staccato whip and crack of the 88-mms, but worst of all was the thunder of the four-barrelled pom-poms. The noise was quite sickening. A blizzard of cannon fire from massed batteries pounded the approaches to Arnhem bridge, and fountains of tracer ricocheted off the buildings. From that moment we took to the back gardens, scrambling over the dividing walls but passing through the houses at times, with only a smile and handshake for the puzzled Dutch families surprised in the act of getting up.

We reached the St Elizabeth hospital without incident and found our field ambulance duly installed there. Handing over my Sten to the others I went inside to find out the situation. The adjutant was in the hall organizing a reception station. He said that the bridge had been captured the night before, but that the enemy had now interposed a force between the 2nd Battalion and themselves. He could tell me nothing of brigade or our squadron headquarters.

Outside I passed on this disquieting news, and went on up the hill again, with the railway sidings on our left and on the right the steep escarpment overlooking the Rhine. The noise of the battle in front was now terrific, and there was heavy traffic moving in the town on the other side of the railway.

When we came to houses again we got into the back gardens on the edge of the escarpment and worked forward cautiously to the top of the rise. Here I was wriggling over a high stone wall when a burst of Spandau crashed out just above my head, and I half fell and was half pulled back on top of Clarkson who was giving me a leg-up. We withdrew quickly a couple of gardens back.

Now we heard a heavy armoured vehicle grinding up the street towards us, so we took up positions and waited. The engine stopped. There was firing further along the road. While I thought out our next move Chepstowe rummaged in his pack and with complete unconcern brought out a loaf of bread and his big tin of spam. He divided them up and the others ate ravenously. 'Come on, have a bite, sir!' he coaxed, but I could not look at it – the very thought of food was repugnant at such a moment.

I had a hurried glance at my plan of the city. We were

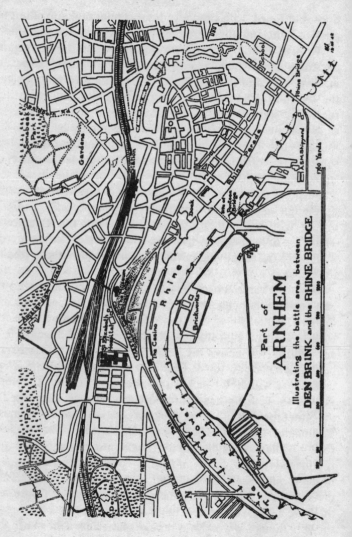

Part of
ARNHEM

Illustrating the battle area between
DEN BRINK and the RHINE BRIDGE

a quarter of a mile beyond the hopsital and still about a mile from the bridge, with the enemy holding the bottleneck in front of us between the railway and the river and evidently watching for us to appear again. Our small party would get no further by this route. I saw that by retracing our steps we might cross the railway line and gain the more open part of the city beyond by a chain of woods, starting with Den Brink park, half a mile west of the St Elizabeth hospital. Here we might link up with the 1st Battalion – for fighting was going on to the north of us in the region of the Amsterdam road – or we might fall in with the 3rd Battalion. I explained the plan to the rest and we set off briskly the way we had come.

We turned north after passing the hospital and entered the chessboard of back streets to the west of it. We were making for the railway near the end of the sidings when we narrowly escaped disaster. An armoured car stood half-concealed in a side road a hundred yards away with a crowd of German infantry in the nearby gardens, fortunately looking in the opposite direction. We ducked back under cover and continued westwards towards Den Brink.

We reached it about twenty minutes later. This park had at some time been a flak site for a heavy battery. The great square sandbagged pits were still there, and the undergrowth had been allowed to advance unchecked. Rhododendron bushes straggled in dark-green islands among tall copper beech trees, and bracken and smaller bushes had grown up thickly, reducing visibility to fifty yards at most.

We spread out and moved into the wood rapidly but carefully, with weapons cocked. We had not gone more than twenty yards when things happened. Someone fired on us from a few yards' range with a Schmeisser machine carbine, then leapt up and ran. His burst missed all of us,

and instinctively I fired a long burst at the green figure in
peaked hat before he dived into a large patch of rhododendron. My shot hit him; the man gasped but plunged
on, making rasping noises between his teeth. My blood
was up, and without further thought I gave chase. I
imagined that the German was a lone sniper hiding up in
the wood. I knew that I had winged him, but he still had
a Schmeisser slung round his neck and we could not go on
in safety with him at large. Chepstowe and I ran to the
right of the rhododendron clump, while I shouted to the
others to go round the left.

Of course it all happened in a flash. The German and I
fired almost simultaneously, and then I was sprinting
round the clump to catch him as he reappeared. I ran on
for about a hundred yards, across a road and into a
clearing, then dropped down on one knee to see where
he had gone. I saw him lying behind a tree and two other
men bending over him. These two were wearing mottled
camouflage smocks and scrimmed helmets and looked not
unlike British paratroopers. I peered for a second unde-
cided, but then one raised his rifle and fired in our
direction. He was wearing black leather equipment, and
as he turned his head I saw the shape of his helmet. I
shouted, 'Hände hoch!' but when he swung his rifle
towards me I gave them a couple of eight-round bursts.
They rolled over without making a sound and lay huddled
together.

I have only the very vaguest impression of what followed. I saw the whole wood running with figures in green
and mottled clothing, men jumping from half-dug
trenches and throwing away picks and shovels, men
scrambling for rifles propped against trees: the place was
alive with Germans dodging and scurrying for the shelter
of solid trunks. It was too late to run for cover myself so I
just hosed with the Sten at anything and everything that

moved. There was no time nor need to aim: they were in a semicircle from twenty to thirty yards away. Two men with a machine-gun, a Spandau, tried to swing it round at me but died over their gun before they ever fired a burst. Two others fell as they dived for trees, another looked out from behind his cover and then crumpled up. I saw the dust fly up in the faces of two others peering over a bank twenty yards to my right, and they disappeared backwards: a single boot came up over the top and stayed there.

I kept thinking to myself, 'Why haven't I been killed yet? Another second perhaps . . . why on earth am I still alive?' A long splinter of wood flew from the tree to my right; a twig kicked up by my knee; the bullets were cracking very near. The Germans were rattled and were loosing off anywhere in my direction. As long as my own miniature blizzard lasted I stood a chance; when my ammunition had gone . . .! I clipped on the fifth and last magazine and almost gave up hope. Then I heard my own Bren thundering away quite close, so leapt to my feet and raced for cover, spraying the Sten in an arc behind me. Clarkson finished off his second magazine and then ran too as I came level with him. Of course he saved my life.

We made that thirty yards in record time. We went over the road and towards a red brick house, then dived for a clump of thickly planted trees. I had two yards to go, then felt the bullet smack into my side. I did the last couple of steps and flopped down gasping.

Corporal Dory and the rest of the party were close by, so we crawled over and joined them. I had great difficulty in breathing and knew that as far as I was concerned the battle of Arnhem was just about over.

'Are you all right, sir?' Dory enquired.

'Bullet in the side,' I gasped. 'Are the rest OK?'

'Stewart's been hit, sir. He's very bad!'

Sapper Stewart was lying beneath a tree, breathing heavily. He had been shot through the upper chest, his face was grey and he was dying fast.

'Corporal Dory!' I hissed. The woods were treacherously silent again. 'You've got to get out of here quickly. Beat it, do you understand? Try and get away without being seen but shoot your way out if you have to. Go on, get out of it!'

He and the others looked at me doubtfully, then got to their knees and set off running, bent double. They did thirty yards, then a rifle cracked and the 2nd Battalion corporal who was with us dropped in his tracks. Clarkson turned and hosed around with the Bren, the others dropped down behind a fold in the ground and were gone. A moment later Clarkson had joined them. I began to feel very much alone. Then I saw the medical orderly a yard to my left.

'What are you doing here?' I enquired angrily.

'You're wounded, sir, and the other man needs medical help. My job is to stay with the wounded.'

We crawled over to Stewart. There was nothing we could do: he was dead. The body of the infantry corporal lay exactly as it had fallen thirty yards away.

'Best get away from here, sir,' the orderly exclaimed after a moment. 'They might try letting us have a few potato-mashers to finish us off!'

We looked around for a suitable hiding-place. Forty yards away to the north was a derelict brick barn covered with ivy. We wormed our way over laboriously, rolled into a ditch beneath the wall and pulled the ivy down on top of us. We were quite comfortable, camouflaged and in fairly good cover. The Germans opened up with a Spandau a moment or two later and sprayed that part of the wood we had just left. Two rifle-grenades landed a little later. But the enemy made no attempt to come and investigate. After a little while half a dozen camouflaged forms crawled out and pulled in their wounded. Their own dead they left where they lay.

As soon as all the commotion had died down the medical orderly came and had a look at my wound. After slitting up my smock and shirt he eased away the blood-soaked garments. There was a neat hole in the middle of my chest. That apparently was the exit wound. He felt gingerly with his hand round the side, then gave a grunt of satisfaction and wiped the blood off his fingers.

'That's all right then, sir!' he exclaimed. 'Gone right through, and a nice clean hole, too.'

I felt very much happier after that. The orderly plugged the holes with field dressings and wound a bandage round. Then he opened his medical pack and gave me ten sulphanilamide tablets to swallow, followed by an injection of morphia from one of my syrettes. I experienced very little pain, only a numbness and difficulty in breathing. As the morphia took effect I felt pleasantly drowsy. We improved our camouflage, then settled down to wait for darkness.

Meanwhile the battle for the main bridge was taking a very unfavourable turn. The Germans had reacted swiftly to the airborne landings and had rushed out troops and armour to intercept our forces. The 2nd Battalion, by taking the southern route, had by-passed the main body of this opposition. Not so the 1st and 3rd Battalions, which both became involved in heavy fighting in the densely wooded country to the north-west and west of the city, and neither was able to link up with the 2nd Battalion at the bridge, though one small group of the 3rd Battalion did get through independently.

The divisional reconnaissance squadron too, which had gone ahead, had lost heavily in their efforts to force a passage through the north-western outskirts, all to no avail. When at last they heard the 2nd Battalion report its arrival, Colonel Gough, the commanding officer, had collected his small remnant, and with the last of his jeeps, had gone down on to the southern route and reached the bridge shortly before midnight.

The 2nd Battalion itself got split by an enemy force which closed in behind the leading companies. These two companies – with whom was the rest of our 'B' Troop under George Irwin – had considerable skirmishing with pockets of German infantry the whole of the way from Oosterbeek to Arnhem bridge. First, one company had to clear Den Brink to the north of them – later, of course, reoccupied by the enemy – before they could pass. The subsequent street fighting in the darkness was slow and difficult, for German patrols would come down side streets and reappear in houses from which they had already been evicted only a short time previously. 'C' Company, after its withdrawal from the railway bridge, never joined up again with the remainder of the battalion but fought an isolated battle near the pontoon bridge, where it was eventually obliterated.

Only two companies of the 2nd Battalion supported by brigade headquarters, some eighty men of the 1st Squadron, RE, and a handful of others arrived in the bridge area, making a total of about four hundred men. These four hundred put up a most epic defence and only succumbed when nine-tenths of their number had been killed or incapacitated by wounds.

* * *

An impression of this heroic battle is gained from the story of the little band of sappers who held the school to the north of Arnhem bridge.

Our 'A' Troop had come on into Arnhem in the rear of the brigade headquarters' party, which followed close on the heels of the 2nd Battalion's advanced companies. In the street fighting in the darkness Paul Mason and his men had had to battle their way through more or less independently, but after beating off an enemy attack from the direction of the waterfront they reached the bridge a little before ten o'clock.

On their arrival they were immediately seized upon to deal with a pillbox which was still holding out at the end of the bridge. 'B' Troop was of course already there, defending a house in the vicinity, but Paul had our flame-throwers.

It was the first time we ourselves had used flame-throwers in action. After knocking a hole in the wall of a house opposite the pillbox the team stuck the nozzle through and gave a good squirt. The result was beyond all expectations. There must have been a lot of ammunition stacked in it, or alongside, for there was a terrific explosion and the pillbox just disappeared in a cloud of oily smoke. That brought the immediate German resistance at the north to a close.

An attempt was now made to cross the bridge and clear the enemy from the other end. Lieutenant Grayburn of the 2nd Battalion – killed later, but posthumously awarded the Victoria Cross for supreme gallantry throughout the action – led his platoon forward despite wounds. It was hopeless. The Germans had an 88-mm and machine-guns firing straight down the bridge, and he and his few survivors were withdrawn.

Thus, instead of the whole brigade with its anti-tank

battery holding a solid perimeter all round the bridge, the four hundred had to be content with denying it to the enemy at their end.

Arnhem bridge was a huge concrete structure with a steel central span on very high piers. The road was carried up to the bridge level by a concrete ramp, about three hundred yards long, ending in a viaduct above the houses near the waterfront. A short way from the bridge four houses lay alongside the eastern side of the ramp. Of these the school, the second from the bridge, was the most important as it controlled a crossroads south-east of it and dominated the other houses near by. There were insufficient men to fortify all four buildings, so Colonel Frost ordered the occupation of the southern three only and gave Paul the task of holding the school and the house just north of it.

As 'A' Troop had been in reserve Paul's two officers had been taken for other duties. But Tony Miles and his party had become attached to him in the general confusion of battle, and Paul's command now consisted of Tony and about fifty other ranks. The party was well armed with six Bren guns, a good number of Stens and an average of two grenades per man. Unfortunately they had no anti-tank weapons as our Piats had gone on the squadron jeeps and none had reached 'A' Troop.

Leaving most of the men to work on the school building Paul took forward a party of eighteen into the office building next door. This was separated from the school by a high wall, and thick shrubbery grew all round it – not very desirable conditions. However, Paul and his men knocked out the windows so that there should be no flying glass and started to prepare the place for defence.

They had only been there a few minutes when they were attacked from the last house in the row. This, we heard later, was a German headquarters, and as it was only fifteen yards from the office building the enemy had crept up unobserved through the undergrowth. The next moment potato-mashers were coming in at all the windows, and there was a chaos of bursting grenades, shouts and the rattle of sub-machine-gun fire. A few of the enemy got into the basement but were quickly ejected with bayonets, Stens and rifle butts.

It was, however, obvious that we could not hope, with our few men, to hold that house as well as the school. Paul first counter-attacked to clear the garden of the Germans while an NCO got the wounded out of the building and over the wall. Then they all withdrew on the school.

The school was a large, strongly constructed U-shaped building with the two wings ending on the concrete ramp. It had a roomy basement, two floors and an attic, but this had a boarded-in roof which introduced a fire risk. Paul decided to fight the battle from the first floor, using the basement for casualties and the attic as an observation post. The stairway between the floors was in the centre of the building.

The ammunition situation was fairly satisfactory, and the men had sufficient food for a further day. Water would be the difficulty, but they managed to get the bath full before the system was damaged and the supply cut off. They had no medical equipment, other than their field and shell dressings, a limited number of morphia syrettes and a supply of benzedrine tablets for relieving exhaustion. A single sapper with some first aid knowledge was put in charge of the 'hospital' downstairs.

Two minor attacks were beaten off during the remainder of the night, but the main battle began at dawn. It opened with heavy fire from the office building, until all the rooms on that side of the school became untenable. As soon as it was light Paul hit on a plan to write off the machine-guns next door. A Bren was fired by remote control from one window while two others were held in readiness in rooms farther down the face. All the enemy guns were successively silenced as they fired on the decoy, and several attempts which the Germans made to salvage them afterwards were frustrated.

Meanwhile the Germans put in an attack on the house to the south of the school and against a building on the crossroads held by a platoon of the 2nd Battalion. To the bedlam of machine-guns, with tracer flickering to and fro and ricocheting off the houses, was added the roar of pom-poms firing from the southern bank. The Bren gunners in the southern wing of the school gave what assistance they could but for the most part held their fire to save ammunition.

It was about this time that some of our own mortar bombs began to drop on the school, and it was at once necessary to let our other posts know that we were still in possession. Someone thought of the old Tunisian battle cry, and a mighty shout 'Ho – Ma-homet!' rang out and was taken up all round the bridgehead. Thereafter it echoed from house to house whenever a garrison had beaten off the enemy's assault – a cry of victory and grim defiance.

The intensity of the battle mounted until, at nine o'clock, the Germans attempted to force a passage from across the bridge with half-track vehicles and armoured cars. Mines had been laid by our infantry on the northern end, but a gap was made when one vehicle blew up, and the rest poured through. Two armoured cars whizzed down the ramps past the school and escaped. Not so the half-tracks, armoured on the sides only. A grenade was dropped into the first vehicle, and it went careering down the road on fire. A second tried to shoot its way through with a Spandau, but the drivers were shot dead and the rest killed as they tried to jump clear. It stood derelict in the middle of the road, forcing the others to stop just out of sight.

Five minutes later they made another attempt to break through, but again the drivers were shot. The first collided with the derelict, setting both on fire. The one following ran into the burning wrecks, and the crew, as they leapt out, were shot down by the Brens. A fifth was dealt with in the same manner. The carnage in the road was appalling; the ramp was littered with dead, the ammunition in the burning half-tracks was exploding and a sickly smell hung in the air.

Two remaining half-tracks tried to get down a gravel pathway between the ramp and the school. Suddenly, to everyone's surprise, one appeared alongside the southern wing. The Germans in it were wiped out in a matter of seconds. The second vehicle then went back and charged down the ramp at speed, but when the driver was shot it crashed into the northern wing of the school and the crew were killed.

After all this there was a lull which lasted over an hour.

At midday the fighting flared up again, and this time the trouble came from the rows of buildings behind the school. From these a machine-gun was now firing in through the staircase windows, preventing communication between the floors; and under cover of this the Germans put in another attack on the crossroads to the south-east. Once again the Bren gunners in the southern wing joined in enthusiastically, whilst others set about wiping out the machine-guns opposite, using the same ruse with a decoy

Bren as before. The assault on the crossroads petered out, and in the late afternoon there was another lull.

Soon after dark the Germans made their first attempt to burn the sappers out of the school buildings. It started with a hail of rifle-grenades from the neighbouring houses into all the windows on the northern face. These small bombs caused enough confusion to allow a German flame-thrower to go into action, and this set fire to the half-tracks resting up against the two wings of the school. As these blazed away the walls became very hot, floorboards began to char and sparks threatened to set the wooden roof alight. Anyone moving outside the building was silhouetted against the flames and came under heavy fire, but eventually two brave men crawled out with large explosive charges and blew each vehicle to pieces. The concussions shook the school to the foundations, but it did the trick.

The enemy now fired the office building immediately to the north, and the strong wind blew showers of burning fragments over the school. All available men were rushed up to the attic with sand, shovels and extinguishers, and a long battle against the flames ensued. The whole area was bright as day and these parties came under constant fire, though covering fire was provided as far as possible from below. At last, after three hours, the flames were under control. Everyone was exhausted from lack of sleep and from working feverishly in the intense heat.

So Monday passed.

In the small hours of Tuesday morning when the fire next door had also died down the enemy launched a new attack, preceded as before by a hail of rifle-grenades through the northern windows. As our men crouched down the Germans swarmed over the wall from the office garden. Then they wilted before the Brens and finally broke and withdrew as they were met with grenades. There was a further lull for half an hour.

Suddenly there was a numbing crash in the southern wing. The passages were filled with clouds of rubble-dust, and then those awful moans which tell of badly wounded men. The south-west room had received a Panzerfaust – a 20-pound anti-tank bomb. Part of the wall came down exposing all the floors, the roof sagged in a tangle of smashed timber and boards, and rubble lay in heaps. All those in the room were wounded and the rest were badly shaken and dazed.

When Paul had recovered sufficiently to have a look round, he was amazed to discern groups of the enemy collecting in the shadow of the trees and bushes outside, thinking they would not be seen. A machine-gun team was setting up its weapon in the garden, to fire at the building to the south. Mortarmen were carrying up their pieces and ammunition. All round the school German infantry were standing about unconcernedly in clusters. There must have been two platoons of them.

Quickly our men were warned. Cautiously they crept up to the windows – new magazines clipped into automatics, pins pulled out of grenades. On the signal, everything was let loose on the Germans below. The men stood up in the windows like avenging furies, flinging their grenades and spraying death, shouting in triumph as the grey crowd melted. Everywhere bodies lay huddled together in knots, others doubled up or splayed out where they had been struck down. Appalled by this disaster the Germans left the defenders alone for the rest of the night.

The few hours of darkness that remained were devoted to building up the defences, moving the wounded below and preparing for the resumption of the assault at first light. By this time our casualties were four killed and twenty-one sufficiently badly wounded to take no further part in the battle – remarkably light really, due to the strength of the building and the dispersal of the garrison in twos and threes throughout the rooms.

Tuesday's dawn was just breaking when the clatter of tracks was heard in the street to the south-east. Someone on the side shouted excitedly:

'Here are our tanks, sir! There are two Churchills outside! The Second Army's here at last!'

This seemed too good to be true, as, indeed, it was. Instead of British Churchills they were two German Mark IIIs, with long-barrelled 75-mm guns.

The two tanks came slowly towards the crossroads, firing shell after shell into the British-held houses near by. Then German infantry were seen working their way along the sides of the streets in support of the tanks, and at once these littered the pavements as they were brought down by our Bren gunners and riflemen. The tanks halted when their infantry failed to get forward, and further advance from that direction was checked.

One of the tanks now turned its attention to the school, while the other supported a new attack going in from the south. High-explosive shells came through the southern face at regular intervals, one every ten seconds or so, and all the rooms at that end had to be evacuated while the shelling lasted. Under cover of this bombardment the Germans set about the systematic reduction of the house to the south, and by midday had succeeded in crushing all resistance in that building. The defenders had fought until it was merely a heap of rubble, then the few survivors were overrun. The Germans were, however, unable to occupy it, for the ruin afforded little cover against fire from the school, and after a while they gave up the attempt.

Then a most unexpected thing happened, again fortifying our men's sense of superiority despite the enemy's desperate efforts to eliminate them. A white flag came round the shell of the office towards the school. The Germans in the headquarters building beyond wished to surrender. They were under fire from our troops in the houses on the other side of the ramp and had had enough. The retention of prisoners in the school was quite out of the question – it would in fact have been contrary to the Geneva Convention – and the request was refused. In the afternoon the party was apparently foolish enough to try and make a bolt for it, and the burst of fire and accompanying cries told their own story. Some say they were shot down by their own people.

Round the bridge itself relays of tanks were attacking along the waterfront, and these were supported by the massed battery of 20-mm flak on the southern bank. Each house strong-point was an independent fortress, for there could be no communication between them except by wireless through battalion headquarters. Frequently they were held by two or three men only, who dodged from room to room when things got too hot in one place. Now each house was gradually reduced to ruins, but the defenders dug themselves in like moles into the rubble, rebuilt their defences each time they were shattered by blast and hung on stubbornly. The 2nd Army could not be long now.

Focke-Wulf 190 fighters came over frequently, circled round and then tried to 'skip-bomb' individual houses. The Germans used their usual methods of ground-to-air recognition – fountains of white Very lights fired from all their advanced positions. These our men quickly learnt to imitate, putting up their own light signals whenever the planes appeared, much to the confusion of the pilots.

Consequently this bombing became more of an embarrassment to the enemy than any real help. There was one Focke-Wulf which came in to bomb very low and was greeted by concentrated Bren and Vickers fire. While taking violent evasive action the pilot hit a church steeple farther up the road and crashed minus a wing. This gave another great boost to morale.

Early in the afternoon the tanks drew off to replenish their ammunition but renewed the battle in still larger numbers at about three o'clock. The school came under heavy mortar fire, tank shelling and an intense machine-gun barrage through the eastern windows which, as before, stopped all movement between the floors. The mortar bombs had delayed fuses, so that they penetrated the roof and caused havoc inside the building. Almost every man had received a wound of some kind by this time. Many suffered terribly owing to the absence of skilled attention but made no complaint. The more serious cases were kept in a state of coma with morphia.

The reason for the new assault was soon apparent. Under cover of the barrage the Germans fired the block of houses to the east from upwind. Quickly the flames got hold and spread down the row, driving out our infantry from the buildings near the crossroads.

During the afternoon the noise of a fierce battle had been heard about a mile to the west, where a relief column from the Oosterbeek area was trying to break through to the bridge. The sound gradually receded as evening approached, but the threat was sufficient to make the Germans redouble their efforts to crush our men quickly.

Two huge Tiger tanks appeared from the north and began to climb the ramp, covering each other with fire and advancing alternately. This was the prelude to a house-clearing drive by German infantry on the far side of the ramp. One Tiger supported this attack while the other dealt with the school. The great 88-mm gun swung round slowly to point at the north-west corner. The first two shells were high explosive, shattering all that side of the building and causing several casualties. The men took shelter in the basement, while Paul watched from the attic for signs of an infantry attack. The Tiger now changed to armour-piercing shot. These went slap through the school from end to end and out the other side, knocking a four-foot hole in every room. The whole structure rocked, the ceilings came down and large cracks appeared in the already damaged walls. Then, when it was only a matter of time before the house collapsed, darkness mercifully intervened. In the flickering twilight of innumerable fires the Tigers withdrew for the night.

Utter exhaustion now laid hold of our men after three days and two nights of continuous battle. No one had had more than a few fitful snatches of sleep in the whole period, and there could be no rest now for the few still capable of fighting. Nor could they be revived with food and water – their last bite and drop had gone. Instead, benzedrine was issued out all round, and thus drugged, the men set about repairing their posts and looking to their weapons. In their condition the benzedrine had peculiar effects. Some saw double as though drunk, while others had queer hallucinations which caused many false alarms during the night. Although there was no attack there were sounds of great activity, and the ever-changing lights on the pall of smoke over the city gave the illusion of movement.

It was now Wednesday morning, their fourth day. Everyone knew it must be decisive one way or the other, for vitality was at a very low ebb. More benzedrine was taken before dawn for the final effort.

As soon as it was light enough for the tanks to operate, three attacks came in one after the other but were beaten back before the infantry could close. The school was now more holes than building, with the rubble banked up to make splinter-proof shelters for the defenders. Red and swollen eyes glared out of gaunt faces black from fire-fighting and the grime of battle. Smocks were torn and ripped, revealing gory dressings. Yet somehow the men contrived to keep their weapons clean, and these they polished and oiled whenever there was a lull in the fighting.

For the rest of the morning the Germans left the school and concentrated instead on groups of the 2nd Battalion still holding the approaches to the bridge. Using a combination of infantry, tanks and self-propelled guns they forced our men out of each building in turn. Then there was a terrific mortar barrage which finally died away to silence. Paul and Tony and the survivors of the original fifty were now the only British troops still holding out north-east of the bridge. They prepared to withstand the last attack.

At three o'clock it began. First a Tiger lumbered into view from the direction of the waterfront. It was followed by a Ferdinand 105-mm self-propelled gun. German infantry moved up in the rear under cover of the shattered houses. The Tiger opened fire with armour-piercing shot at the corners of the building, then the Ferdinand followed suit with high explosive at eighty yards' range. This brought down the remainder of the southern face. As the shelling continued against the rest of the structure those who could again retired to the basement. Now the upper storeys caught fire. The explosives had been stored on the second floor. The plastic HE flared up and then detonated. That demolished the roof and the work of destruction was complete. Everything was now blazing fiercely, and it was imperative to get the wounded out at once. Paul decided that the only thing to be done was for the able-bodied to shoot their way out, to gain time for the wounded to be moved.

In the basement there were fourteen men still capable of action and twenty-five totally incapacitated. Tony volunteered to lead a break-out party of six, each armed with a Bren gun. Two others were to stay with Paul to cover the evacuation while the remaining six got the wounded into the garden. The parties were assembled and given their instructions. Then Tony led his men out into the open air.

The enemy's attention was held by the flaming building, and the party gained the shelter of the burnt-out offices without incident. There they took up position while the wounded were swiftly but carefully brought out. It was a heavy task and took some time. When the last man was out the party pushed on again towards the German headquarters house, but as they started to climb over the high wall they were seen, and came under machine-gun fire. The Germans now opened up on the garden with mortars, and Tony and eight of the fourteen were hit. Mortar bombs now dropped amongst the badly wounded, killing one and further injuring others. At once Paul ordered Tony to surrender with the other wounded, while he himself led the remaining six with the Brens in a last effort to get away.

They reached the street behind and surprised a German platoon resting by a couple of tanks. Emptying their Brens into the grey they made a dash for it, but they were scattered by machine-gun fire and eventually taken prisoner. Paul's attempt to feign death was brought to an end when a German stuck a bayonet into his seat.

But the defence of the bridge was not yet over. About a hundred and forty men, the remnant of the 2nd Battalion and brigade headquarters, were concentrated in and around a building near the waterfront; nearly half of these were casualties, including Colonel Frost.

During Wednesday night the last fortress caught fire, and after several hours of unavailing effort by the garrison suddenly became a raging inferno. A desperate sortie to gain another lodgment was met and dispersed by a withering blast of tracer, and the medical officers had to surrender the seriously wounded to save them from the flames.

Some survivors continued to hold out beneath the ramp and managed to cling to an improvised redoubt until Thursday morning. German pioneers, who tried to lay charges on the roadway above during darkness, had been stopped by some dauntless officers and men who crawled out and shot them down. But with the coming of daylight tanks deployed in front of the emplacement, and in a short time had blown the barricades to pieces.

And so organized resistance came to an end. Some evaded capture for a while, but all were rounded up during the day.

Even then many escaped at the first opportunity, including Paul and Tony and two 'A' Troop NCOs, who found themselves together in a transit camp at Emmerich – a German town on the Rhine, just above the point where it divides into the Waal and Neder Rijn. These four prised the bars from a small window with their jack-knives and walked all night down-river to the frontier. There they lay up for a day and then stole a boat which carried them into the British lines at Nijmegen.

18
The Last Stand
17–26 September, 1944

What went wrong with the Arnhem operation? The answer certainly does not lie in easy clichés about 'dispersion of force' and 'defeat in detail'.

Success at Arnhem entirely depended on German opposition being slight, and in all the circumstances this was a justifiable gamble. There was no time for a deliberate co-ordinated attack if the bridge was to be captured before the enemy had decided to destroy it, at the same time cutting their own communications with the south. The only hope lay in a rapid advance on a broad front, seizing any opportunity for independent groups to slip through to the bridge quickly, however small these groups might be in the first place. If there were much resistance the operation must fail anyway. But in this sense the plan was fully successful. The bridge was secured intact and was held long beyond the time given for the link-up by the ground forces.

There were two major misfortunes. The first was the presence of an SS Panzer corps which was moving down to the Aachen sector from a refit area in northern Germany and Denmark. We were to learn that part of it had already passed through when we landed; and it was this battle group that held up the 2nd Army, and had cut, time and again, our slender corridor through Eindhoven and Nijmegen. The remainder of this armour was quickly diverted to Arnhem and was then followed by whatever other formations could be scraped together.

The final blow was the sudden break in the weather.

Incessant rain impeded the ground operations, and low clouds in England threw the air-lifts completely out of gear. In the later allocation of aircraft, priority had to be given from the south northwards – to assure the break-out and advance of 30th Corps – and Arnhem had to be served last.

The full story of this battle can never be told, for it was not a co-ordinated action but a succession of innumerable group combats. The account that follows can only give a general picture – even those who took part had little consciousness of time, and retain only a series of impressions.

In the area of the landing zones things were still going according to plan on that first night of Sunday the 17th of September. While the 1st Parachute Brigade were battling towards the centre of Arnhem the Air Landing Brigade spread their outposts to secure the dropping zones. With more than two square miles to protect they had to do it with a number of widely separated company strong-points.

The Border Regiment guarded the southern zone on which we had dropped and on which the 4th Parachute Brigade were due to arrive the next day, while the King's Own Scottish Borderers held the main glider landing zone farther north. Only half the battalion of South Staffs had been brought over on the first day, and these now formed a mobile reserve.

During Sunday night the Border Regiment found a German garrison in Renkum, just north of the Rhine, and after surrounding the village in the darkness cleaned up the lot at first light. But the King's Own Scottish Borderers to the north were not so fortunate. On Monday morning the Germans counter-attacked from the direction of Ede and overran a company holding a wood. There were no survivors, and it took two counter-attacks to restore the position.

German pressure from the north continued to increase during Monday, but the landing zones were held. Messerschmitts and Focke-Wulfs came over early and strafed the wreckage of gliders already on the ground, as though these were full of reinforcements just landed. It is possible that the enemy discovered the time of arrival of the 4th Parachute Brigade, for their planes turned up at the exact time appointed for the drop. But the 4th Brigade's departure from England was delayed by fog, and they did not land until the afternoon.

As in our case the 4th were escorted by a great concentration of fighters and ground-attack aircraft, but opposition to the actual landing was much heavier. Two or three of the Dakotas caught fire and plunged earthwards, trailing smoke and a few fluttering parachutes. Several of the men were wounded in the air, but most of the brigade got down safely and the Germans withdrew at their approach. There is something very awe-inspiring about a massed parachute descent, and the enemy contented themselves with sweeping the dropping zone with fire from a safe distance.

Meanwhile the position of the 1st Parachute Brigade in various quarters of Arnhem was very confused, owing to the division and further sub-division of the units into separate fighting cells. The 3rd Battalion had run into armoured cars and mortar fire on the Utrecht road, but one company had made a detour to the left and advanced down the railway, eventually reaching the bridge about a platoon strong.

The 1st Battalion had been sent round to the north to get into Arnhem down the Amsterdam road. But they too had encountered strong enemy outposts, and in the black darkness of thick woods had been compelled to laager there for the night.

At about midnight the rest of the 3rd Battalion were pulled out of their positions silently and switched on to the lower road to follow the 2nd Battalion's route. Accompanied by the Brigadier they moved down past Oosterbeek Station, but the Germans had now reoccupied the brick railway-arch over the lower road, and the battalion went on across the meadows to the cart track alongside the river.

Part of the battalion lost contact as they filed along in the pitch darkness, but dawn found the leading company, battalion headquarters and half of our 'C' Troop advancing along the tow-path east of the railway bridge. They now came under heavy fire but gradually fought their way forward to the vicinity of the Rhine Casino, on a level with the St Elizabeth hospital. During the morning a flak battery opened up from across the river, but this was later silenced by Brens, mortars and some excellent shooting by the 75s of the Light Regiment, RA, from Oosterbeek. Then enemy tanks appeared. Towards evening some of the battalion got up into the town near the hospital against intense opposition and mortar fire. Here they made contact with the 1st Battalion who had battled through from the north-western outskirts after a fierce engagement with a strong enemy force in Den Brink. But no further progress could be made that day.

During the night the battalions reorganized for a last supreme effort. At dawn on Tuesday they again moved forward, the 1st up the hill past the hospital and the 3rd along the riverside. They rushed the open spaces in waves, and as each yard was gained the shattered platoons closed their ranks and plunged on again. With great valour the

1st Battalion reached the Museum, but burnt away in the attempt. Below, the 3rd gained the dock area, but there was no cover by the river, and they were shot to pieces from the south bank and by tanks which attacked them from all directions.

In the end both battalions were too weak to go farther. They could see the battle at the bridge where everything seemed to be on fire; the defenders there heard them shout their battle cry, 'Ho – Ma-homet', but none got through.

A relief column which the divisional commander despatched had no better success. It consisted of the South Staffs, and of the 11th Battalion, Parachute Regiment, from the 4th Brigade. They made steady progress along the lower road into the city, but resistance stiffened with each yard gained, and the drive lost momentum. Without armoured support this type of fighting could only be slow and costly. The high-walled back-gardens, the layout of the streets and the knowledge that time was against us, all favoured the defence. Flank protection had to be provided along the route with small parties dispersed in individual houses, and these garrisons found themselves isolated when the main column had passed through. Apart from the considerable drain of casualties all these factors sapped the strength of the formation and gradually brought the attack to a standstill. The South Staffs reached the Museum but were then overrun by tanks and had to withdraw. They again dislodged the enemy from Den Brink but were heavily mortared before they could dig in, and again driven back. Tanks had also got in amongst the 11th Battalion, who became engaged in a desperate battle without any opportunity of advancing. At last the attempt was abandoned, and what was left of the column was ordered to retire to Oosterbeek.

The remnants of the 1st and 3rd Battalions were withdrawn at the same time. They were amalgamated to become the '31st' Battalion which, even so, numbered less than seven officers and a hundred and fifty men – all that was now left of the 1st Brigade.

These were grouped with the survivors of the South Staffs and 11th Battalion to form 'Lonsdale Force', named after the second in command of the 11th who now took charge. The four commanding officers and our brigadier had all been killed or badly wounded.

The other two battalions of the 4th Brigade, the 10th and 156th, were meanwhile fighting across the Utrecht railway line towards the Ede road; firstly to relieve the German pressure there, and secondly to secure the landing zone in that area for the Polish glider element arriving that afternoon. The country was densely wooded, and the 156th had severe losses in successive attacks against strongly entrenched positions, finally being nearly obliterated by an enemy counter-attack. The 10th Battalion was similarly reduced and was only able to clear the southern edge of the landing zone, which thus became a bullet-swept no-man's-land between the Germans and ourselves.

Another mishap in this operation was the almost complete failure, for the first day or two, of wireless communication between the division and airborne corps headquarters. One result of this was that dropping zones could not be altered to suit the changed circumstances.

The RAF did their first re-supply drop on Tuesday morning. Owing to a timing error due to bad communications with our fighter bases on the Continent the huge escort of previous days was lacking, and the Stirlings and Dakotas came under flak and air attack all the way from the coast to Oosterbeek. Casualties in crews and aircraft were heavy, particularly during the drop; yet the pilots refused to take evasive action until their task was completed. But we no longer controlled many of the dropping points; and as the ground signals of our hard-pressed troops were not seen the greater portion of the supplies fell into enemy hands.

The Polish Brigade's glider element also fared badly in the afternoon, as they too missed the rendezvous with their fighter cover. At three o'clock the drone of many planes was heard, and the Stirlings and Horsas appeared in the east. Then everyone was horrified to see another flock of aircraft racing in from the north, overtaking the slow-moving tugs. The chatter of cannon and machine-guns sounded very ugly up there in the sunny sky. A Stirling side-slipped out of formation and went down a ball of flame. Its Horsa corkscrewed to earth. Another broke up in mid-air, catapulting several large, dark objects into space. Other gliders cast-off and came in to land steeply, blazing from end to end.

The Focke-Wulfs came down again and again to rake those gliders that had got down safely and the crews working frantically to unload jeeps and guns. The Germans on the northern end of the landing zone joined in with machine-guns and mortars and then counter-attacked.

But despite their losses the Poles managed to salvage a few of the guns. These were a welcome addition, for there were now only about a dozen anti-tank guns left in the division. The 1st Battery had lost half its guns in Arnhem, while the 4th had had most of its equipment destroyed when it was caught on the move by German tanks.

On Tuesday evening orders were given for a general withdrawal on Oosterbeek. Strong concentrations of German armour were reported to be moving down from the north only twelve hours' march away, and reorganization within a perimeter defence was essential.

So on Tuesday night began the battle of Oosterbeek: a battle of unimaginable savagery, an inferno of shell and heavy mortar bombardment, a hell of attack and counter-attack in woods bewitched by artillery fire to become a labyrinth of tangled shrubbery and fallen trees, where a man could lose himself within fifty yards of his hole. There was no rest in Oosterbeek; days and nights came and went in a sort of grey twilight seen through red and smarting eyes, when nothing mattered except the life that tried to survive in a narrow world, six feet long and four feet deep in the ground. Those that died lay for ever in their pits; the shelling and mortaring made it impossible to bury the dead.

The position which the division took up lay within a rectangle about a mile long by half a mile wide, bound by the residential districts of Hartenstein, Sonnenberg, Heveadorp and Oosterbeek. Broadly speaking the Air Landing Brigade held the western side of the perimeter, the 4th Brigade and Lonsdale Force the east and the divisional troops the northern sector. Divisional headquarters were centred on the Hartenstein Hotel. The men of the Glider Pilot Regiment (who became an organized fighting formation on landing), were the divisional reserve for reinforcement or counter-attack.

The Light Regiment, RA, with their 75-mm howitzers, occupied the area of Oosterbeek church. Here they not only provided artillery support all round the perimeter but had to beat off many German tank and infantry attacks on their own front as well.

The above rough distribution of troops takes no account of the mixing of the units, nor of the transfers which often had to be made from one formation to another to meet each crisis as it arose. All units were under continuous attack while the perimeter was being formed, and for some time the Germans were in between the 4th and the Air Landing Brigades.

The enemy bombardment started early in the morning of Wednesday the 20th of September and went on with few intermissions for six days and nights. The Germans had four artillery regiments pounding this tiny area, apart from innumerable mortar batteries of all calibres. It was so small that it could be swept by automatic fire from all directions. Yet in general it remained unchanged until the end, despite every enemy effort to pinch out the sides. There was many a fierce battle just to retain the ruins of a house, or perhaps a mere twenty yards of ground, for any one failure jeopardized the whole.

Everyone looked forward eagerly to the badly needed reinforcement of the Polish Parachute Brigade, already a day overdue. The division waited throughout Wednesday in expectation only to receive the disheartening news that the Poles were still fog-bound at their aerodromes in the north of England. The original plan had been for them to land directly south of Arnhem bridge, but as this was no longer practicable – and wireless communication had now improved – it was arranged that they should drop near Driel, across the river opposite the perimeter. There was a ferry at Heveadorp – a barge drawn across on a cable – and it was hoped to get the brigade over by this means.

In the meantime our line was so extended that it was impossible to prevent infiltration by enemy snipers who now became a very special menace. These men showed great initiative and bravery and wormed their way into the midst of our positions where they would pick off our men even in their pits. The life and death hunt to locate the killers was a major preoccupation. Men were continuously on the watch for any tell-tale rustle of a branch following a rifle shot, and then the rattle of a Bren would often bring a body tumbling out of a tree. At times the search would end in a frightened boy of the Hitler Youth dragged out from his hide and propelled with loathing at bayonet point into the divisional POW pen.

The prisoners were collected in a large tennis enclosure behind the Hartenstein Hotel where they were given picks and shovels to dig themselves under cover. But later, when they could no longer be fed and were in imminent danger, they were sent back to their own lines under a white flag.

On Wednesday night the expected German armoured reinforcement began to arrive. It came chiefly from the SS Panzer Division 'Liebstandarte Adolf Hitler' and SS Grenadier Division 'Frundsberg', both powerfully armed after refit with Tiger tanks and well supported by self-propelled guns.

The main German thrusts were made from the north-west and then from the east and west across the neck of the perimeter. At first there were infantry assaults covered by artillery and mortar bombardment, but these met with no success – our men charged the attacking waves with Brens and bayoneted rifles, firing from the hip. Finding that his infantry could make no headway whatsoever the enemy thereafter used them as cover to his tanks and employed the Tigers and SP guns to try and batter us into submission.

Some of the fiercest fighting occurred near Oosterbeek church and the main dressing station, where the Germans drove down the road from the direction of Arnhem. Here we were holding some houses on a crossroads a few score yards in advance of the MDS. When the Germans forced us out of these we could not retire on the MDS but had to go right back several hundred yards beyond it. The enemy then had no compunction about firing his mortars from behind the 'neutral' cover, so that it was essential to recapture the original crossroads. Only after being regained and lost twice did they remain finally in our hands.

The condition of the wounded in these dressing stations and first-aid posts was appalling. The dressing stations became more and more congested. Floors and basements were jammed with stretcher cases, while the walking-wounded sat huddled in the passages. Sooner or later every building was hit by shells or mortars and many caught fire.

Through it all the surgeons and medical staff performed a heroic work under every possible handicap. Lighting and water became the chief problem. Major operations had often to be carried out by torchlight; and, for water, recourse was had to old wells and even to rainwater from the puddles. Drugs, dressings and anaesthetics were totally inadequate. Lastly, for much of the time there was no food; for, with the limited air supply, rations within the perimeter were cut to one-sixth or less.

Twice during the battle a stage was reached when fighting had to be suspended for the sake of the wounded. During these two one-hour truces, British and German medical orderlies mingled under the Red Cross, to sweep the no-man's-land and clear the aid posts near the trenches. Moreover when the MDS near the church was set on fire the Germans agreed to the wounded there being moved into Arnhem.

The Dutch were beyond all praise in the assistance they gave our casualties. Young men and girls wearing white-painted helmets and overalls bearing large red crosses ran about the streets under fire moving wounded to safety.

Others prepared their cellars as aid posts and gave willingly of everything they had. Many of them died during the days and nights of intense fighting. These citizens of Oosterbeek, and of Arnhem too, had seen their whole world crash in ruins, yet they never once reproached us but looked upon this tribulation as part of the price they would have to pay for freedom. In Arnhem I saw several of our dead lying where they fell, covered by a snow-white sheet and a heap of flowers. Our admiration for these people was too deep to be expressed.

The Polish Parachute Brigade arrived at last on Thursday afternoon. This time there was again a strong fighter screen and the Poles dropped, without undue interference, on the other side of the river. Soon, however, the German artillery got on to them, and columns of black smoke rose from burning houses in Driel.

Divisional headquarters' signalmen intoned the call signs monotonously into their radio sets, but there was no reply from the Poles across the river. From the flare-up of automatic fire it was evident that the Germans were attacking them.

Unfortunately also it was at about this time that, on our side of the river, the Germans got control of Heveadorp and gradually closed in behind the division on the northern bank. In any event the ferry site had lost its value, for the barge had been sunk by gunfire.

When it was dark an officer from divisional headquarters slipped through to the river and swam across with a message from Major-General Urquhart to the Polish commander. He returned the next day with the news that two weak battalions – numbering in all about seven hundred and fifty men – were established in Driel but that the third had gone astray and had not yet made contact.

The brigade would cross that night if the means could be found.

The task of bringing the Poles across fell to the 9th Field Company, RE. All they had at first were half a dozen rubber reconnaissance boats, and as these only took two persons, of whom one would have to row the boat back, only one man could be ferried over on each trip. An attempt to draw the boats across on signal cable failed: the strong current broke the wire, and one boat was carried two miles downstream before it gained the far side. The ferry service went on laboriously all night, but by dawn on Saturday only fifty Poles had reached the north bank. After collecting at Oosterbeek church they went straight into action with the Air Landing Brigade.

On Saturday night the ferry was continued. The sappers used every sort of improvisation, and by great ingenuity and resource a further hundred and fifty were brought over. The river was lit up by parachute flares from the German lines, and under fire the whole time. Many of the Poles were drowned, but the timely reinforcement provided by this gallant band of two hundred eased a critical situation and was greatly encouraging to the exhausted division.

Earlier in the day two of our Cromwell tanks had at last broken through independently to Driel: and now, with their assistance, the Poles remaining on the southern bank withstood all attacks and held open some slight communication with the outside world.

The battle in the forest went on without respite and with a steady, irreplaceable drain of casualties. Day by day the units had dwindled with a relentlessness that preyed on the nerves. Commanders had to think of battalions in terms of fifty men or less, and platoons had no further meaning. The 10th Battalion had entirely ceased to exist, and in one counter-attck the KOSB had lost four officers killed and eight wounded, with other ranks in proportion.

Where the Germans attacked again and again with fresh, rested troops they were met by grim and hungry warriors who had forgotten the meaning of sleep in the unending roar of shells or of mortar bombs bursting in the trees above them. There was just one long blast of chaotic noise, of howling shrapnel and crackling tracer, and it was death to put one's head out of cover.

The enemy general himself had boasted that he would sweep the last British soldier from the north bank by Thursday night. It was now Sunday and we were still standing as firm as ever. During the whole battle the troops never once lost faith in themselves.

The Germans brought up a propaganda unit and set up loudspeakers at night a hundred yards or so from our lines.

'Remember your wives and sweethearts you left at home!' the wireless blared. 'You are no good to them dead! Save yourselves by honourable surrender, gentlemen of the 1st Airborne Division!' A list of our senior officers already in their hands would be followed by a more threatening tone. 'There aren't any Red Devils now! There are only dead men waiting to be finished off!'

It merely served to infuriate and stimulate our men, and every record was greeted with laughter, catcalls and abuse.

What really saved them towards the end was the Second Army's artillery. The medium regiments got within range when the Waal was reached at Nijmegen, and the first barrage came down on Friday night. Its accuracy was impressive, considering that the guns were firing at extreme range, and then only from the map. Soon the field regiments joined in as well. When a wireless net was established the CRA of the airborne division was able to direct the shoots; German tank concentrations were dispersed, attacks were broken up while they were still forming and enemy batteries were engaged. Towards the end the wireless link became so effective that infantry commanders on the spot could radio an SOS and get instant artillery support. It all added immensely to the feeling amongst our men that help was at hand.

On Sunday afternoon, just a week after our landing, the first complete unit of the 30th Corps reached the river. They were the 4th Dorsets of the 43rd Division and they had orders to cross over that night in assault boats which were coming up after dark. When the Dorsets were over the rest of the Polish Brigade was to follow.

The boats had numerous delays on the road, and it was very late by the time they were launched. They were under fire and bombardments as before, and by dawn only two companies of the Dorsets had crossed. These found themselves somewhat to the west of the divisional perimeter, but they managed to hold on throughout Monday against repeated tank attacks, though not without loss.

In the meantime the High Command had been weighing up the situation and had come to the conclusion that the operation must be abandoned. In the early hours of Monday the 25th of September an officer brought this decision over to General Urquhart who then issued his orders for a withdrawal across the river that night.

During Monday afternoon the western suburbs of Arnhem were heavily bombed by squadrons of Marauders. This was to block the roads with rubble and so prevent any large-scale attack while the evacuation was on. Arrangements were also made for every available gun in 30th Corps to put down a 'box barrage' round the perimeter throughout the night.

Three Canadian field companies were employed on the evacuation, two from points on the river bank north-east of Driel, and the third with some pontoon equipment on a feint a few miles farther west. For the main operation the two companies had fourteen storm boats and a number of the canvas assault boats.

The companies were shelled while they moved up after dark from Valburg four miles to the south, as the enemy observed them from the high ground around Arnhem and projected flares over the area. Then at the launching site they had to negotiate two separate floodbanks with steep sides twenty feet high. It was a night of drenching rain, and the banks became more and more slippery, so that some boats were badly damaged before reaching the water.

The Germans realized that a crossing was being undertaken, and shelled, mortared and machine-gunned the banks and the river itself, now illuminated by fires and flares in an otherwise dense night. Bren guns on the southern bank fired lines of tracer to guide the boat crews, while our own shells whipped and sighed overhead to land on the encircling enemy positions. The lashing rain, bitter wind and, finally, the inferno of the covering barrage all helped to keep down the enemy's fire and resulted in far fewer casualties than had been thought possible.

The first boat was launched about nine o'clock, but after its rough handling it filled and sank at once. The second set off with its crew a quarter of an hour later but received a direct mortar hit in midstream. Half an hour afterwards, however, the third boat crossed successfully and soon returned with fifteen Airborne troops. The next was swamped on the return trip by a mortar near miss, and only five persons emerged from the river alive. Nevertheless the service got into its stride and by half-past three was working at full capacity. Danger and often tragic loss were ignored in this feverish race against the dawn – the Canadians fighting their boats back and forth, sometimes with paddles only, while fitters slaved on the beaches under fire and rain repairing the outboard motors.

Within the perimeter the withdrawal was carried out smoothly and in unhurried order – the men were too utterly exhausted for haste. The enemy artillery bombardment had intensified when night fell, and now the earth was rocking with the volcanic eruptions of heavy shells. The troops – those that could still walk – left their pits to face the hazards of the forest; stumbling over fallen trunks, past burning trees, grovelling before the shell bursts and occasional stream of tracer, keeping contact for the most part by holding the coat-tail of the man in front. They had to by-pass enemy posts between themselves and the river, and boots had been muffled with rags and bits of blanket – though the barrage and the downpour drowned all other sounds.

The control of the moving lines was organized by the glider pilots, who acted as traffic police from the forest to the beaches. Unruffled by the holocaust around them they would step from the shadows to guide the men onwards, whilst others marshalled the parties on the meadows to await their turn at the waterside.

Group by group the men waded out to the boats which swirled in from the darkness. Then the dash across the river; crouching low as the tracer stabbed around them and the water heaved to the mortar bombs; grounding at last on the other side to tumble out on to the bank and safety. Shells were falling here too, but they seemed almost insignificant now.

About three hundred men were still left on the north bank when daylight brought the evacuation to an end. They included a number of the Dorsets who had provided the rearguard. Many, however, managed to hide and were later helped to escape by the Dutch Underground.

Two thousand men of the 1st Airborne Division went down the road to Nijmegen and were then flown back to England. Two thousand out of the original force of over ten thousand strong. They had left behind them fifteen hundred dead and nearly five thousand five hundred severely wounded – three thousand of them in the Ooster-beek 'perimeter' . . .

That was Arnhem – a tragedy but a name that will live for ever.

19

The End of the Road

September 1944

I have little idea how I came to the 'Hoogstede', a rest home for old people at the western end of the Utrecht road and on the south side of Den Brink.

On that first Monday the medical orderly and I had lain in the ditch under the ivy until dusk. During my conscious periods I had been aware of a great deal of fighting near by, of mortars and machine-guns firing heavily and of German tanks and armoured cars moving up and down on the road a couple of hundred yards away. I remember trying to crawl with my arm round the orderly's neck, but the rest is confused, until at some time I was placed on a stretcher, lifted over a low hedge and carried into this house. It seems that I arrived outside the garden draped between the orderly and another of our men. They had been trying to get me back to Oosterbeek when they saw the red cross flying from the roof.

I was taken down some steps into the basement, and two Dutch nurses came and had a look at me. One, speaking perfect English, asked me where I was hurt. Then I was carried along a passage into a room and put on to a bed. Several people came in and held a lengthy conversation over me in hushed tones. I gathered that they thought I was in a bad way. I hastened to tell them that I was far from giving up the ghost yet. After that two more nurses came and removed my boots, battledress and blood-soaked underclothes and gave me a suit of pyjamas – bright yellow ones!

There were about twenty-five old people in the place,

many of them bed-ridden. Everyone had been moved down to the basement. Five nurses looked after the patients. Four of them were young girls; the fifth, the Sister of the Home, was a charming woman of about twenty-seven, well educated and efficient to the point of devotion. I discovered later that it was her bed I was occupying, and she slept on a mattress on the floor. She was like a guardian angel that night, and I probably owe her more than I shall ever know. I felt worse than I had before; I was cold and numb and the presence of death seemed to lurk in the darkness. I was thankful when the first streaks of light appeared and the coming of day brought a new lease of life.

The day was uneventful as far as we were concerned. The orderly assisted in the basement 'wards' where there were already three other British wounded, as well as two wounded German SS men. I wondered whether I had anything to do with these two being there; both were suffering from a generous peppering of 9-mm about the legs. There was the noise of considerable fighting about a quarter of a mile away. Mortar bombs landed quite close, shattering the windows upstairs, and some aircraft flew overhead and machine-gunned farther down the road towards Oosterbeek; but it was impossible to tell who was who, or which way the battle was going. Once or twice German armoured cars whizzed by going west, and I even heard the unmistakable note of a jeep-engine, followed by one of our own light-weight motor-cycles. I grew quite excited then, feeling sure that our men had arrived at last, but the Sister told me they were driven by Germans, and had black crosses painted over our Airborne Pegasus signs.

All continued to go well until early on the following afternoon. There had been unusually heavy German activity in the neighbourhood all the morning, but we were quite unprepared for what now happened. Suddenly there was a stupendous explosion, the sound of falling masonry, and the whole basement was filled with rubble-dust and smoke. A German Panzerfaust had blown a ten-foot hole into the passage farther along from my room. This was immediately followed by a stream of machine-gun bullets from a Spandau at close range. Under cover of this fire, two brave Germans crawled up to the shattered wall and started lobbing grenades through the hole into the basement. The noise was quite indescribable. Broken glass had showered on to my bed. Many old women started to scream, others to pray out loud. By amazing good fortune the bomb had missed the rooms with their crowded occupants and had expended its force in the passage, which the grenades and the hail of bullets had also chewed up badly, exposing the floorboards of the room above. One old man had his arm smashed, and others were shaken up by the concussions, but that was about all. Not knowing what was happening – and being really frightened myself at this appalling noise – I feared dreadfully for these good people and was amazed on being told what little damage had been caused.

There were now shouts from outside and I knew we were surrounded.

'Kommen Sie aus!' a German shouted down into the basement. 'Kommen Sie aus mit Hände hoch!'

The Sister ran out and explained in German that this was a hospital and went on to point out in what I took to be very strong language that they had violated international law. She drew their attention to the large signboard standing outside the building, showing it to be a nursing home, and to the flag flying from the roof. The nurses had made this by painting the red cross on a sheet with their lipsticks.

Two German SS infantrymen entered the basement and had a look for themselves. They were fierce-looking gentlemen in mottle-camouflaged clothing, scrimmed helmets and with a row of potato-masher grenades stuffed into their belts. The leader carried a Panzerfaust tucked under his right arm in the ready position, as though to warn us what to expect if we misbehaved. The other advanced behind and covered everyone with sweeps of his Schmeisser machine-carbine. When they saw that we were in reality quite defenceless and harmless they were most apologetic and said they would send their doctor to attend to us. Ten minutes later this personage himself arrived. He was a blond youth of about twenty-five who wore his SS peaked forage cap at a jaunty angle, was dressed in the same mottled-camouflaged clothing as the men but had a red-cross armband round his left sleeve. He had a quick look at all the wounded and said he would send an ambulance to take us up to the German hospital. It really began to look as though I could not avoid becoming a prisoner.

We heard nothing more about the ambulance that afternoon. A jeep arrived at about four and took the two wounded Germans away on stretchers. But towards evening they took our medical orderly off under guard to a prisoner of war cage and posted sentries outside the house. They wanted to have the guards inside, but the Sister stood firm and said it was against international law to have armed men in a hospital. After four years of occupation she knew how to deal with these people: she was splendid. However, at six o'clock the sentries were withdrawn, and we were left in peace again.

It was about eight o'clock that the Sister came to me in

great excitement and said that some men of the Dutch
Underground Movement had come to take us to the
British hospital. She had been up to the St Elizabeth
hospital to get one of our doctors as we needed proper
medical attention, but this solution would be much the
best.

Six stalwart youths appeared, all wearing long white
overalls bearing correspondingly large red crosses. They
had been doing stretcher-bearer duties in the streets
during the battle and had two stretchers and a parachutist's trolley. We were swathed in blankets up to the eyes
to 'look as though we were civilians', made as comfortable
as possible on our various means of conveyance, and then
set off at a good pace.

It was a good half-mile carry to the hospital, but those
Dutch lads made easy work of it. We passed through the
shattered streets, by still smouldering houses, a derelict
and bullet-pocked tram, past groups of SS infantry standing on the street corners, and once or twice a wrecked
anti-tank gun and little groups of dead. Several of our
jeeps, now in the service of the Waffen SS, went by in
convoy, crammed with armed men. Nobody paid the least
attention to us, and we made this rather extraordinary
journey without incident.

We went up the hill towards the St Elizabeth hospital
and saw how the full fury of the battle had been let loose
there. On the right, where the escarpment falls to the
lower road, the trees and bushes on the cliff side had been
ripped and torn by mortar bombs. Long slivers of blackened wood lay about the road, among the potholes and
stone setts of the torn-up pavé. A huge but tattered red-
cross flag flapped idly from the hospital roof, yet the red-
brick walls were starred with splinter splashes, and all the
upper windows were gone. Glass carpeted the street. One

fondly imagines that hopitals are immune from the horrors of war, that there is a power in the red cross which breathes peace, security, faith into all who shelter beneath it. But here nothing was sacred, no sanctuary untouched.

I was carried up the long bank of steps into the central hall and down the corridors to where our few doctors were struggling to keep pace with the stream of wounded. The Dutch youths said good-bye – they had risked a lot on our behalf. Our own medical orderlies took over and whisked us into the operating theatre for examination, after which I was carried along a dark passage and put to bed by the light of a torch. I had the impression of a row of beds in front of and behind my own, stretching end to end down the side of the passage into the tunnel of total darkness. Somebody stirred and groaned farther down the row, a pathetic little whisper of sound from what seemed far away. Flickering points of candle light came towards me down the corridor as an orderly and a Dutch nurse brought a tray of drugs.

'Is that Lieutenant Terrick you've just brought in?' That was our brigadier's voice from a nearby bed.

'Yes, sir,' I replied.

'Have you come from the bridge? Were you with Colonel Frost's party?'

'No, sir. I was on my own. I was sent to the railway bridge.'

'Oh, I see. I am trying to find someone who can give me news of what is happening down at the bridge. The last I had was twelve hours ago. They were still holding on then but very hard-pressed. Where have you been hit?'

'Bullet through the chest, sir; gone right through, thank goodness! How about you, sir?'

'Oh, I got peppered by a grenade in the back. Nothing very much.'

I slept well that night, supremely confident that now I was in good hands everything was going to be all right. The Second Army would reach the Rhine within a day or two and soon be across.

The next day I heard the adventures of the 16th Parachute Field Ambulance. Everything had gone well until the Monday morning when they were cut off from our force holding Arnhem bridge. On Tuesday the South Staffs and the relief column had tried to get through but had become heavily embroiled. The Germans had set up a mortar just behind the hospital and lobbed bombs over the roof; they were utterly unscrupulous. There had been sniping and Sten and Schmeisser skirmishes – all the unpleasantness of battle breaking around the neutral walls. But worst of all was when the enemy set up machine-guns to fire on fixed lines through the corridors and out on to the road beyond. The stone passages magnified the roar of the guns, and everything was bedlam while the streams of tracer licked down the corridors. Finally, there was an incident. A German SS colonel strode in and announced that three doctors were to be handed over to be shot. Grenades had been thrown from the hospital premises at German troops – an unheard of, infamous, violation of the Convention. As the culprits could not be found three doctors would pay the penalty. The CO of the field ambulance stood his ground; he pointed out all the many breaches by the SS troops and said that if the SS persisted in this outrageous behaviour he would have to answer for his actions before an international court. As it was the matter was being reported to Geneva. At length the German withdrew his demand but removed as prisoners all those of the medical staff not actively engaged at that moment in the operating theatres. The field ambulance was working on night and day shifts, and the night shift was now off duty after a hard twelve hours' work. In spite of all protests the night shift was carried off. Then SS sentries were placed in every ward with machine-carbines and fixed bayonets to see that no more of these so-called incidents occurred. They had their belts stuffed with potato-mashers and were obviously enjoying the situation. One had a red doll, meaning us, skewered on his bayonet. The sentries were withdrawn on Wednesday afternoon, but everyone in the hospital was now virtually a prisoner, even if we persuaded ourselves otherwise.

Each day we had a visit from some senior member of the SS staff and once by the German general himself. He was a funny little portly man, his rotundity exaggerated by a black leather motoring jacket. He wore the camouflaged SS overalls on top of his own baggy trousers and jackboots with a black forage cap perched on his head. He strode pompously down the ward, talking loudly in German. His interpreter turned to the British doctors following behind and spoke so that all could hear.

'The General-Oberst congratulates you on the efficiency of your hospital. You must make more room. The General-Oberst says he is going to finish off your division this afternoon, and many more wounded will come here.'

But his boast was not fulfilled.

Six days went by. The noise of the Oosterbeek battle was terrific, ever growing in intensity. For hours on end the ground trembled as in an earthquake, and the inferno growled on and on like a continuous mutter of thunder three miles away. Sometimes a column of tanks – Tigers and huge self-propelled guns for the most part – rumbled down the hill outside, shaking the whole building. A battery of guns fired intermittently from the high ground above the hospital, and the shells cracked over our heads.

They always seemed to begin just as one was dropping off to sleep, and the sudden clatter of rapid fire would startle one violently awake, causing unexpected agony. We learnt to hate those guns, and our thoughts went out to our comrades in Oosterbeek.

Our Dutch stretcher-bearers visited us daily and brought news of the outside world. The leader was a captain in the 'Underground' so I gave him all my maps of North Holland. He spoke good English, as did his attractive wife.

'The Germans are very afraid of sabotage in Holland,' he said, 'and we keep them busy. Your RAF drop us supplies of guns, ammunition and explosives, but not enough. In my band we have only one Sten gun and we have to draw lots for it every time we go out. It is a pity, but it makes keen competition!'

On Monday the 25th of September we knew that something unusual was in the air. For the past two days we had been getting British medium shells close to the hospital, presumably searching for the battery of guns further up the hill. The 4.5s roared overhead to land with devastating crumps a quarter of a mile away. It was a nerve-racking sensation, lying in bed unable to move while the shells rushed down upon us – especially as they were our own shells.

On Monday afteroon our bombers droned over and plastered the eastern part of the city. Our medical order-lies gave us a running commentary and expressed uncon-trolled delight as plumes of black smoke rose from the German quarter. But suddenly we heard with horror the avalanche of bombs sighing down on us. Then the ward was rocking; the explosions rippled across the ground, thundered to a climax and then passed by. I found myself rigid with terror and prickly with sweat. Another stick whistled down, cut a path of destruction towards us, blasted the house across the street and then thundered away towards the railway station. Glass was falling, some of the nurses screamed, and acrid smoke poured in through broken windows.

'Phew! That was close!' I heard myself saying.

'Yes, it's getting beyond a joke! Careless blokes, these Yanks!' The man in the next bed was a Canadian officer attached to the South Staffs. He was badly wounded in the thighs and could move even less than I.

'Everybody all right along here?' A medical orderly moved quietly down the line of beds.

'Was the hospital hit? Anybody hurt?' I enquired.

'No, sir. The nearest bomb was on the far side of the buildings across the street; knocked them for six, it did. Lots of plaster down in the big ward, but no one hurt, thank God!'

This bombing, although we did not know it then, was part of the softening-up before the withdrawal of our troops across the Rhine.

During the afternoon the Germans ordered the complete evacuation of all civilians in the western outskirts of Arnhem south of the railway line. It seemed harsh at the time but, as events turned out, it was just as well.

The evacuation order was posted at 4 P.M. By 6 P.M. every man, woman and child had to be out of the area on pain of death. Thus started a tragic exodus of families setting out with only what they could carry on a long road usually ending in misery and hunger.

Our nurses in the St Elizabeth hospital were heart-broken that they too had to go. They had worked hard to make our lot easier, and now felt that they were being robbed of the one chance to do something in the Allied cause. Many wept bitterly when they came to say good-bye, and the thought of these girls on the road with their suitcases and bundles filled us with hatred for the SS.

The Germans eventually allowed ten nurses to remain to look after the civilian casualties, but the hospital seemed very quiet after the others had gone.

The artillery bombardment started soon after dusk. It began with a murmur like the first whisper of a storm. The guns growled behind Elst, and the air rustled softly as the shells sighed over and crumped in the western suburbs. Then they came in a deluge; the southern sky danced with light, shells screamed and rumbled in terrible orchestration, and the ground shook under the torrent of explosive. We held our breath, while the outskirts of Arnhem were reduced to a welter of craters and rubble.

It was at the height of the bombardment that Brigadier Lathbury walked out of the hospital and made his escape. He had taken off his badges of rank soon after being wounded and was registered in the hospital files as a private. If the enemy had discovered his real identity he would have been removed to the German infirmary in the north of the town. The Brigadier was in high spirits when the bombardment began. We all believed that it was the preliminary to a crossing by the Second Army.

He came round to say good-bye. He thought it was dangerous to stay in the hospital as the enemy might move all the wounded eastwards as soon as our men approached. His plan was to get into the woods north of Arnhem and lie up until our forces arrived. All the Germans in the neighbourhood were taking shelter during the bombardment, so he was able to slip out of a side door unobserved and make off in the smoke and flickering darkness of the night.

His subsequent adventures are another story, but he shortly rejoined our forces in company with hundreds of others, thanks to an elaborate escape system organized by the Dutch. Brigadier Hackett of the 4th Brigade was another who, after being very severely wounded at Oosterbeek and later admitted to the St Elizabeth hospital, was spirited away by the Dutch under the very noses of the Germans. For several months they nursed him back to health and then passed him through to safety.

The bombardment died away just before daylight, and I dropped off to sleep with the return of blissful peace, not realizing what had happened. When I awoke everything was quiet, and the morning was fresh as though exhilarated by the storm. But Germans still walked about outside, and it suddenly dawned on me that our men had withdrawn. Another unpleasant fact followed in the same train of thought – we were now prisoners of war.

During the afternoon our walking-wounded were marched up from Oosterbeek under SS guard. It was a scene I shall never forget. The men were in an indescribable state but never once lost their high morale or cheerful bearing. Even though in great pain from untreated wounds they sang all the way and marched in step. I heard the singing while they were still half a mile away and I thought it was a battalion of SS marching through the town. Then the tune sounded familiar, so British and so very un-German. It grew and grew in volume as the column approached. The medical orderlies passed round the word that a thousand walking-wounded were arriving at the hospital, and I have never been so proud to belong to those men as I was now. It was as if they were victorious. The Germans were awed by the sight, and inwardly I knew that these men were unconquerable.

But their triumphant song belied their pitiful appearance. I have seen some heart-rending sights in the wake of war but I was completely shaken when these men rolled, staggered and reeled into the St Elizabeth hospital. They were hardly men, they were like animals in rags, swathed in revolting, evil-smelling bandages, caked in mud and dried blood, red eyes glowing like coals in drawn and haggard faces, tight-lipped and bearded; so changed as to be unrecognizable.

'Why, hullo, sir!' A voice challenged me from a batch of new arrivals. I stared and searched the group for the speaker. Eight apparitions leaned on sticks, and gazed on me with sunken, sub-human eyes.

'I *am* glad you're all right, sir. I thought you were a goner!'

A small hunchbacked figure like one of the witches from *Macbeth* was addressing me. His clothing had been ripped away at the shoulder, now tightly strapped in brown-stained bandages, with a piece of rag for a sling. At last I perceived the man behind the grizzly ginger beard.

'Chepstowe! I didn't know you! How are you?'

'Oh, me shoulder's nothing, sir! I'm all right! Clarkson's outside. Got a bullet in the arm and some cuts on his head. After you sent us off we barricaded ourselves in a house until the South Staffs came and then we went back to Oosterbeek.'

The others told me about Chepstowe's shoulder. The RAF had dropped a container of rations right in his trench, breaking his collar-bone. His comrades thought it was poetic justice.

A medical orderly cut short any further conversation, and the group were hurried away to have their wounds dressed. I never saw Chepstowe again.

Poor old Paddy was brought in later on a stretcher, and we were able to have a few words while his bed was being prepared.

He was one of those left on the north bank when the evacuation was abandoned at daylight. He had tried to swim the river, but the current was too strong, and he only just managed to struggle out again. He was hit in the thigh by a Spandau when trying to rush back across the meadows.

His news was very heavy – a long list of people known to be casualties, and an even longer one of missing. Martin Brush and Ted Boyse were dead; Joe Wallace was very seriously wounded and still in danger; Tim Hollings had been wounded and taken prisoner; of the whole squadron only Tom Slater and about a dozen men were known to have crossed the Rhine to safety.

That night all the walking-wounded were moved by lorry as soon as it was dark. The rest of us were told that ambulances would be coming to take us to another hospital at Apeldoorn to the north. We felt extremely reluctant to leave the Rhine for we still hoped desperately that a crossing would be made and that we should be free again before the week was out. Apeldoorn, only twenty miles away, sounded like a penal colony at the ends of the earth.

The complete evacuation of the hospital, except for a dozen very badly wounded, came sooner than we thought. On the evening of Wednesday the 27th of September six ambulances arrived, and our medical staff were ordered to prepare us to move at once. German orderlies clumped into the ward with stretchers, bundled us out of our comfortable beds into filthy-looking blankets and then carted us outside. It was very cold without adequate clothing or covering, and the ambulances were no bigger than bakers' vans, with very little springing. They carried four patients in two tiers, with only the barest clearance.

The journey began badly with our vehicle refusing to

start. At last we got under way and jolted up the street, dodging those potholes the driver saw in time and taking the rest in our stride. A paratrooper above me cursed the driver with everything he knew.

It was dark by the time we reached Apeldoorn. The doors opened at last after what had seemed an eternity of bumps and stabs of pain. I was carried inside a large lighted building and dumped in the hall. Armed SS troopers stood all around, and a few of our own medical orderlies were trying to sort out the general chaos. I got a glimpse into a room opposite and saw wounded men lying without blankets on an inch or two of straw. The stench of rotting wounds was very strong. After the peace and efficiency of the St Elizabeth hospital this place looked appalling. A harassed orderly came and looked at me, and then I was carried upstairs and into a large, cold, bare room. There was no straw on the ground here, and several other men were lying on the floor with only a single blanket over them. The Germans said they needed my stretcher, so I too was tipped off on to the ground along with the other unwanted bodies and left to fend for myself.

Things improved a little the next day. Working all night the Air Landing Brigade's field ambulance managed to create some order out of this tragic mess. We were in an empty barracks, but by searching all the other buildings in the compound our orderlies had found enough beds for the more serious cases. During the morning the Germans sent a cartload of straw, and this filled sufficient palliasses to get everyone off the stone floor. Blankets arrived within a day or two, and when, by the end of a week, each of us had a bed, a mattress and three blankets, it could almost be called a hospital.

The Queen Wilhelmina cavalry barracks had been

occupied by the Luftwaffe earlier on and had been hastily opened up to accommodate as many as possible of our five thousand wounded. We heard from the Germans that they themselves had suffered over twenty thousand casualties during the ten-day battle, and all the hospitals around Arnhem, including the three existing ones at Apeldoorn, were crammed beyond capacity.

The wounded kept pouring in from Oosterbeek, many of them in a pitiful state from lack of attention, from thirst and hunger and from living under the most dreadful conditions. Drugs were very short, and in this the Germans could do little to help. The remnants of all three field ambulances were now here, and everyone who could gave a hand. Gangs of walking-wounded were detailed for cookhouse fatigues, for potato-digging to supplement our minute ration of bread and soup and as part-time orderlies in the wards.

It was two days after my arrival that the first batch was sent off to Germany. Though few were yet properly fit to travel, a thousand of the walking cases were loaded into cattle wagons at the railway station, locked in and then made to endure a five-day train journey on top of all their suffering. Three doctors were allowed to accompany the party, but without freedom of movement they could not do much. Two days later a further five hundred were sent under the same conditions.

But our men still maintained their spirit and cheerfulness. Our SS guards had been relieved by some elderly men of a pioneer battalion. When the wounded were marched down to the station they started off singing, and then gradually lengthened the pace until they were moving at the customary Airborne 'forced-march' step. This was too much for their ancient guards who soon lost all semblance of control and were in a state of collapse by the time the station was reached.

The Dutch were very good to us the whole time we were in Apeldoorn. The Germans had sent to Amsterdam to enlist the help of Dutch surgical teams, but when one of these arrived they would only give their services for the British wounded and would not lift a finger for the Germans. We had books and tobacco smuggled into the hospital, as well as a daily news broadsheet from the BBC European programme. Much of this came through the civilian hospital, where patients from our barracks were often sent for X-ray or special treatment and were regularly visited by our padres and others. The Germans knew it was going on and hated the Dutch for befriending us and insulting them on every possible occasion; and they awaited their opportunity to take reprisals.

It came shortly in a particularly brutal manner. The German High Command decided to construct a defence line on the Ijssel, using Dutch labour. The Burgomaster of Apeldoorn was given two days in which to produce four thousand workers, the equivalent in fact of the total population including women and children. The two days expired, and the numbers were not forthcoming. The next day the Gestapo arrived in motor coaches and, after closing the town, took forty 'hostages' and shot them. Our doctors saw the bodies lying round the town on the main thoroughfares, each bearing a card in Dutch, 'Warning! This might have been YOU. Do not another time disobey the orders of the High Command!'

We heard reports daily that the Second Army was massing on the Rhine, and on clear mornings we could hear the gunfire plainly. When it was very loud we told ourselves that a crossing had been made. Our rocket-firing Typhoons flew over continuously and shot up

German transport moving on the road, or an engine trying to sneak through on the line to Amsterdam. The flak put up a fine display against our planes, but we never saw any hit. The air assault increased every day, and we were sure that it was the prelude to a new offensive. If only we could remain in Apeldoorn for a little longer! But the enemy had other ideas.

One night a commission of six German doctors arrived and began sorting out our stretcher cases. Seventy were to go on a hospital train leaving within a day or two. Our own surgeons accompanied the Germans round the wards and tried to put the worst complexion on each case. One of the Germans examined me and seemed satisfied on being told that I had been shot through the chest. I was labelled 'Not to be transported', and breathed a great sigh of relief.

However, the next day there was a very different story. Not seventy, but five hundred, stretcher cases were required; the whole hospital was to be evacuated, except for about twenty who would go to the civilian hospital in the town. A special ambulance train had been sent from Germany to take us. Our spirits sank very low. The train was to be loaded by six o'clock that night, and it was already midday.

Half a dozen German ambulances ferried the wounded from the hospital to the train all the afternoon. Once again there was the springless, jolting agony of the mile run down to the station, but I was very pleasantly surprised by the train itself. The coach was fitted with three-tier steel bunks down either side for twenty patients and a German medical orderly and had full equipment for serving meals. After the indifferent handling we had received from the SS the train orderlies manoeuvred our stretchers round the corners with expert care. They were mostly elderly men who had seen the suffering of both wars, and recognized their duty to the wounded, whether friend or foe. Our little man, Karl Mütz, had lost two sons on the Russian front and now felt no bitterness; only a hopeless grief and loneliness and a longing that it all might end.

The German general inspected us as soon as the last man was aboard. He was accompanied by a posse of doctors and the ambulance-train staff. There were a couple of nurses – two strapping Nordic Fräuleins who seemed to delight in ripping the dressings off our wounds and applying a most virulent antiseptic.

The general expressed considerable satisfaction that the loading had gone so smoothly and was now ready to despatch us amid cheers to the Third Reich. But there was a hitch. The little German station-master in magnificent blue uniform and red peaked hat came padding up in considerable agitation. One small item had been overlooked. There was no engine, and one could not be expected for another twenty-four hours.

Those were anxious hours that we spent in Apeldoorn station, listening apprehensively for the coming of rocket-firing Typhoons, Mitchells and Marauders. Our train was well marked with red crosses, but right alongside us – of course, by design – lay a German flak train. It had specially constructed coaches with a four-barrelled 20-mm pom-pom on the roof of each and the crew's living accommodation below.

We used to watch the gun crews practising, swinging their pieces on well-oiled bearings. Sometimes they had to do the real thing.

'Achtung! Flieger Alarm!' And the crew would put on their steel helmets and take up action stations. As our Typhoons flew over, weaving backwards and forwards, the crew would follow them with their guns, shouting out the range as it was intoned by the men on the range-finder and looking very tight-lipped and nervous the while. Our men roared with laughter and called out ribald remarks. But it was only after the planes had turned for home that the gunners let drive. Ten four-barrelled guns all blazing away at once make a hellish noise; our windows rattled, and we became taut in anticipation of the 'Tiffies' peeling off and roaring down with their rocket bombs. A most unpleasant sensation, and I felt glad I was on the bottom bunk.

We finally got away on the third night. Our engine turned up on the second, but the RAF bombed the bridges over the Ijssel that afternoon, delaying us another day. When the train pulled out of Apeldoorn and gathered speed away from our men across the Rhine I knew that all hope had gone and we must now bear a short period of captivity as cheerfully as possible. I lay awake most of the night listening to the wheels drumming on the track, gloating over my misfortune – 'You've had it . . . you've had it . . . you've had it.'

The officer above me – Davis of the 1st Battalion – was making preparations to escape, to jump the train before we reached the frontier. I wished I felt well enough and had the courage to do the same. He had been shot by several machine-gun bullets through the upper part of both thighs. He could scarcely crawl a yard, let alone walk to safety, but determined to go just the same. I heard him pulling on his trousers painfully; he begged a jacket from a more seriously wounded comrade and got me to put on his boots. I listened to him wriggling on the middle bunk, watched him crane his head out of the window – calculating our speed and how it was best to land. He was a paratrooper and would probably bring it off where others might fail. I dozed off for a couple of hours, and when I awoke again his bed was empty; only the curtain flapping furiously out of the open window showed which way he had gone. I closed the window and inwardly wished him luck; he was a very brave man.

After that I couldn't sleep any more. Before daylight we would have crossed the German frontier, and something would have died in every one of us; the light of freedom would have gone out. Well, I had managed to dodge it up till now, and I had known all along that I could not last for ever. My luck was out, that was all. We had come a long way, and this was the end of the road.

I sensed this feeling was shared by many that night on the train; we had suffered ill fortune but not defeat. There certainly was no despondency, only resignation. For us the war was over.

Index

War – now available in paperback from Grafton Books

Alexander Baron
From the City, From the Plough   £1.95 ☐

Norman Mailer
The Naked and the Dead   £2.95 ☐

Tim O'Brien
If I Die in a Combat Zone   £1.95 ☐

James Webb
Fields of Fire   £2.95 ☐
A Sense of Honour   £2.95 ☐

John McAleer and Billy Dickson
Unit Pride   £2.50 ☐

J P W Mallalieu
Very Ordinary Seaman   £1.95 ☐

Nicholas Monsarrat
HMS Marlborough Will Enter Harbour   £1.50 ☐
Three Corvettes   £1.50 ☐

Dan van der Vat
The Last Corsair (illustrated)   £2.50 ☐
The Ship that Changed the World (illustrated)   £3.50 ☐

Erich Maria Remarque
All Quiet on the Western Front   £2.50 ☐

Robert Kee
A Crowd Is Not Company   £1.95 ☐

Etty Hillesum
Etty: A Diary 1941–3   £2.50 ☐

Leon Uris
Battle Cry   £2.95 ☐

To order direct from the publisher just tick the titles you want
and fill in the order form.   **GF1981**

True war – now available in paperback from Grafton Books

To order direct from the publisher just tick the titles you want and fill in the order form.

True war – now available in paperback from
Grafton Books

To order direct from the publisher just tick the titles you want
and fill in the order form.   GF2181

All these books are available at your local bookshop or newsagent, or can be ordered direct from the publisher.

To order direct from the publishers just tick the titles you want and fill in the form below.

Name _____

Address _____

_____

Send to:
Grafton Cash Sales
PO Box 11, Falmouth, Cornwall TR10 9EN.

Please enclose remittance to the value of the cover price plus:

UK 60p for the first book, 25p for the second book plus 15p per copy for each additional book ordered to a maximum charge of £1.90.

BFPO 60p for the first book, 25p for the second book plus 15p per copy for the next 7 books, thereafter 9p per book.

Overseas including Eire £1.25 for the first book, 75p for second book and 28p for each additional book.

Grafton Books reserve the right to show new retail prices on covers, which may differ from those previously advertised in the text or elsewhere.